DEVELOPMENT OF THE HILL AREAS

About the Author

G.L. Dobhal (*b.* 1936) was a Senior Reader in Economics in Shyam Lal College, University of Delhi since 1970 and retired in 2001. Earlier, he served as a Lecturer in Economics in Shambhu Dayal (Post-graduate) College, Ghaziabad under Meerut University, Meerut.

Dr. Dobhal was awarded M.Phil and Ph.D. by Jawaharlal Nehru University, New Delhi. His field of specialisation has been regional development and planning. He takes keen interest in the problems of development of the hill areas and has contributed articles in leading journals.

DEVELOPMENT OF THE HILL AREAS
A Case Study of Pauri Garhwal District

G.L. Dobhal

CONCEPT PUBLISHING COMPANY, NEW DELHI-110059

Cataloging in Publication Data—DK
Courtesy: D.K. Agencies (P) Ltd. <docinfo@dkagencies.com>

Dobhal, G. L. (Girdhari Lal), 1936-
Development of the hill areas : a case study of Pauri Garhwal District/ G.L. Dobhal.
p. cm.
Reprint. Originally published: 1987.
Originally presented as the author's thesis (M. Phil.—Jawaharlal Nehru University, 1973) under the title: Pauri Garhwal : a regional study.
Includes bibliographical references (p.)
Includes index.
ISBN 818069223X

1. Rural development—India—Pauri Garhwal (District).
I. Title. II. Title: Pauri Garhwal : a regional study.

DDC 307.141 209 542 21

ISBN 81-8069-223-X

First Published 1986
Reprinted 2005

Published and Printed by
Ashok Kumar Mittal
Concept Publishing Company
A/15-16, Commercial Block, Mohan Garden
New Delhi-110059 (India)

Phones: 25351460, 25351794
Fax: 091-11-25357103
E-mail: publishingBco nceptpub.com

DEDICATED

TO

MY PARENTS

Preface

The Himalayas have from time immemorial constituted a subject of profound and unique interest by the distinguished explorers and investigators. The Hill region of Uttar Pradesh considered as one of the holiest part of it and of the country, has as well remained a perennial source of attraction and inspiration, among others, by its sanctuaries of Badrinath, Kedarnath, Gangotri and Yamnotri. It seems quite paradoxical and incredible that no comprehensive, accurate and scientific account of the area and the people has been written. Nevertheless, it is a fact that with the exception of a few brief accounts mostly by the Britishers, there is hardly any regional study whether at meso or micro-level, worth the name. It is with a view to filling this important lacuna in our knowledge of this region, that the present study was undertaken.

The study entitled "Development of the Hill Areas - A Case Study of Pauri Garhwal District" grew from my earlier study of Pauri Garhwal District, one of the eight districts of the Hill Region of Uttar Pradesh. The study of the Hill region as a whole was presented and approved as a thesis for the M.Phil. degree of Jawaharlal Nehru University in 1973. The study brought out the salient features of the Hill region's economy, characteristics of underdevelopment due to peculiar features of the topography, resource base, population and its attributes and above all the outmigration resulting in the heavy dependence of the region on moneyorder remittances. A study of these features affecting the economy cannot be understood and appreciated fully by using the secondary data at district level. To fill this gap, Pauri Garhwal District of Hill region is studied in detail using 169 patwari circles (groups of villages) to bring out the spatial profile of the economy. This is followed by extensive fieldwork to compile secondary data, not ordinarily available at the district level, and sample survey of 218 households in 42 villages to enquire into the levels of living under conditions of outmigration and moneyorder remittances. The study had to be conducted under the constraints of non-availability of large-scale maps. The entire data of 3,236 inhabited settlements were compiled, aggregated and analysed patwari circlewise (groups of villages). Likewise, the primary data on land-use and cropping pattern were compiled in local units of measurement. To the extent the data base permitted, the techniques of analysis have been blended by combining cartographic and quantitative techniques with those of the field observation method.

The study focusses on the following. First, an overall study of the economy of the Hill region is presented as a backdrop, revealing the characteristics of underdevelopment and resource potentials. These characteristics of underdevelopment have been evaluated in detail through a micro-level study of Pauri Garhwal District. The spatial patterns and variations of its structure have been analysed; the complex relationship between physical, economic and social structure of the economy examined and agricultural, horticultural, industrial and other potentialities assessed. Thirdly, the spatial processes that are at work such as the impact of outmigration and inflow of moneyorder remittances on the regional economy, have been analysed. Fourthly, a synthesis of these led us to attempt regional differentiation of the development process leading on to the identification and characterisation of typologies of development within the district. Finally, the spatial development strategy for the development of the Hill areas in general and for the district in particular, has been worked out.

The study is by no means exhaustive to cover all the dimensions of development, yet to the limited knowledge of the research scholar, and his humble submissions, it is a first micro-level study of the region. It is hoped that this modest attempt brings into focus the regional realities more meaningfully than the earlier attempts and would stimulate interest of the academic community and others genuinely interested in the development of the region.

The responsibility for errors and oversights is entirely mine. I am deeply indebted to Professor L.S. Bhat of the Indian Statistical Institute for his invaluable guidance, suggestions and encouragement in bringing out the work in its present form.

I thank Professor Moonis Raza of the Centre for the study of Regional Development, Jawaharlal Nehru University, New Delhi (now Vice-chancellor, Delhi University), Professor G.S. Bhalla of the C.R.D., J.N.U., New Delhi and Professor C.D. Deshpande, Editor, Annals of the National Association of Geographers, India, for their suggestions and encouragement at various stages of the work. I thank Professor A.T.A. Learmonth, Open University, U.K. for going through the entire draft and offering invaluable comments and suggestions. I thank Dr. Amitabh Kundu of the C.R.D., J.N.U., New Delhi who has provided valuable comments and suggestions in statistical analysis. I am indebted to Shri A.N. Sharma of the Indian Statistical Institute, New Delhi and Shri Bachi Ram of the Department of Human Geography, Delhi School of Economics, University of Delhi for their assistance in cartographic work. Grateful thanks are due to Dr. K.V. Sundaram for his comments and suggestions in his capacity as Consultant to the Indian Council of Social Science Research for evaluating the study for publication. Finally, I thank the Indian Council of Social Science Research, New Delhi for their liberal financial assistance towards my field-travel and also for the liberal grant towards the publication of this book.

October 12, 1986 G.L. Dobhal

CONTENTS

List of Tables

List of Figures

Glossary

Abbal lands	The best quality of lands.
Angu	*Fraxinus micrantha.*
Anwala	*Emblica officinalis.*
Bagaar	Rugged terrain.
Baib	A variety of grass, *Eulaliopsis binata.*
Bakeli	A tanning raw material.
Banj	Oak, *Quercus incana.*
Bhaber	Waterless and boulder country at the foot of the Hills. Bhaber grass is used for rope-making.
Bhang	Hemp, *Cannabis sativa.*
Bhangela	Hempen cloth.
Bhimal (Bhyunl)	A plant. Its fibres are used in rope-making and floor matting. *Grewia oppositifolia.*
Bhat	Soyabean, *Glycine soja.*
Bichhu	A variety of wild grass, used in rope-manufacturing. *Gerardiana palmata.*
Binao	*Rhododen dren arborem.*
Bugyal	Highest summer pastures.
Charas	Resinous exudation of hemp.
Chipko	Hug the tree. A non-violent movement by the people of Uttarakhand to protect the trees against fellings.
Chir	*Pinus longifolio.*
Chua	*Amaranthus frumentaceus.*
Dandas	Small hills.
Deodar	A variety of tree. Its wood is used for manufacturing pen holders and pencils. *Cedrus deodara.*
Dhaura	A tanning raw material. Gives softness and yellow colour to the leather.
Doyam	Second class lands.
Gad, Gadhera	Glen, ravine with water.
Gaddies	The valleys carved out by small, seasonal streams and comprise of narrow flat lands and bordered by a series of terraces.

Gohat	Horsegram, <u>Dolichos bitlorus.</u>
Gul	Leat, small water-channels.
Haldu	<u>Adina cordifolia.</u>
Jhangora	<u>Oplismenus frumentaceus.</u>
Kaphal	A tanning raw material, <u>Myrica lapida.</u>
Katil, khil	Intermittent cultivation in virgin soil.
Kauni	<u>Panicum italicum.</u>
Khair	<u>Aeacia catechu.</u>
Kharaks	Temporary sheds of herd boys.
Kharif	Autumn crop.
Kharsoo	Species of oak, <u>Quercus semicarpifolia.</u>
Khunkri	A sharp-edged weapon, made of iron, usually kept by Gorkhas.
Kilmora	<u>Beriberries asiatica.</u>
Kunja	<u>Rosa moschatta.</u>
Kuri	Lantana grass, <u>Nyetanthes arbortristis.</u>
Kurumula	A local insect, causes destruction of crops.
Mahua	A tanning raw material, gives hardness to the leather.
Malu	A reddish coloured creeper, used in rope manufacturing—<u>Vibernum continifolium.</u>
Mandua	Ragi, <u>Eleusine coracana.</u>
Munj	A variety of grass used in rope-making, <u>Saccharum bengaleuse.</u>
Maru	<u>Quercus dilatata.</u>
Myrabolam	A tanning raw material.
Nali	240 Sq. yds. or 4 lbs.
Ogal	Buckwheat.
Padam	<u>Prunus comuta.</u>
Padera	A variety of grass.
Palla or Pharkha	Temporary movable cattle-shed.
Pancher	Temporary irrigable land.
Pargana	Principal division of the district.
Patti	Revenue sub-division of the pargana.
Payars	Highest pastures.
Rabi	Spring crop.
Rambans	A variety of wild tree whose fibres are used is making fishing nets.
Raunsala	<u>Abeis pindrow.</u>
Reh	A tanning raw material.
Ringal	A type of cane similar to bamboo, used in mat and basket making. <u>Arundinaria.</u>

Sabai	A variety of grass and a raw material component of the paper industry.
Sal	_Shorea robusta._
Sandan	_Enginia dallierglodes._
Sar	Set of fields for rotation.
Seras	First class irrigated lands.
Silli	Shady.
Simul	A tree growing scattered all over the hills. _Salmalia malabarica._
Shimar	Water-logged land.
Shisham	_Dalbergia sissoo._
Tailo	Sunny side
Talaon	Irrigated and cultivated low lands.
Tarai	Marshy malarious country immediately below the Bhabers.
Tailonj	A variety of oak, _Querous diatotes._
Thaner	_Laxus baccata_
Tisala	Triennial.
Tun	_Cedrela toona._
Tur	_Cajanus flevus._
Upraon	Dry cultivated upland slopes.
Urd	Rayed kidney beans, _phaseolus radiatus._

ONE

Introduction

The present Chapter comprises of two parts. Part I highlights the growing significance of the concept of regional development planning, conceptual and theoretical background and an appraisal of regional planning in India. In Part II, the aims, objects and the methodology adopted have been discussed.

The formulation and implementation of economic and social development planning both in developed and developing countries give rise to new problems and considerations and discovers new dimensions. One of these dimensions is the concept of regional development planning in its various forms and applications.[1] It is a direct outcome of an *ad hoc* treatment of spatial dimensions in the sectoral-temporal planning.

Regional development implies "a process resulting in a secular growth of regional output or real income".[2] It takes into consideration the integration of spatial and functional aspects of development both at the national and regional levels. It encompasses multiple dimensions[3] - the dimensions relating to administrative levels, sectors of the economy, physical environment, political structure etc. In Indian context, regional analysts have identified macro regions (groups of states or parts of them), meso regions (state or intra-state) and micro regions (district, development block or tahsil or in some cases clusters of villages) within them.

Regional development implies multi-level planning with its manifold links and strong interrelationships between national, sectoral and regional levels. How the process of development takes place? There are two alternative approaches. The first is the regionalisation of the national plan, either disaggregating it in its regional plans or by distributing among the regions the projects envisaged in the national plan. The second is the formulation of regional plans and aggregating the targets of various sectors of the regional economies to make up an integrated national development plan. Both the processes i.e., of working from the top to downward and from the grass-roots level upwards are complementary and supportive rather than competitive and substitutive.

Regional development planning can play a vital role in the formation of specialised regional economies within a country of large-size and sharp contrasts in resource-endowment and levels of development as in India. It can contribute to the socio-economic integration within the country taking into account objective scientific criteria, the level of development achieved, the administrative boundaries, the development potentials and possibilities and the specialised functions within the region. Against a background of social welfare, social justice and egalitarian principles, it should be related to a system of traditions, values and culture. It should pay attention to intra-regional inequalities reflecting social stratification within a region. It should play the role of redistributive mechanism aiming at long-run processes of gradual and continuous internal change, the breaking down of the vicious pattern of external dependence and integration of vertical and horizontal patterns of development. Further, it should lead to rational decision making through equalising the economic, political and social weight of various groups and reconciling social interests and ensuring balanced development of various regions.

Of late, the concept of regional development has acquired importance for several reasons. First, with the process of development, socio-economic problems have become more and more complex partly to their constantly changing structure and partly to corresponding revaluation entailed in change. Secondly, spatial dimension of regional development is another which by no means be underestimated. Existing development potential in developing countries is often cramped by the legacy of the past—the acute spatial disequilibrium and disproportion in spatial structure so often concomitant with a dualistic structure.[4] A dualistic economy - social, economic or technological - aggravates inter-regional discrepancies, countributes to persistent spatial disequilibrium and becomes an integral part of the factors and causes of underdevelopment. However, it is not the "disequilibrium" or "polarisation" or "dualism" which poses an urgent problem but rather its degree, causes and those factors which determine its perpetuation and thus impede growth. Thirdly, spatial incidence of social and economic growth has an inevitable impact on the growth of the economy. It implies an integrated approach to the economic, social and physical aspects of development both at the national and regional levels. Fourthly, social aspects of regional development are as important as economic, technical and physical aspects. The need is especially felt in view of changes, transformations and interactions between regions that accompany the development process. In both the "core" and "periphery" areas, social problems are created, perpetuated and aggravated leading on to the complexity of social structure due to intensification of social differentiation.

In the light of role and significance detailed in the preceding pages, the objectives of the regional development could be outlined. They would, however, vary from nation to nation or even among different regions of a country within the national framework. The major objectives would be to carve out the structure of the economy most suited to the region and spatial organisation of the regional economy in such a way that it serves to achieve the goal of maximum utilization of resources, development of lagging or depressed regions for providing at least minimum basic needs and reduction of inter-regional disparities.

It has been emphasized that the techniques of regional development planning should be to integrate theory and practice. These, in large part, are an extension of development in general economics which occurred during the 1940s namely a revitalisation of location theory, international and inter-regional multiplier theory, inter-industry input-output analysis and mathematical programming.[5] Walter Isard and Cumberland emphasize comparative cost analysis, industrial complex analysis, the input output method and cost-benefit analysis.[6] Recently, there has been an emergence of accounting analysis.[7] Analogous to the national accounting system, the regional accounting system has been considered as a technique of regional analysis.[8] All these techniques of analysis have become vital in regional development planning in a variety of ways. The application of each of the foregoing techniques would, however, depend upon the nature and size of the region, the object of the study and the qualitative and quantitative aspect of the available data.

I

REGIONAL DEVELOPMENT : THEORETICAL AND CONCEPTUAL BACKGROUND

On account of the ambiguity of the regional concept, its multidisciplinary content and the complexity of the subject, itself covering physical, social and economic elements, a general theory of regional development has still to be formulated. The theories in regional development have generally been evolved by extension or adaptation of theories in other fields especially from economics. However, an analytical treatment has been made in regard to the existing theories.

The Earlier Location Theories

The earliest formulation of locational theories were based on the ideas of Von Thunen[9] and Weber.[10] It is only recently that a serious attempt has been made to integrate the two approaches, notably by Isard.[11] Based upon a large number of assumptions, Von Thunen postulated six concentric zones of agricultural activities by considering the relationship of three factors : transport cost, selling price and production cost. He concluded that the number of profitable options decreases with distance from the city market. However, the modern methods of transportation and technological development have radically changed his visualised pattern. The formation of concentric zones is not inevitable as a large number of factors such as demand function for agricultural products, the agricultural inputs, technology and ecological conditions etc., might distort the concentric zones of product. This is particularly so in the regions like the hilly areas, where micro-level variations are large. Whether, it is along a railway or road or a river almost parallel belts of land-use would appear.[12]

In contrast to Von Thunen approach, Weber enunciated a systematic deductive theory of industrial location. The pulling of the industry into different geographical regions, was according to him, due to both the regional (primary) as well as agglomerating and deglomerating (secondary) factors. The theory, based upon unconvincing, over-simplified and unreal assumptions and over-burdened with technical considerations did not provide a definite explanation of industrial location in its entirety. It did not take into account the non-economic factors which influence the cost structure and make difficult to determine the location of an altogether new industry in underdeveloped regions. Some theoretical apparatus is necessary to analyse the component parts of an industry from the standpoint of costs.[13]

Supplementing the work of Weber, Sargant Florence made an inductive analysis of industrial location. The genesis of his work revolved around three concepts : the location quotient, co-efficient of localisation and the co-efficient of linkages. He observed, "the relation of an industry to an area is not so important as the relation of an industry to the distribution of the occupied population as a whole.[14] It, however, does not throw light on the correct allocations of industries among different regions. The co-efficient of localisation varies from country to country, according to local conditions and factor endowments.

The Central Place Theory

The earlier location theories were, however, not relevant to a multi-town economy characterised by extremely complex functional diversities, size variations and inter-connections. A theoretical framework for the study of such a complex system is provided by the work of a German geographer, Walter Christaller in 1933.[15] The work with modifications by Losch has come to be recognised as "Central Place Theory".[16]

The theory, based on the assumptions of uniformity of the physical and cultural landscapes in an unbounded unit area, existence of accessibility conditions in all directions and the prevalence of rational consumer behaviour postulates that the distribution of human settlements in any settled area (rural or urban) is not disorderly but has a distinct relationship among the number, size and pattern of settlements. As such development viewed as a process of innovation as well as growth does not appear everywhere at the same time but manifests itself at favoured points from which it tends to propogate outwards. A favoured point possessing gravitational pull is akin to a nucleus around which crystallisation of mass takes place. On the other side, it is also the focal and distribution point for goods and services to its rural hinterland. The relationship is, therefore, complementary and supportive rather than competitive. The points or the settlements performing these functions are, therefore, called "Central Places" and the services performed purely for a surrounding area are called "Central Functions".

Both the central places and central functions are closely related and can be ranked according to notional scale of ordering. The central functions (or human activities) are organised in space, horizontally as well as vertically in regularly spaced clusters forming triangular lattices. The functions at lower order central places are located at gravity centres of triangles formed by places at the next order centres. Under the hypothetical conditions of the theory each goods offered at a central place will carve out its marked area through the interplay of three factors viz., demand functions, economies of scale and cost of production. Since the assumption of rational behaviour that each consumer will satisfy his demand for goods and services at the nearest centre, the market area (or hinterland) around a central place will be circular but ultimately if the whole plain is covered by a system of central places, the market areas will be hexagonal, the geometrical figure closest to a circle having no interestitial unserved space.

The size of the hexagon depends upon the size of service areas of the central places viz., the small hexagons are the service areas for the lower central places and larger hexagons represent service areas for the next higher order central places. The lower order central places nest within the higher order central places. Whatever be the order of central place, it performs a function to the central place itself first, and then to the area surrounding it. The higher order central places are higher in respect to the number of activities, range of goods produced, volume of business, trading areas and specialisation than the lower order ones. They supply all goods which are supplied by the lower order centres but in addition a number of grades of wider ranges and specialised functions for themselves. Obviously, they are more widely spaced than the lower order ones.

Based upon the different orders of central places and their respective service areas (or hinterlands), Christaller postulated the concept of hierarchy - a hierarchy of central places from higher order central places to lower order central places, the former having bigger hinterlands and performing a large number of functions than the latter. In fact, the distance of higher order central places is a function of lower order central places. The pattern of nesting of the service areas and location-spacing of successive lower order centres is arranged under three different conditions, each giving rise to a characteristic pattern of hierarchy, in turn for the "marketing principle", the "transport principle", and the "administrative principle", each of which operating according to their respective K-value.[17] K-value (K = 3) under "marketing principle" indicates the rate at which the successively lower order market areas increase in a given hierarchy. The "transport principle" would operate by a rule of fours (K = 4) ensuring that a maximum number of important centres are located along the major transport routes minimising thereby the cost of the transport network. The hexagonal system under "administrative principle" would emerge by a rule of seven (K = 7) evolving a distinct network of central places and their corresponding complementary regions resulting thereby an efficient administrative control of settlements.

In order to determine the centrality, Christaller preferred telephone density to population as the criterion, although other criteria could also be used. It has, however, been observed that the centrality is proportional both to the hinterland and to the number of functions performed.

Christaller introduced the concepts of "range of good" and "threshold". The former fixes an upper limit beyond which the consumers would not travel for the satisfaction of a particular good ensuring positive demand while the latter fixes a lower limit below which there are insufficient consumers to support the particular function ensuring thereby normal profits. In contrast to Christaller's concept of "range of good", Berry and Garrison[18] introduced the term "threshold" to describe the amount of purchasing power to support a function or service. Threshold populations depend upon the size of population not only of the settlements but also of its hinterland and vary along a continuum weighing both the subjective and objective considerations.

August Losch modified the Christaller's model by demonstrating a complete economic landscape on the basis of a general concept of hierarchies. In spite of many similarities with Christaller's model, Losch's model is a departure in many respects. Both Christaller and Losch agree that triangular pattern of settlement distribution and hexagonal shaped market areas represents an optimum for a single good in an unbounded plain, with equal access in all directions. Both assumed homogeneous and even demand for goods as the starting premise. Both neglect the supply of and demand for agricultural inputs and outputs. However, as against Christaller's approach, Losch begins with lowest threshold good and subsequently builds upward; there is an alternative concentration and dispersal of centres in different sectors in his economic landscape of complex hexagonal market areas; that the model is for the geography of secondary, market-oriented manufacturing activities; and lastly his K-system does not produce rigid hierarchy as the hierarchic centres, at the same level, provide the same number of functions but do not provide the same kind of functions.

From the foregoing analysis, the following points emerge. It is postulated that there is regularity in spacing of different orders of central places. While Christaller postulates uniform spacing, Losch visualises closer spacing in "settlement rich" and wider spacing in "settlement poor" sectors for the same order of central places. Since the assumed triangular lattice is a purely theoretical concept based upon isotropic surface premise, distortion in spacing of central places is expected in reality owing to agglomeration, resource localisation and time lags in the process of settlement evolution. The distortions would be augmented further in a hilly region with sharp physiographic features, inaccessibility conditions and dispersed settlement and population structure.

The hexagonal shapes of market areas maintained by both Christaller and Losch prove to be purely theoretical. The pattern of initial spatial organisation would, in fact, determine the shape of market areas. The hexagonal shape will be distorted in reality with the deviations in the spacing of settlements and variations in population density. In an area like the Hill region of Uttar Pradesh where interactions among people, to a large extent, take place in north-south directions along the river valleys, and where low density of population and sprinkled settlement structure are the characteristic features, the search for the hexagonal shape of market area boundaries is futile.

The generic base of central place theory is the hierarchical vertical functional organisation of the central places. This element, lying at the heart of central place theory, has evoked greatest interest and empirical verification of hierarchy have been attempted for several regions. Christaller's fixed K-system, binding the central places and their market areas in functional organisation suggest a rigid hierarchical framework. Nevertheless, by relaxing even the underlying assumptions of isotropic plain in view of the physical and other spatial dimensions of the Hill area, the hierarchical organisation of the central places is likely to hold good. The basic concepts of "range" and "threshold" for the establishment of goods and services, resulting from the interplay of three factors - demand function, transport cost and economies of scale, are enough to substantiate the inevitability of the hierarchical organisation of centres. This, in turn, would give rise to a cluster of activities in a hierarchical order of central places, nesting the market areas. Nevertheless, despite the limited applicability of these models, they provide the necessary framework for a planned regional development. At least on normative levels, the theory could be used for working out a locational model of central places in regions - developed or developing; rural or urban; and hilly or plains.

Growth Pole Theory

The growth pole concept was introduced first by Perroux[19] in 1955 and extended by Boudeville[20] and Hagerstrand[21] and Friedman[22] and others. The theory assumes that economic activities necessarily take place in geographical space; that they cluster together to generate internal and external economies; and if allowed uncontrolled would create spatial disequilibrium, congestion and diseconomies and finally that autonomous processes could be directed through policy intervention to rectify disequilibrium conditions.

By using deductive method, Perroux considered a growth pole as a centre in abstract economic space from which

centrifugal forces emanate and to which centripetal forces are attracted. Each centre being a centre of attraction and repulsion has its own field which is set in the field of other centres. The forces which he conceived were essentially economic; the generators of these forces were basically firms and industries and the foci of change were urban centres. Economic development never occurs uniformly over space and tends to be concentrated in certain parts which thereby develop as growth poles or growth centres.

There are three important aspects of the theory. First is inter-industry interdependence akin to Leontief input-output model which presumes development process as essentially unbalanced, interdependent and automatic once inter-industry linkages are well established. The firms or industries establish, grow and concentrate, accelerating thereby the development process by agglomerative economies, technological changes and psychological factors. The second aspect is the innovatory character of the firm which is generally a large economic unit in size, dynamic in character and propulsive in nature. It belongs to a rapidly growing sector, forms a nucleus and generates growth impulses in environment. It is technologically advanced also and operates in high income elasticity market for its product.[23] The relationship between growth pole to its surrounding area or hinterland is the third aspect of the theory. The growth pole mechanism emphasizes not only concentration but dispersion of economic activities in the surrounding areas. The idea of centrifugal spread of economic prosperity is analogous to the functional relationship between a large city and its surrounding hinterland as viewed by Lampard.[24] Hoselitz[25] classified the role of city as one of "generative" and "parasitic" on the basis of whether or not they stimulated economic growth in a wider region in which it is located. The role is not only economic but envelopes commercial, political, socio-cultural dimensions as well.

Boudeville[26] applied this theory to geographical space and contended that only those nodal points can be identified growth poles in which are located propulsive firms/industries. Myrdal's[27] "backwash" and "spread" effects as the favourable and unfavourable effects[28] respectively are the end results of interactions between the growth poles and their surrounding areas. These are further testified by the "core-periphery" dichotomy of Friedman.[29]

The process of development, as Indian experience demonstrates, is not automatic and creates conditions of spatial disequilibrium. The model is static and is concerned less with the spatial dimensions of the region. The existing socio-economic and spatial characteristics of the region would have to be considered before such a model is adopted. In regions of wide diversities like the Hill region, the multiplier effects would not take place in the desired directions due to leakages; the hinterland might not be ready to participate in the innovation process and the economic dualism might be developed in the hinterland.

Export-base Theory

The theory is an adaptation from the general theory of income determination in economics. It revolves around three facets - the export base, the non-basic or residentiary activities and the multiplier. The export base which denotes collectively the exportable condition of a region, is a primary determining factor of the rate of growth, levels of absolute per capita income and the development of residentiary, secondary and tertiary activities.[30] The residentiary, a consequence of export-base, refers to the industry developed for the local market where the consumer population resides. The ratio between export activities and residentiary activities, measured in terms of income, employment and output is called a multiplier. The integral component of the theory lies in the process of development of the export-base in the following way. The export-base because of its locational advantages is instrumental in reducing the processing and transport costs of the exportable commodities. Reduced costs enable the export-base to shape the nodal points. The nodal points gradually emerge as the trading centres and foci of other activities. Creation of infrastructure, services and amenities becomes inevitable. This gives an impetus to the development of subsidiary industries of residentiary varieties requiring more investment,[31] through a multiplier process similar to familiar investment multiplier and foreign trade multiplier in national income models. The whole process of growth of exports however, presupposes major developments in transportation, increase in income and demand in other regions, adaptation of technological developments and government's role in creating social overhead benefits in the region.

The theory does not provide sufficient scope for internal growth sequences. By establishing the "export-base" in a predominantly agricultural region of the hills, it is not inevitable that harmonious interrelationships among different sectors of the regional economy would be developed and functional and spatial aspects integrated. Moreover, the residentiary employment does not adapt passively and automatically to the strategic "region-building" industries that have external trade relationships. Nor services can be viewed as entirely dependent.

Therefore, in such an area the interrelationships among the various kinds of activities within a region, including the complicated "multiplier effects" are critical in the regional economic growth.

Tiebout[32] points out that the export-base, as visualised by North depends also on the size of the region under study; the levels of income in surrounding areas; the smooth functioning of the internal mechanism in terms of autonomous activities and finally on the non-economic considerations. Considering these factors, the export-base would not be a sufficient condition of growth of the Hill region. The vast geographical area and variability in resource structure would lead to an unbalanced development of the spatial structure. The large intra-regional and inter-regional disparities in income would adversely affect the demand conditions for output. Lack of entrepreneurial skill and ability would restrict the smooth functioning of autonomous activities. The costs of inputs would go up on account of inaccessibility conditions and lack of infrastructure. The socio-cultural dimensions would outweigh the economic considerations, and finally, the limited size of market might inhibit specialisation.

Since the regional economies are relatively more open-ended than the national economies, they are not subject to the constraints of international trade. The growth of any sub-national unit, as the theory points out, is tied to development within the national economy and in some cases to changes in international trade as well. The changing patterns of national demand and investments, on the other hand, receive an appropriately central position in the analysis of regional growth. Therefore, the aggregation of industries and activities in the Hill region would have to be viewed in terms of the total relationships including inter-regional relationships and nodal centre to hinterland relationships as well as in terms of ties to the state and national economy as a whole. To what extent the Hill region's economy has the linkages with these area levels is an important consideration in formulating long-term and short-term development strategies.

Growth Diffusion Theory

Myrdal and Hirschman, the chief exponents of "Growth Diffusion Theory" contended that social process in developing countries tends to be dominated by the vicious circle[33] which keeps the economy in a low level of equilibrium, perpetuating itself and culminating in economic stagnation. Myrdal's model comprises of three important elements. First is the principle of circular and cumulative causation, implying a circular constellation of forces tending to act or react upon one another in such a way as to keep a country in a state of poverty.[34] Taking inspiration from Rostow[35], Myrdal optimistically asserts that the economy can be pulled out of "vicious circle" and from its cumulative downward movement and pushed forward to a "virtuous circle" and to its cumulative upward movement by various measures. The second element of his model is the concept of equilibrium. Myrdal argues that the notion of stable equilibrium is a false analogy as there is no such tendency towards automatic self-stabilization in the social system. On account of supporting the exogeneous changes, the equilibrium will be unstable. The third and the most significant element of his theory is the spatial interaction between the growing and the stagnating regions as an explanation of differential regional growth. The cumulative process of growth results into the "spread" and "backwash" effects as positive and negative factors in the "lucky" and "unlucky" regions respectively. The spread effects would be felt strongest in the highly developed regions due to a corresponding development of transportation and communication, higher levels of education and a more dynamic communion of ideas and values. In contrast to these phenomena, the stagnating regions experience backwash effects in terms of outflows of skilled and enterprising workers, locally generated capital, raw materials and other natural resources. Both these aspects are relevant in the context of the Hill region's economy **mutatis mutandis.**

In examining the spatial interaction, Hirschman calls the "North" the region exercising growth and "South"[36] as the one that remained behind corresponding to "growing" and "stagnating" regions of Myrdal. The former has come into being with the special receptivity to innovation and enterprise in addition to its locational advantages and industrial atmosphere; while the latter remained in the trap of economic backwardness. The key role of differential growth is accorded to spatial interaction in the form of "trickling down" and "polarisation" effects.[37]

Myrdal-Hirschman regional income inequality approach is useful in analysing spatial concentration of economic growth as the basis for the formulation of a development model for a region. Considering the relevance of the theory in the context of the development of the Hill region, it is observed that sharp inter-regional and intra-regional disparities persist in the State of U.P. The less developed regions of the Hills, is stagnating under the operation of a large number of negative factors leading to the convergence of growth. The existence of strong growth poles outside the region and negligible inside it, has virtually brought about strong backwash effects. There has been to a considerable extent, an outflow of human and natural resources from the region. The outmigration of the people is selective both in age and sex. Consequently, the economy subsists on the moneyorder remittances from these outmigrants living outside the region. Any regional development model for the Hill region, should therefore, take into account not only the existing inter-regional inequalities but also the causation process operating and leading to it.

Theory of Functional Spatial Organisation

The genesis of the theory of functional spatial organisation centres round three aspects viz., the spatial, the functional and the interconnections between the two. The spatial element is emphasized while considering the areal distribution of varied phenomena. It is in space that critical development in the evolution of patterns and functional organisations have been taking place within a total setting of resources and culture over a period of time. It is through the functional connections that race as a whole developed locational and internal organisations with roots in specific places.[38] The second aspect is the functional organisation, the evolution of which have been envisaged through different stages whereby a region's economy starts getting organised initially around such settlements whose function is to serve the surrounding area which in turn sustains it, giving rise to organisation of larger functional regions and finally to a more complex and specialised type. The third aspect of the theory is the interconnection between the two. Because of the areal organisation of the earth's surface relatively discontinuous and fragmentary, it gives rise to two types of interconnections as parallel and nodal, the former among units/areas of relative homogeneity and the latter among the relative heterogeneity. These inter-connections lead on to an areal structure comprising of a nested orders of areal functional organisation arranged in a functional hierarchy.

The theory of functional spatial organisation by integrating spatial and functional linkages conceives of the creation of growth foci all over the region at convenient locations. An hierarchy of growth foci, functionally linked with other larger or smaller clusters, send socio-economic impulses to clusters lower in hierarchy and receive similar impulses from centres higher in hierarchy. The desirability of such nodes is more imperative in the context of Hill area with vast regional disparities and inequalities, poor infrastructure facilities, unconnected settlement pattern and inadequate trading and services centres and the poor linkages.

A review of various theories examined in the preceding pages highlights the fact that none of the theories developed so far presents an adequate explanation as the basis for the regional development planning. Each one of them is partial and treats the discipline from one or the other angle. The central place theory as enunciated by Christaller and later expanded and formalised by Losch and Berry is largely concerned with spatial location and distribution of clusters of human activity marked by concentration. Perroux-Boudeville's concept of growth pole was marked by geographical spatial orientation leading to centralised concentration of industrial and other activities. The theory of spatial diffusion as demonstrated by Myrdal-Hirschman-Hagerstrand stands between the two and integrates into a spatial theory of development whose dimensions are spatial, sectoral and temporal. The theory of export-base and its multiplier effects in terms of residentiary activities is only partial for its failure in terms of its sectoral integration. Finally, the theory of functional spatial organisation, while integrating spatial and functional aspects emphasizes the emergence of nodalities - the foci of regional growth. In the light of this, it would, therefore, be pertinent to examine the relevancy or otherwise of these theories in the background of the various features of the regional economy one is contemplating.

REGIONAL DEVELOPMENT - THE INDIAN EXPERIENCE

Balanced regional development has always been one of the stated main objectives of economic planning in India. The First Five Year Plan followed a strategy of balanced growth of the economy and gave topmost priority to agricultural development while at the same time emphasizing the vital role of industries in decentralised sector. Community Development Programme as a part of the strategy was, therefore, launched in 1952 to initiate the process of transformation of social and economic life of villages through a change in outlook and methods of production of rural population. Taking the block as the unit, the programme sought to bring about an improvement in all aspects of life, by providing a uniform pattern of administration for development throughout the length and breadth of the country.

The Second Plan admitted that "in any comprehensive plan of development, it is axiomatic that the special needs of the less developed areas should receive due attention. The pattern of investment must be so devised as to lead to balanced regional development."[39] The Third Plan programmes were so prepared as tc "reduce disparities of development between different states although in the nature of things this process must take time."[40] Accordingly, the Third Plan included schemes to enlarge the possibilities of development of areas which have in the past been relatively backward. As such, Intensive Agricultural Development Programme as one of the schemes, was started during the Third Plan, in recognition of the failure of the global approach to rural development inherent in Community Development Programme. It was distinguished by two features- the package approach and concentration of efforts. The idea was to provide a package of improved inputs and services in selected districts which promised higher growth. In the industrial front three important steps were directed. First, weightage was given for backward states in the allocation of central assistance; secondly, backwardness of a state or an area was taken into consideration as one of the factors in location of central sector projects; and thirdly, special assistance was made available to backward areas like Nagaland and Eastern U.P.

Notwithstanding the above efforts, regional disparities increased during 1951-66. It became inevitable for the government to set up two Working Groups, one for the identification of industrially backward areas and the second for suggesting an elaborate set of fiscal and financial incentives for encouraging the setting up of industrial units.[41] In July, 1969, the Lead Bank Scheme was also introduced to bring in the commercial banks as catalytic and responsible agents in area approach to development. They were considered instrumental in conducting overall surveys of the existing infrastructural facilities, identification of growth centres, estimation of credit gap, expanding the banking structure and finally effectively participating and stimulating the process of Integrated Area Development.

In the Fourth and the Fifth Five Year Plans, several measures were undertaken in order to give effect to the policy of correcting inter-regional imbalances. The backward areas were identified and grouped into two categories: first, were the areas with unfavourable physio-geographic conditions, terrain and climate such as drought-prone areas, tribal areas and the hill areas; and the second consisted of the economically backward areas marked by adverse land-man ratio, lack of infrastructure and inadequate development of resource potentials. The criteria of allocation of central assistance to the backward states was also modified. Central projects subject to techno-economic feasibility and viability for drought-prone areas and tribal areas were undertaken and special allocation of central assistance for Hill areas were made. The Central Government also initiated projects which laid particular emphasis on the mobilisation of credit and provision of agricultural inputs and development of essential economic infrastructure for small farmers, marginal farmers and agricultural labourers in particular and the community in general. It has also been encouraging private enterprises by means of central subsidy, fiscal incentives and concessional finance from financial institutions for private investment in backward areas. The State Government have in addition played a supplementary role for establishing promotional and financial institutions.

The Sixth Plan, laid emphasis on the strategy of "Integrated Area Approach" in backward areas. Such a strategy has been pursued in the developed countries of the west to deal with "problem areas" by selected measures.[42] However, these measures could not remove the root cause of underdevelopment. It is for this reason that the approach is gradually gaining wider recognition.[43]

The concept of Integrated Area Development can be defined as comprehensive planning for the economic and social development of a specified geographical area. The term integrated refers to two types of integration - functional and spatial. Functional integration means co-ordinated expansion of various social and economic services needed for the development of area e.g., transportation, communication, banking, health etc. It is based upon the idea of complementarity between various sectors and does not view the problems of rural and urban in isolation. Spatial integration, on the other hand, seeks to utilise the linkages between various levels of urban or rural centres (or growth points - rural or urban) through which space economy is organised for the development of the region.

An objective evaluation of the Five Year Plans would, however, reveal that the balanced regional development, as one of the principal accepted objectives of economic planning in India, was in practice, ignored right from the inception of planning. The Community Development Programme failed as it was ambitious both in scope and geographical coverage and followed a strategy of global character. The rural development was considered in isolation and did not encompass urban areas within its purview. The neglect of spatial dimension of rural development and the optimum location of economic and social services was also glaring. Even the adoption of a new strategy of I.A.D.P. during 1960s, as a prelude to the much applauded green revolution, and considered as a marked improvement over the Community Development Programme in terms of both the package and concentration of efforts approach, could not bring about balanced regional development. Instead, the existing gulf of income disparities widened between the irrigated and dry areas on the one hand and between rich and marginal farmers on the other in every state. The programme, confining itself to agricultural development did not integrate rural and urban development.

The industrial development presented a more distorted picture of regional development in India. Both Hazari[44] and Dutt[45] highlighted that the inefficacy of the existing Industrial Licensing Policy led not only to the growth of monopoly capital, economic concentration and disparities in income and wealth, but was also unable to help the industrially backward states, culminating into the growth of regional disparities. Moreover, the locational concentration of licences in the metropolitan towns and cities led to urban-rural dichotomy. While the growth centres experienced rapid, sustained and cumulative economic growth, the neighbouring regions experience outflow of the people, capital and resources.

Despite several measures undertaken by the Government during Fourth and Fifth Five Year Plans, no noticeable regional development has taken place. The revised formula for central assistance could not tilt the balance in favour of backward states. Most of the development measures are specially meant to help drought-prone, hilly or tribal areas. The localisation of large central projects by way of subsidized investments, in specified districts/areas has neither accelerated the dispersal process nor improved the lot of these economies. Moreover, the spread effects are low and surrounding areas continue to remain poor and underdeveloped because of the slow growth of ancillary industries. Very few entrepreneurs have approached the public sector institutions for concessional finance. Consequently, the dualistic economic structure persists.

The approach to the "Integrated Area Development" has been a subject of vehement criticism. It implies multi-level and decentralised planning to overall development of the economy. The economic theory relating to area development is still inadequately developed[46] and requires considerable research in concepts and techniques of analysis. It involves phased procedures and programmes such as identification and delineation of viable areas of development, determination of objectives, formulation of strategy, data collection and their analysis by suitable analytical techniques and finally the formulation of the development plan. It requires a clear and concrete definition of area as apart from a region.[47] The areal unit such as a district[48] should be operationally sound, economically viable and technically feasible.[49] Objectives set should represent the collective welfare of the people living in the area, and should be realistic and operational. The objectives pursued at area level and national level should not be conflicting and impinge the formulation of the plan. Lastly, planning at the area level being more concrete, requires multi-disciplinary teams comprising of engineers, sociologists, psychologists, economists, regional scientists.[50] It is like an apparatus which serves the watershed hinterland in much the same way as the circulatory system serves the human body.[51]

II

DESIGN OF STUDY

The study aims first, at understanding the complex relationship between the physical, economic and social structure of the region's economy, in the light of ecological and other man-environment relationships as framework of understanding of the varied activities of the people; secondly, assessing the agricultural, horticultural, industrial and other potentialities of the region; thirdly, identifying the processes of regional development, in terms of growth promoting and growth retarding factors and the levels of development; in particular evaluating the nature and extent of the moneyorder flows and outmigration and their impact on the socio-economic conditions of the people; and finally to working out a spatial development strategy for integrated development of the Hill areas in general and the district under study in particular.

Hypotheses

The hypotheses tested were: (i) a low level of functional organisation of a region reflects a low level of regional development; (ii) in areas with sharp contrasts in regional structure, the spatial pattern of development is highly selective between areas leading to intra-regional imbalances in development; (iii) in Hill areas, desirable integration of land-uses and settlements implies physical planning with strong emphasis on man-environment relationships; (iv) social aspects of planning are as important as economic aspects of planning under conditions of subsistence economy; and (v) the vicious circle of poverty is still dominant by the operation of a number of negative factors, keeping the economy at a low level of equilibrium.

Review of Literature

Literature, both theoretical and empirical on regional development is somewhat scarce as the concept is of a very

recent origin. It is only very recently that a few empirical studies on regional planning have been made in India. Such regional studies are at three levels - macro level, meso-level and micro-level. Chief among the macro-level studies include those of the Registrar General, India (Economic Regionalisation of India - Problems and Approaches, 1961); Regional Survey Unit, Indian Statistical Institute (South India Macro-Regional Study, 1962); Rao (Regional planning in India, 1963); Bhat (Regional planning in India, 1972) and Town and Country Planning Organisation (South East Resource Region, 1969). Among the meso-level studies, the important ones include those of National Council of Applied Economic Research (Techno-economic Survey, Uttar Pradesh, 1955-56); Wanmali (East Maharashtra, 1970); Andhra Pradesh Government (Rayalaseema, 1971) and Gokhale Institute (Marathwada, 1975). The more useful information in the context of a regional study at district level is contained in various micro-level studies carried out by National Council of Applied Economic Research (Moradabad, 1968); Prakasa Rao (Muzaffarnagar, 1969) and National Institute of Rural Development (Raichur, 1955). Studies below district level are those of National Institute of Rural Development (Miryalguda, 1974; Suryapet, 1974; Pauri Tahsil, 1974) and Bhat (Karnal Tahsil, 1975). It is however, more difficult to find proper regional plans, carried right through to implementation, evaluation and modifications based on the evaluation.

There is an acute gap of information on the various aspects of the Hill region's economy. Nevertheless, the background knowledge was provided by such official publications as the various Settlement Reports, Gazetteers, Codes of Customary Laws, Land Tenures and the Census Reports compiled mostly during the British period. Traill's earliest account "Statistical Sketch of Kumaon, 1828" is an indispensable one. E.T. Atkinson's 3 volume work "The Himalayan Districts of North West Provinces of India (1882-86)" is a comprehensive and accurate account on the area and the people. It is on such sources that most of the subsequent accounts rely heavily. Besides, there are the historical accounts detailed in the works of Williams (1874), Oakley (1905), Pate Ram (1917), Tewary (1923), Raturi (1928), Sankrityayan (1959) and Dabral (1966-76). Dabral's 8 volume work is a very exhaustive and valuable account of the region. Most of the information on geographical, economic and social aspects of the Hill region is available in unpublished form in doctoral theses. Pant's "Social Economy of the Himalayans" (1935) and Dhoundiyal's "Economic Life of Garhwal" (1945) are the main earlier works authentically portraying the socio-economic life of the people. More details of the social aspect of the Hill region are available in the writings of sociologists.

While the works of Gairola (1922), Blunt (1931), Joshi (1955) and Sanwal (1976) aimed at an analysis of the caste structure, those of the Saxena (1955), Majumdar (1962), Berreman (1963) have focussed on the customary laws of the polyandrous people of the Himalayas. Sanwal's "Social Stratification in Rural Kumaon" is an outstanding contribution. Added to these are the extremely rich folklore containing a body of information. Upreti (1894), Vaishnava (1938) and Budhisagar (1964) have given a vivid description of these. Last but not the least is the G.A. Grierson's "Linguistic Survey of India", Volume IX, 1916, which provides invaluable linguistic and historical data.

Units of Study

Considering the limitations of data and large-scale maps and the need for indepth study of the spatial patterns and processes of man-environment relationship in a less developed hilly region, it was considered necessary to use 169 patties [52] or patwari circles as the units of data compilation (Figure 1). A list of these patwari circles is given in Appendix I. On an average each patwari circle has a geographical area of 15 $km.^2$ with 19 settlements and 3,000 population.

Data-Base

Both primary and secondary data were collected from time to time in 10 field visits from various sources at different places. The important places visited included inter alia Lucknow, Kanpur, Kotdwara, Dogadda, Lansdowne, Pauri, Srinagar, Rudraprayag, Chamoli, Hardwar, Rishikesh, Tehri, Kalagarh, Ramnagar, Nainital, the 14 Block Headquarters and 42 sample villages. Secondary data collected pertained to the population census, land-use, cropping, moneyorder remittances, forest products, industry, agriculture, horticulture, animal husbandry, transport and other miscellaneous items. The land-use and cropping data related to 3,568 villages inclusive of 332 uninbabited settlements. Besides, postal data relating to inflow and outflow of moneyorder remittances were compiled from Pauri and Lansdowne Head Post Offices and Kalagarh Sub-post Office. These data related to 54 Sub-post Offices and 274 Branch Post Offices connecting with over 4,000 postal villages. The primary data were collected for 42 sample villages and 218 households with the help of specially prepared schedules and questionnaires. The village schedule was administered with a view to collecting data on village resources, accessibility conditions to services and amenities, felt needs of the villagers, the development problems of the villages etc. The household questionnaires pertained to the collection of data on agricultural and allied activities, agricultural production and incomes, consumer expenditures, outmigration, moneyorder remittances etc. A copy of both village and household questionnaires, is appended. (Appendix II).

Methodology

For the analysis of the present study, a combination of cartographic, quantitative and field work methods was used. The topographical map of 1" = 1 mile has been used as the basis. An attempt has been made to analyse the features of the area under study. The spatial patterns of distribution of population, land-use, cropping pattern, services and facilities, inflow of moneyorder remittances etc., have been analysed by the use of different cartographic techniques such as choropleth, isopleth, pie diagram etc.

Various quantitative methods deemed feasible and essential were used for the analysis of spatial association of different variables. Lack of both qualitative and quantitative data restricts the application of sophisticated mathematical and statistical tools of analysis. Novertheless, in the analysis of levels of development prinicpal component analysis was used.

The cartographic and quantitative methods were supplemented by field work by conducting a survey of 42 sample villages and tracts with the help of specially prepared schedules and questionnaires. Because of the special nature of the study, samples were not randomly drawn. Instead, purposive sampling, based upon the crop combination regions, demarcated through the application of the Thomas Method was resorted to. The choice of samples from these regions was followed after a detailed analysis of the secondary data of 3,236 villages on the existing settlment structure and functions in addition to the proper consideration of accessibility conditions, altitudinal variations and the geographical area. Due care was also taken that the size of samples was adequately representative of each of Tahsil, Block and Kanungo Circle in the distrct.

The household samples where survey was conducted numbered 218. The criterion for choosing household samples was the range of variation of the size of operational holdings owned. The range of variation was classified into 5 categories on the basis of an analysis of the district level data. Ordinarily 5 sample househols, one from each category in each sample village were chosen except where the range of variation in the size of operational holdings or the size of population of the sample village was large. The number of sample households surveyed in each category are given above.

S.No.	Operational holdings category	No. of households
(i)	Less than 0.25 hectare (12.5 Nalis* or less)	44
(ii)	0.25 - 0.50 hectare (12.5 to 25.0 Nalis)	53
(iii)	0.50 - 1.00 hectare (25.0 - 50.0 Nalis)	63
(iv)	1.00 - 2.00 hectares (50.0 - 100.0 Nalis)	41
(v)	2.00 - and above hectares (100.0 Nalis and above)	17
	All categories	218

* Nali is the local name of unit of measurement of land.

Data collected through household survey were analysed by tabulation and interpreted against the background of the regional structure, patterns and variations in respect of physical landscape, resources, settlement and population distribution and composite grouping of patties on the basis of several attributes. Such an approach has brought out several features of development/underdevelopment and the factors responsible for them. These have been summarised in the form of guidelines for formulating a spatial development strategy for the region under study.

NOTES AND REFERENCES

1. U.N.O. : Regional Planning - **Report of the Sixth Interregional Seminar on Development Planning,** New York, 1973, Chapter I, p.3.
2. Krutilla, John V: Criteria for evaluating Regional Development; **American Economic Review,** May, 1955.
3. Isard, W. & Cumberland, J.H. : **Regional Economic Planning** (Ed.) - Techniques of analysis for less developed areas; O.E.E.C., Paris, 1961, pp. 19-20.
4. U.N.O. op. cit. Chapter II, pp.12-16.
5. Meyer, John R.: "Regional Economics - A Survey" in American Economic Association : **Surveys of Economic**

Theory - Growth and Development, St. Martin's Press, New York, Vol.II, 1965.
6. Isard, Walter & Cumberland, J.H. op. cit. p.26-37.
7. Hoover, Edger M. & Chinitz, Benjamin : Role of Accounts in the Economic Study of Regions : in **Regional Development and Planning - A Reader** by Friedman, J. & Alonso, W., pp. 612-615.
8. The United Nations System of National Accounts is now being prepared by most countries. But regional accounts at a level below that of the country have not been evolved so far in a manner which would be of value to the regions. In India, the proposals for regional accounts have been finalised in the Final Report of the Committee on Regional Accounts, Government of India (1976).
9. Von Thunen, Johanan H. : **Isolated State,** Oxford University Press, London, 1966. (Translated by Wartenburgh, C.M.)
10. Weber, Alfred : **Theory of Location of Industries** (Trans) 1929. He was a German economist whose original work was first published in 1909 in german language. It was translated into English in 1929 by Karl J. Friedrich under this title.
11. Isard, Walter : **Location of Space Economy,** 1956.
12. Michael Chisholm: **Rural Settlement and Land-use,** pp. 34-35.
13. Balakrishna, R. : Limitations of the Deductive Theories of Industrial Location: **Indian Journal of Economics,** October, 1946.
14. Sargant Florence: **Investment, Location and Size of Plant,** p.34.
15. Christaller, W: **Central Places in Southern Germany,** (translated by C.W. Baskin), New Jersey, 1966.
16. Losch, A.: **The Economics of Location,** New Haven, 1954.
17. Bhat, L.S. et. al. : **Micro Level Planning,** K.B. Publishers, New Delhi, 1976.
18. Berry, B.J.L. & Garrison, W.L. : The Functional Basis of Central Places Hierarchy; **Economic Geography,** 1958, Vol.34, pp.145-154.
19. Perroux, F.: Economic Space - Theory and Application, **Quarterly Journal of Economics,** Vol.64, February, 1950.
20. Boudeville, J.R.: **Problems of Regional Planning,** Edinburg, 1964.
21. Hagerstrand, T.: **Innovation Diffusion as a Spatial Process,** Chicago Press, Chicago, 1967.
22. Friedman, John : **Regional Development Policy - A Case Study of Venezuela,** The M.I.T. Press, Cambridge, 1966, pp.10-13.
23. Misra, R.P.: **Regional Development Planning in India - A**

New Strategy, Vikas Publishing House, Delhi, 1974, p.183.

24. Lampard, Eric A. : The History of cities in the Economically Advanced Area; **Economic Development and Cultural Change,** No.3, January, 1955, pp.81-137. See also **Economic Development and Cultural Change,** Vol.3, Nos. 1 & 2, October, 1954 and January, 1955.
25. Hoselitz, B.F.: Generative and parasitic cities; **Sociological Aspects of Economic Growth,** Free Press, New York, 1966, Chapter VIII, pp. 184-214.
26. Boudeville, J.R. : op. cit.
27. Myrdal, Gunnar : **Economic Theory and Underdeveloped Regions,** London, 1967. See also Myrdal's **Asian Drama - An Enquiry into the Poverty of Nations,** Penguin, Mass. 1968, Vol.III, Appendix 2, pp.1843-1940.
28. Hirschman, A.O. : **The Strategy of Economic Development,** New Haven, 1969, Chapter 10, pp.183-202.
29. Friedman, John : op.cit. pp.10-13.
30. North, Douglass C.: Location Theory and Regional Economic Growth; in **Regional Development and Planning—A Reader** by Friedman J. and Alonso, W., M.I.T. Press, pp.240-255.
31. North, D.C. : op.cit. pp.250-251.
He has listed four types of industries viz.
(i) materials oriented industries, located at the source of material like sugarbeet refining, flour milling, lumbering etc. (ii) service industries to the export industries e.g., foundaries and establishments making machine tools, specialised agricultural implements; (iii) residentiary industry producing for local consumption; (iv) footloose industries where transfer costs are not of significant importance. A great many of such industries may develop by chance in some location.
32. Tiebout, Charles M.: Exports and Regional Economic Growth, in **Regional Development and Planning - A Reader** by Friedman, J. and Alonso, W., M.I.T. Press, Cambridge, Mass 1964, pp.256-260.
33. The concept is being thoroughly discussed in a number of works, chief among them being: Nurkse, R: **Problems of Capital Formation in Underdeveloped countries;** Leibenstein, Harvey: **Economic Backwardness and Economic Growth;** Benjamin Higgins: **Economic Development;** Singer, H.W.: **Economic Programme in Underdeveloped countries;** Meier, G.M. and Baldwin, R.E.: **Economic Development: Theory, History, Policy ;** Lewis, W.A.: **Theory of Economic Growth;** etc.
34. Nurkse, R: **Capital Formation in Underdeveloped Countries,** Oxford, 1953, Chapter I, p.7
35. Rostow, W.W.: **The Stages of Economic Growth,**

Cambridge, New York, 1960. And also his earlier work, **The Process of Economic Growth,** W.W.Norton & Company, Inc., New York, 1953.

36. This terminology was suggested by Hirschman in view of the fact that a large number of lagging areas at least in the Northern Hemisphere, appear to be located in southern parts of the countries to which they belong.
37. These effects correspond exactly to "spread" and "backwash" effects as explained by Myrdal. Nevertheless, there are considerable differences in emphasis and conclusions.
38. Philbrick, Allen K.: **Principles of Areal Functional Organisation in Regional Human Geography,** Economic Geography, Vol.33, No.4, October, 1957, p.300.
39. Government of India, Planning Commission: **Second Five Year Plan,** 1956, p.36.
40. Government of India, Planning Commission: **Third Five Year Plan,** 1961, p.9.
41. In 1968, two Working Groups under the chairmenship of B.D. Pande and N.N. Wanchoo were set up by the Planning Commission. The objectives of the Working Groups were the "identification of industrially backward areas" and bringing out simultaneously an elaborate set of fiscal and financial incentives for setting up industrial units in the demarcated areas.
42. O.E.C.D.: **Regional Factor in Economic Development;** Chapters VI and VII, Paris, 1970.
43. O.E.C.D.: **Multi-disciplinary Aspects of Regional Development,** Paris, 1969, p.21.
44. Hazari, R.K.: Industrial Planning and Licensing Policy, Final Report, 1967.
45. Government of India: **Report of Industrial Licensing Policy Inquiry Committee,** July, 1969.
46. O.E.C.D.: **Multi-disciplinary Aspects of Regional Development,** Paris, 1969, p.21.
47. The concept "area" and "region" are interchangeably used. In the context of India with reference to Integrated Area Development, however, it is used for a smaller spatial unit of the country, namely district, taluk/tahsil or a block of villages. In this sense "area planning" becomes synonymous with local or grassroot planning.
48. National Council of Applied Economic Research: **District Planning-Moradabad,** New Delhi, 1968.
49. Singh, Daulat et al. : "Dynamics of Integrated Area Development in India", **Indian Journal of Agricultural Economics,** Vol.XXVIII, No.4, October/November, 1973, p.33.

50. Institute of Social Studies: **Development and Change,** the Hague, 1970-71, p.3.
51. Singh, Daulat et al. : op.cit. p.33.
52. The term **patti** is the original native name. Prior to the British occupation of the territory in 1815, the Garhwal princes used to appoint, at their discretion, suitable persons as "Thatwan" or "Thokdar" for a group of villages, irrespective of their geographical locations for the convenience of revenue allocation and collection and called them as "Thok" or "Thaat". They in turn had the discretion to appoint "Malguzar" or "Padhan" for the respective village(s). The group of villages thus classified came to be known as patti. Whereas, the classification into Parganas (Kanungo circle) was introduced by Traill in his First Settlement Report in 1816; the arrangement of Patties, according to their geographical contiguity was made by Beckett in 1860, dividing the entire district into 11 Parganas and 86 patties. The present 169 patties (Patwari circles) as the units of our study, came into existence on Ist July, 1966 by bifurcating the existing patties.

TWO

Salient Characteristics of the Hill Region.

INTRODUCTION

Uttar Pradesh, the most populous state accounts for 16.1 per cent of the total population and 9 per cent of the total area of the country. It contributes over 11 per cent towards the national income by employing over 78 per cent of the working force. Agriculture from where 50.8 per cent of the domestic product originates, forms the backbone of the state. Within the state, however, there are wide variations and sharp differentiations in climatic conditions, topographical features, soil characteristics, surface and ground-water availability and resource and settlement structure etc. All these have significant implications on the levels of socio-economic development contributing to regional imbalances. It is on the basis of intra-state variations that the state has been divided into five economic regions viz., Hill region, Western region, Central region, Eastern region and Bundelkhand region. An analysis of the intra-state variations in respect of physical, resource and settlement structure etc., reveals that the Hill region possesses a unique personality and an independent entity. It has a deep-rooted history; a separate geographical identify in comparison with the rest of Uttar Pradesh; distinct socio-cultural dimensions; sharp physiographic features and fragmented and emerging cultural landscape patterns. It represents unity in the midst of intra-regional diversities.

Historical background

The Hill region referred to by different names[1] possesses a deep-rooted history. It has been traced back in Vedic, Jain and Pali literature; in the literary classics of Panini, Patanjali and Kalidasa; in the records of the empires of Mauryas, Kanishkas and Guptas; in the travelogue of Huang Tsang and in the sanctuaries of Badrinath and Kedarnath established by Guru Sankaracharya. Katyuri dynasty was the first historical dynasty who ruled for 500 years up to 1223 A.D. It was succeeded by Panwar[2] and Chand dynasties (1223-1804 A.D.). Gorkhas' tyrannical rule lasted for 12 years (1803-1815 A.D.) until it became a part of British territory in 1815. By 1840, the entire Hill region was constituted by three distinct parts: Dehradun district under Meerut division; Tehri Garhwal district under the Tehri prince; Garhwal, Almora and Nainital districts under Kumaon division. Presently, the Hill region consists of the Garhwal and Kumaon divisions, the former comprising of five districts of Dehradun, Tehri Garhwal, Uttarkashi, Garhwal and Chamoli and the latter comprising of three districts of Almora, Pithoragarh and Nainital.

Physical structure

The Hill region lies between 28°.50' N. and 31°.30' N. latitudes and 78°.20' E. to 80°.05' E. longitudes. It is bounded by Tibet on the north; Nepal on the east; Himachal Pradesh on the west and Bijnor, Moradabad, Rampur and Pilibhit districts on the south (Figure 2). Physiographically, the Hill region comprises from south to north, in ascending order, the Tarai Bhaber; Bhaber and Dun Valleys; the Sub-himalayas or the Siwaliks; the Lower-himalayas; and the Higher-himalayas. Tarai Bhaber is a broad belt of over 15 kilometres in width, running parallel to the foot of the outermost Himalayas. It is characterised by the grassy and swampy plains; marshes and fans; oozing streams and water-choked morasses and tropical and insalubrious climate. The Bhaber, ranging between 300 to 600 metres above mean sea level with its elevation increasing from east to west, comprises of a small belt of plain land of a width between 6 to 24 kilometres. The Sub-himalayas or the Siwalik hills, with an average height of 1,225 metres, have been divided into a number of hills. The Lower-himalayas, extends from west to east like a spinal chord. The northern most part of the region is called the Higher-himalayas mostly lying above 3,000 metres with ranges averaging 1,850 metres above mean sea level and a width of above 50 kilometres. The topography, in general, is highly rugged with difficult precipitous slopes. It is characterised by innumerable spurs, horned peaks, high ridges, glaciers, snowclad mountains, hanging and narrow valleys and torrential rapids.

Geology

Geologically, this is a little explored region. The Higher-himalayan zone has a glaciated topography with many moraines. The Lower-himalayan zone is composed of granite and other crystalline rocks. The Sub-himalayan zone is built entirely of Siwalik sediments with great thickness of rocks, clay and conglomerates. Bhaber is made up mainly of gravel with in-

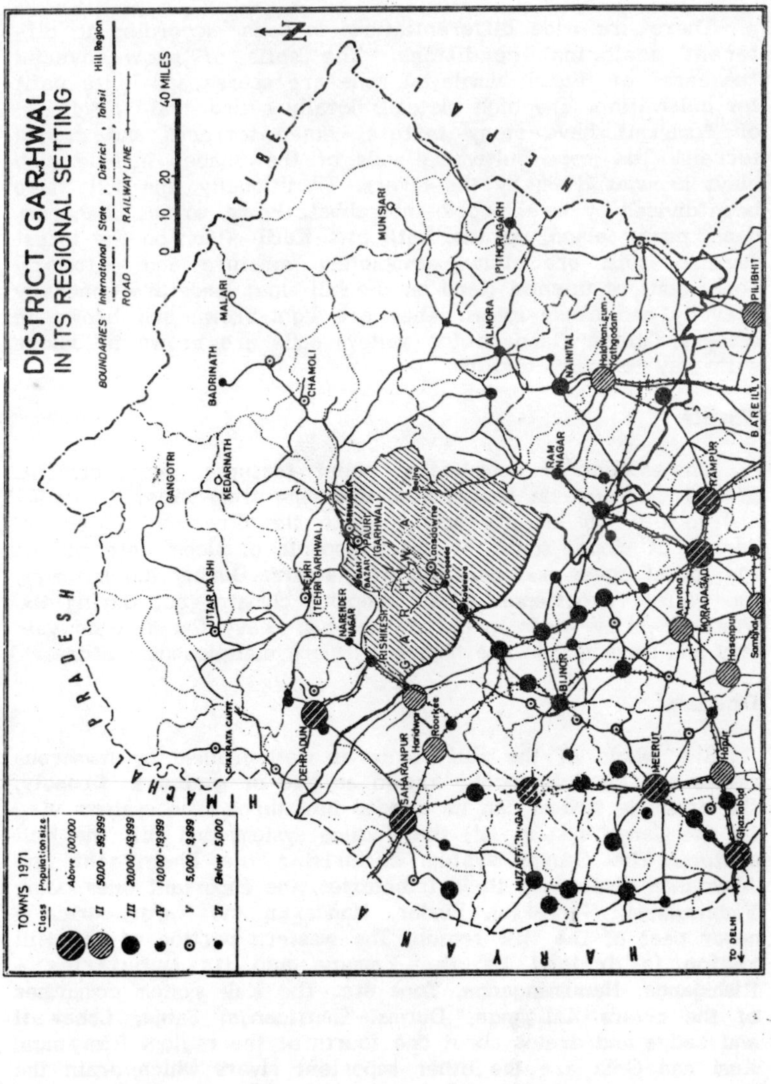
DISTRICT GARHWAL
IN ITS REGIONAL SETTING
BOUNDARIES: International, State, District, Tahsil
Hill Region
ROAD
RAILWAY LINE
0 10 20 40 MILES
N
TOWNS 1971
Class Population size
I Above 100,000
II 50,00 - 99,999
III 20,000 - 49,999
IV 10,000 - 19,999
V 5,000 - 9,999
VI Below 5,000
TIBET
NEPAL
HIMACHAL PRADESH
HARYANA
UTTAR KASHI
GANGOTRI
KEDARNATH
BADRINATH
MALARI
MUNSIARI
CHAMOLI
PITHORAGARH
ALMORA
NAINITAL
RAM NAGAR
TEHRI (TEHRI GARHWAL)
NARENDER NAGAR
PAURI (GARHWAL)
Lansdowne
Kotdwara
RISHIKESH
DEHRADUN
CHAKRATA CANTT.
SAHARANPUR
Hardwar
Roorkee
BIJNOR
MUZAFFARNAGAR
MEERUT
Ghaziabad
Hapur
Hasanpur
Amroha
MORADABAD
RAMPUR
BAREILLY
PILIBHIT
TO DELHI

Fig.2

tecalations of sand and clay[3] and has a close affinity to upper Siwalik conglomerates[4]. It resembles convergent alluvial fans of dry deltas[5].

Soils

There are wide differentiations in soils, according to different ecological conditions. The soils of snow-covered "bagaars" of Higher-himalayan zone are sparse and quite unfit for cultivation. The high plateaus locally called "rath", "ghaar" or "dhangu" have stony texture, steep terraces and rugged terrain. The more cultivable soils of the Bhaber include rich clays brought down by the rivers. Traditionally, the soils have been divided by local people into **abbal, doyam, soyam, chaharam, dang, pang, talaon, upraon, katil** etc. **Katil** (land on the forest margins) soils are stony, completely immature and extremely poor. Soils of **upraon** (land on the hill side) lands are generally gravelly and sandy loams. They are light-brown and brown in colour. **Talaon** (land in the valley) soils are brown in colour with clay to loamy texture.

Climate

On account of complicated relief features, micro-climates are of considerable importance, differing from valley to valley and locality to locality according to the direction of ridges, degree of slope, sunny or shady aspects of slope, intensity of the forest cover and nearness of glaciers. During the summers, the valleys experience a hot tropical climate, but during the winters, valley-winds in narrow valleys, heavy fog in wide valleys and snowfalls in the higher hills are conspicuous features.

Drainage

The whole of the Hill region is well drained by numerous rivers and rivulets locally known as **gad** or **gadhera**. Broadly, the drainage system can be divided into three main systems viz., (i) the Ganga system; (ii) the Yamuna system; and (iii) the Kali system. The Ganga system comprising the Bhagirathi and Alaknanda rivers and their tributaries, the important ones being Vishnuganga, Nandakini, Pindar, Mandakini and Nayar, drain a major part of the Hill region. The western portion of the Hill region is drained by the Yamuna and its tributaries - Rishiganga, Hanumanganga, Tons etc. The Kali system comprises of the rivers Kaliganga, Dorma, Gauriganga, Sarju, Lohawati and Ladya and drains about one fourth of the region. Ramganga, Kosi and Gola are the other important rivers which drain the eastern part of the region.

Water resources

In its drainage system, in its rivers and rivulets; in its lakes and tals; in its springs and glaciers lie the resource potentials especially for economic power generation. The river courses are marked by steep gradients, deep gorges, rapids and falls which facilitate the power generation. Intensive cultivation through irrigation has also scope at the meeting point of the rivers with the plains as in the Bhaber.

Mineral resources

After 1947, many techno-economic[6], geo-chemical and geological surveys have been carried out by different governmental agencies such as N.C.A.E.R., Geological Survey of India, Atomic Energy Department etc. As a result, different mineral deposits have been established in various parts of the Hill region. Districtwise details are given in Table 2.1 below:

TABLE 2.1
Mineral Resources of the Hill region

S.No.	Name of the district	Mineral resources
1.	Pauri Garhwal	Copper, Gypsum, Iron, Limestone Phosphatic shales and Mica.
2.	Chamoli	Asbestos, Copper, Iron, Limestone and Sulphur.
3.	Tehri Garhwal	Dolomite, Gypsum, Iron, High Calcium Limestone, Mangesite, Mica and Uranium.
4.	Uttarkashi	Copper, Magnesite and Sandstone.
5.	Almora	Copper, Graphite, Limestone, Magnesite, Sandstone, Sulphur and Talc.
6.	Pithoragarh	Copper, Lead, Limestone, Magnesite and Zinc.
7.	Nainital	Copper, Graphite, Iron, Limestone and Magnesite.
8.	Dehradun	Copper, Dolomite, Graphite, Gypsum, Marble, Limestone, High calcium Limestone and Sandstone.

Forest resources

The total forest cover in U.P. in 1975-76 was estimated to be 51,300 square kilometres or 17.42 per cent of the total geographical area of 294,366 sq. kms. Out of 51,300 km^2, the Hill region covered 34,207 km^2 and the rest by the plains (33.34 per cent). In 1970-71, a major portion of the forested area (79 per cent) of the Hill region were Reserved Forests and the remaining were civil and soyam forests, panchayat forests, cantonment and private forests. An analysis of intra-regional variations in the distribution of forests (Table 2.2) reveals that Uttarkashi district has the largest area under forests followed by Chamoli district.

The large forested area of the Hill region because of altitudinal variations, has given rise to vertical zonations of the vegetal cover in the region. The region can be divided broadly into four zones. First, the Sub-tropical zone (below 1,200 metres), comprises the Bhaber and Siwalik area, possesses hot to temperate climates. The important species are **sal, kanju, semal, haldu, khair, sessum, toon** and **saandan.** In the wet hollows and along the streams, cane brakes and bamboo brakes are also found. The second is the Temperate zone (1,200 metres to 1,800 metres). While **chir pine** is the dominant tree, other species of importance are **banj oak, kharsoo oak** and **maru oak.** The third zone (1,800 metres to 3,000 metres) is called the Sub-alpine zone. The **banj, tilonj** and **kharsoo** are the chief species of the zone. The Alpine zone (over 3,000 metres) has very little vegetation on account of cold climatic conditions. The chief species found are **padam, bhoj** and **thaner.**

A large variety of major and minor forest products come from the Hill region. The major products are timber and fuel. They contribute annually between 50 per cent to 75 per cent of the total out-turn of the state. The minor products include all kinds of other forest products such as grasses and bamboos; waxes and dyes; fibres and flosses; gums and resins; herbs and medicinal plants; lac and shellac; edible wild plants and fatty oils; and a host of others. The region has the monopoly of producing ringals, resin, gypsum and bhaber-grass in U.P. Some of the minor products such as katha, gums, resins, lac etc. are of national and international commercial significance. Both the major and minor forest products annually fetch a sizeable revenue in crores of rupees to the state government.

Notwithstanding these contributions, the Hill region in recent years has become poorer climatically, economically and aesthetically on account of indiscriminate cutting of forests due to a lack of imagination and farsightedness. During the last 15 years, 25 per cent of the Himalayan forests have been damaged.[7] Ramganga Dam Reservoir would need to be desilted after only 40 years because of large-scale soil erosion in its

TABLE 2.2

Distribution of forested area in the Hill Region

S. No.	Name of the District	Total Geog. Area (Sq.kms)	Area under Forests				
			Forest Deptt.	Revenue Department	Panch-ayat Forests	Private Forests	Total Forest Area
1.	Uttarkashi	8,000	6,952.19	-	-	-	6,952.19 (21.37)
2.	Chamoli	9,100	3,845.87	1,043.00	677.18	-	5,566.05 (17.22)
3.	Pithoragarh	7,200	758.54	1,284.00	303.60	-	2,346.14 (7.27)
4.	Almora	7,000	2,107.97	1,929.00	770.71	-	4,807.68 (14.79)
5.	Pauri Garhwal	5,400	2,528.01	1,806.00	112.90	-	4,446.91 (13.38)
6.	Tehri Garhwal	4,400	2,695.54	-	-	-	2,695.54 (8.38)
7.	Nainital	6,800	3,609.75	203.00	206.01	-	4,018.76 (12.29)
8.	Dehradun	3,100	1,539.58	-	-	165.00	1,695.58 (5.30)
	HILL REGION	51,000	24,028.45	6,265.00	2,070.40	165.00	32,528.85 (100.00)

Note: Figures in parenthesis are in percentage to the total forest area in the Hill region.

catchment areas comprising of Dronagiri and Dudhatoli in Garhwal hills.[8] In Terai area, sub-soil water has gone to 8 to 10 metres deep as against 5 metres deep only a decade ago. It has also been estimated that in the absence of forests, the flow of water from the streams has decreased 7 to 13 times the normal rate of flow with long periods of nearly dry channels.[9] The region has become poorer economically because of large-scale drainage of forest resources to the plains areas without much reciprocal advantage to it. It has become poorer aesthetically because of fast vanishing flora and fauna.[10] The ecological balance has thus been disturbed. All these factors have created a pessimistic atmoshpere of neglect, exploitation, frustration, uncertainty and a threat to the very existence of the people of the region, culminating into the emergence of a Chipko Movement.[11]

DEMOGRAPHIC AND SETTLEMENT STRUCTURE

Population

The total population of the Hill region, according to 1971 Census was 3,822,000. It increased at the rate of 21.67 per cent during 1961-71 as against 17.90 per cent during the earlier decade. Districtwise details are given in the following Table 2.3.

Urban Population

It would be observed from the following Table 2.3 that the urban population constituted 14.68 per cent of the total population. It ranged from 2.65 per cent in Tehri Garhwal district to 47.08 per cent in Dehradun district. The urban population dwells in 33 towns of which Dehradun is the only Class I city and Haldwani-cum-Kathgodam the only Class II city. These two cities share among them nearly 45.60 per cent of the urban population. Besides, there were 4 Class III towns, 8 Class IV towns, 11 Class V towns and 8 Class VI towns. These towns in their distribution show a linear pattern along the important road linking the plains with centres and areas of tourist and religious importance.

Scheduled Population

The Scheduled population in the Hill region in 1971 was 7,54,000 of which scheduled caste population constituted 16.05 per cent and the rest 3.68 as Scheduled tribe population. The range of variations among the districts was not much.

TABLE 2.3

Population of the Hill region - Rural and Urban, 1971

Sl. No.	Name of the district	Total popula-tion	Rural Popu-tion	Per cent	Urban Popula-tion	Per cent
1.	Uttarkashi	147,805	141,785	95.93	6,020	4.07
2.	Chamoli	292,571	280,365	95.81	12,206	4.17
3.	Tehri Garhwal	397,385	386,862	97.35	10,523	2.65
4.	Pauri Garhwal	553,028	518,181	93.70	34,847	6.30
5.	Pithoragarh	313,747	301,805	93.20	11,942	3.80
6.	Almora	750,038	710,926	94.79	39,112	5.21
7.	Nainital	790,080	615,201	77.87	174,879	22.13
8.	Dehradun	577,306	305,529	52.92	271,777	47.08
	HILL region	3,821,960	3,260,654	85.32	561,306	14.68

Settlement Structure

Most of the settlements in the Hill region are dispersed, small in size and vary considerably. 63.68 per cent of the total rural settlements in the region were having population of less than 200 persons each and accommodated about 27.83 per cent of the rural population. About 28.61 per cent of the settlements had a population between 200 and 499 persons each and 39.88 per cent of the rural population was living in these villages. The next size-class viz., 500-999 persons covered 6.12 per cent of the settlements and 18.54 per cent of population only. The percentage of relatively large settlements (over 1,000 population) was only 2.29 and about 13.75 per cent of the rural population lived in those 238 settlements.

Occupational Pattern

In 1971, the total working population accounted for 40.15 per cent of the total population. As could be seen from Table 2.4, agriculture and allied activities occupied 77.00 per cent of the workers which among different districts ranged between 38.89 and 92.19. Cultivators formed the major segment of the workers in primary sector. The percentage of agricultural labourers was very small in all the districts excepting Dehradun and Nainital districts. Because of the relatively small expansion of non-agricultural activities in the region the working population engaged in secondary activities was also small. The services sector absorbed 18.40 per cent in the Hill region and varied from 8.33 per cent in Uttarkashi district to 50.22 per cent in Dehradun district.

TABLE 2.4

Occupational structure in the Hill region - 1971

S. No.	Name of the District	Total No. of workers	Occupational Categories (Percentage)									
			Primary			Secondary			Tertiary			
			I	II	III	IV	V(a)	V(b)	VI	VII	VIII	IX
1.	Uttarkashi	93,921	85.90	1.00	1.55	0.04	0.72	1.09	1.37	1.05	0.15	7.13
2.	Chamoli	169,747	86.52	0.43	0.19	0.01	1.72	0.33	0.42	0.90	0.32	9.16
3.	Tehri Garhwal	204,581	90.96	0.55	0.68	0.03	1.09	0.51	0.23	0.87	0.21	4.87
4.	Pauri Garhwal	251,093	78.01	1.30	1.62	0.03	0.83	0.66	0.56	1.58	0.76	14.65
5.	Pithoragarh	125,942	79.54	1.28	0.73	0.04	2.10	0.47	1.00	1.69	0.58	12.57
6.	Almora	291,343	82.44	1.70	0.97	0.05	1.12	0.77	0.52	1.79	0.69	9.95
7.	Nainital	264,924	45.56	18.45	4.39	0.53	2.05	5.15	1.81	6.34	3.60	10.12
8.	Dehradun	201,050	28.36	8.20	2.33	0.18	2.47	6.82	1.42	7.93	3.84	38.45
	HILL REGION	1,602,601	70.36	4.87	1.70	0.13	1.51	2.15	0.89	3.02	1.43	13.95

I. Cultivators
II. Agricultural Labourers
III. Forestry, hunting etc.
IV. Mining and Quarrying
V.(a) Manufacturing other than households.
V.(b) Households industry.
VI. Construction
VII. Transport and Communications.
VIII. Trade and Commerce.
IX. Other Services.

Density of Population

The density of population is very low consistently all over the Hill region and averaged 75 persons per km.^{2} The lowest density is in Uttarkashi district with 19 persons per km.^{2} which goes upto 189 persons per km.^{2} in Dehradun district.

Sex-ratio

An outstanding characteristic of the Hill region is its imbalanced sex ratio (i.e. more females than the males) more marked in rural areas than in the urban areas. Overall sex ratio of the region is 966 females per 1,000 males while the rural and urban ratios are 1,016 and 719 females per 1,000 males respectively. Districtwise variations are concealed by the averages of the Hill region. In general, these figures, reflect the outmigration characteristics.

Literacy

The Hill region has an overall literacy rate of 31.02 per cent. The variations range between 45.06 per cent, the highest in Dehradun district and 19.05 per cent, the lowest in the Tehri Garhwal district. The overall male literacy is 45.58 per cent ranged from 36.69 per cent and 53.64 per cent in the same districts. Similarly, the overall female literacy is 15.96 per cent. It varies between 4.34 per cent in Tehri Garhwal to 33.85 per cent in Nainital district. Without the necessary infrastructure and economic inputs high literacy rate has not contributed significantly to the wellbeing of the people.

Work Participation

A significant demographic characteristic of the Hill region is its high work participation, prominently in the rural areas. The total work participation rate for the Hill region, in 1971 was 41.93 per cent and ranged between 33.53 per cent in Nainital district to 63.54 per cent in Uttarkashi district. The male work participation rate (52.29 per cent) was relatively much higher than the female work participation rate (31.22 per cent). The former ranged from 47.64 per cent in Pauri Garhwal district to 65.36 per cent in Uttarkashi district and the latter between 7.72 per cent in Nainital district to 61.52 per cent in Uttarkashi district.

The outmigration of male members of the family perforces the female population to work in the field or in nearby towns. Besides, non-competitive nature of female labour, the nature of the family structure, inaccessibility of transportation and communication, low level of urbanization and secondary activities contribute towards confinement of woman work-force in rural sector. This is confirmed by the extent of association between sex ratio and female work participation (Table 2.5).

TABLE 2.5
Rank Coefficient of Correlation between female work participation and other variables in Hill region

S.No.	Correlate ;	rs at District level
1.	Rural Literacy and Female Work Participation	-0.523
2.	Urban Literacy and Female Work Participation	+0.191
3.	Overall Literacy and Female Work Participation	-0.809
4.	Rural Sex Ratio and Female Work Participation	+0.453
5.	Urban Sex Ratio and Female Work Participation	-0.905
6.	Total Sex Ratio and Female Work Participation	+0.358
7.	Combined Scheduled Caste and Scheduled Tribe Population and Female Work Participation	-0.381
8.	Scheduled Caste Population and Female Work Participation	+0.143
9.	Scheduled Tribe Population and Female Work Participation	-0.238
10.	Rural Male and Female Work Participation	+0.096
11.	Urban Male and Female Work Participation	+0.691
12.	Overall Male and Female Work Participation	+0.358

A perusal of Table 2.5 reveals that it is possible to establish some relationships at this disaggregative level.[12] The differences in female participation rates are possible to explain in terms of (i) disparate levels of literacy and (ii) differing sex ratio. It is not however, possible to explain in terms of varying proportions of Scheduled Caste and Scheduled Tribe population and dissimilarities in male work participation. The female work participation does also show a marked negative relationship with literacy though with urban literacy, it does not. The relationship between female participation rates and the sex ratio is strongly positive though there is a negative correlation between urban sex ratio and female work participation. The argument that where women outnumber men, the former have to carry a great responsibility for the family's livelihood is confirmed. There is a positive correlation between male and female work participation in the urban sector but not in the case of rural sector. We may conclude that female work participation tends to act independently of male participation in the rural area and in terms of the district as a whole but not in the urban sector.

LAND-USE AND CROPPING PATTERN

Nature and Type of Cultivation

The nature and type of cultivation in the Hill region differs significantly from those of the plains area due to variations in physiographic, climatic, agronomic and other factors. Three types of cultivation are prominent throughout the region.[13] They are, the **katil** cultivation, the **upraon** cultivation and the **talaon** cultivation. The talaon cultivation may further be considered of three types viz., the **sera** cultivation, the **pancher** cultivation and the **shimar** cultivation.

Land-use Pattern

Of the total geographical area of 51,104 km^2, 16.5 per cent lies under snow and 63.8 per cent under forests. Only 16 per cent of the area is under cultivation. According to Agricultural Census,[14] out of the total area of 638,000 hectares under operational holdings in the Hill region, 92.7 per cent was under the category of "Net Area Sown" and 1.3 per cent under "Current Fallow". The fallow land other than current fallows was hardly 1.4 per cent. Similarly, culturable waste was only 1.1 per cent in the region. Finally, the land not available for cultivation covered only 2.5 per cent of the total area. Intra-regional variations in respect of each of the categories are not significant. The scope of increasing cultivated land is severally limited by increasing pressure of population and acute scarcity of cultivable land, making thereby a strong case for intensive cultivation.

Cropping Pattern

An analysis of cropping pattern reveals that in the Hill region, major concentration is on the production of foodgrains and a little is devoted towards the production of commercial crops. Prominent crops are wheat, mandua and paddy. They together accounted for 73 to 84 per cent of the total cropped area among different districts. The percentage of area under wheat, mandua and paddy accounted for 31.8, 25.9 and 24.7 respectively. The remaining area was devoted to small millets, oilseeds, pulses and other miscellaneous crops. With the exception of Dehradun and Nainital, other districts devoted less than 5 per cent on the production of non-food crops.

Land Holdings

Holdings are very small in size. A large number of operational holdings (2,33,000 or 33.1 per cent) figure in the size-group of "less than 0.50 hectare" and covered an area of 9.6 per cent in the Hill region. The districtwise variation of holdings in this class ranged from 19.1 per cent in Uttarkashi district to 47.6 per cent in Dehradun district. While those of area ranged from 2.4 per cent in Nainital district to 14.5 per cent in Chamoli district. Similarly in the size-group of 0.50 hectare to 1.00 hectare, the Hill region covered 29.2 per cent of the holdings with 19.6 per cent of area. In the higher size-classes although the percentages of holdings were low yet they covered higher percentages of area. The districtwise variations were also small.

Area under Irrigation

Irrigated area in the Hill region has 127,000 hectares (21.5 per cent) out of a total of 591,000 hectares under net area sown and is mainly by leats (**guls**) from smaller streams.

INDUSTRIAL AND TOURIST POTENTIALITIES

Industrial Potentialities

The Hill region possesses vast potentialities in respect of industry and tourism development. They are based more on forests, livestocks, horticulture and less on crop cultivation.

Forest-based potentialities

A number of industries based on major and minor products of forests can be developed. The important among them are: saw mills, wooden furniture, paper manufacturing, sportsgoods, stationery articles, geometrical instruments, resin and turpentine, certain essential oils, ayurvedic medicines and scores of others. The grasses such as Bhaber grass (**bhabhar, baib** and **sabai**), **khus-khus, munj, koran** can be utilised variously. Bamboos and canes, possessing over 90 varieties are of universal utility and can be used in many ways.

Mineral-based potentialities

Mineral resources (refer Table 2.1) can be used for the maufacture of glass bottles, glass tubeware and pressedwares, glass shells, tubes, scientific glass apparatus; crockeries, insulators, chemical procelain, industrial ceramics and artware

ceramics; glass ampoules, glass mirrors, clinical thermometers, spectacle lenses, cement and chemical industries; marble chips and marble-powder; soap and calcium silicate, plaster of paris and dolomite bricks and others. The possibility of establishment of glass factory cannot be ruled out.

Horticulture Based Potentialities

The Hill region is gifted with various ecological habitats because of sharp climatic and altitudinal variations. All types of temperate, tropical and sub-tropical forests and vegetables can be grown successfully. The region is suitable for the growth of mushrooms, asparagus, saffron, spices, ginger, turmeric; ornamental shrubs and flower plants; bulbs and tubers etc. Potentialities for setting up fruit-processing, rice-milling, rice-bran manufacturing, cattle and poultry-feed manufacturing can also be explored.

Miscellaneous Industries

Industries like dairy farming, wooden manufacturing and manufacturing of footwear, leather goods, rubber toys and articles, have ample scope for development. Besides, service-based industries like automobile repairing plant, can-making, cold storage plant, jobbing workshops, medicine manufacturing would automatically be induced.

Presently, region possesses neither the medium scale nor the large-scale industries of any significance. So is the case with cottage and household industries. However, with the governmental efforts, some industrial units have been established. others are coming up and proposals for a few others are mooted. Nevertheless, industrial development in the Hill region is handicapped by topographical and geo-physical constraints, inadequate transport, power, finance and other infrastructural facilities; and human, social and political impediments. Dearth of properly-trained and motivated people at entrepreneurial, managerial and technical levels has increasingly been felt.

Tourist Potentialities

Nature has bestowed on the region all kinds of tourist attractions: religious shrines and glittering snow-clad mountains; perpetual rivers and lofty mountains; attractive springs and rhythmic waterfalls; beautiful lakes and natural passes; magnificent landscape and picturesque forests; deep gorges and snowy glaciers; flourishing fields and salubrious climate; valleys of flowers[15] and wonderful **bugyals** and **payars**[16] and a multitude of fauna and flora. The region has been called **Tapobhumi** or **Devbhumi** - land of sages - for abounding in invaluable spiritual treasures. It is a land of Panchbadri[17], Panchkedar[18] and Panchprayag[19]; and of Gangotri and Yamnotri. It has been the sacred place for performance of religious yagnas and rites. Thousands of temples, big and small of different sects bear testimony to these facts and provide tourist attractions of great potentials. The need is strongly felt to develop the industry by removing the existing bottlenecks inhibiting its development.

INFRASTRUCTURE

Although the Hill region is a strategic one yet it lacks in basic infrastructure and other services and amenities such as roads, educational facilities, power, medical and other health facilities.

Roads

Motorable roads constitute about 35 per cent of the total length of roads, the rest being the bridle roads maintained by the Public Works Department, Forest Department and District Boards. The road construction drive is making headway in the region but there is a still a high proportion of villages which are more than 5 kilometres from the pucca roads.

Education

The educational facilities are also meagre. The educational institutions at primary, secondary and university levels are low in relation to population. Their number has since increased. In terms of institutions of higher learning, the region had only 22 degree/post-graduate colleges. Over 75 per cent of the colleges are arts and science colleges. Pantnagar Agricultural University, Rudrapur confines its activities mainly to the plains area. The setting up of Kumaon and Garhwal Universities has led to an impetus to the educational development programme in recent years.

Power

Despite vast hydro-electric potentials, Hill region is the least electrified region of U.P. as out of 15,000 villages only 15 per cent of them were electrified by 1975-76. The per capita consumption of energy is not only low but also varied widely among different uses. The proposed Tehri Dam and other hydro-electric projects are likely to boost up the power-generation programme.

Medical and Health Facilities

In the Hill region, medical facilities in terms of population facility ratio are relatively greater as compared with other regions of U.P. Considering the hilly terrain, mountainous topography and its inaccessibility conditions even the existing facilities seem to be quite meagre. This is quite clear from the fact that the number of hospitals and dispensaries per lakh of population was only 8.95 in 1976-77 in the Hill region and varied very little among the districts. Similarly, the variations in respect of the number of beds per lakh of population were only 121.35 and ranged widely between 63.64 in Uttarkashi to 212.06 in Dehradun district. The percentage of total which were more than 5 kilometres from the allopathic hospitals/dispensaries was very high (83 per cent) in the region.

SOCIO-CULTURAL DIMENSIONS

The socio-cultural dimensions place the Hill region relatively on a distinct footing. The existing class structure, caste hierarchy, the family system and structure, religion, customs, traditions, language, dialects, the folk lores, the folk dances and other characteristics are all harmoniously blended into a distinctive socio-cultural pattern and depict man-environment relationships. Deeply engrained into these socio-cultural institutions, they reflect the cultural cadres in terms of values, motivations, incentives and attitudes and are mutually so entwined and interrelated as to form an intricate process. Besides, the Hill region is also featured by nomadism, semi-nomadism and special tribal culture. Gujjars as the nomadic herdsmen are both settled agriculturists and seasonal nomads. Their settlements are mainly confined to the plains regions. Their entire way of life and social structure is attuned and harmonised to nomadism. The graziers of Dudhatoli[20] in Pauri Garhwal district lead a semi-nomadic life and have evolved a system locally called "Kharak System" to keep their herds of cattle intact and feed them properly during their summer migratory system. Bhotiyas, Boxas, Jaunsaris, Bagis and Tharus are the five scheduled tribes recognised in the Hill region. Bhotiyas are the semi-nomadic and culturally distinct tribals of high altitudes (over 3,000 metres) of the border districts of Pithoragarh, Chamoli and Uttarkashi. While both Boxas and Tharus are the tribals of the plains of Nainital and Tarai-Bhaber, the Jaunsaris and Bagis are those of Jaunsar Bawar in Dehradun district. No other tribal culture has aroused so much keen academic interest as those of the Jaunsar Bawar for its system of polyandry. Each of these features in area specific within the Hill region.

The foregoing spatial profile of the region's economy and analysis of intra-regional variations in terms of physical and resource structure; demographic and settlement structure; land-use and cropping patterns; industrial and tourist potentials; infrastructure and other services and facilities and socio-cultural dimensions strongly indicate that the Hill region in itself possesses a unique personality for the purposes of regional development planning. Deeply entrenched in its historical antecedents, religious background, political and socio-cultural institutions, it has evolved through centuries an identity of its own. The various characteristic features as portrayed in the preceding pages vividly reflect its entity. The complexities, diversities and variations in respect of physiography, geology, climate and soils are distinctly marked throughout the region. Its resource structure highlights the existence of considerable water, minerals and forest potentials. They are fairly distributed in space and await prospective exploitation. Among these, the forest resource, rich and variable both in quality and quantity, forms the backbone of the region on account of its substantial contribution towards income, output and employment in addition to a host of other direct and indirect contributions. The demographic structure shows that the region is characterised by small-sized settlements and low growth rates of population, large proportion of rural population with little urbanisation, low density of population, imbalanced sex ratios, high levels of literacy and work participation rate. The settlement structure reveals that most of the settlements are dispersed, small in size and vary considerably with little interactions among them. Occupationally, most of the workers are engaged in agriculture and its allied activities. Cultivators form the major segment of the workers in primary sector. There is a general lack of secondary and tertiary activities. The nature and type of cultivation differs significantly from those of the plains due to wide differentiations in physical and other features. Agriculture is pursued mainly for the production of food crops and very little proportion of land is devoted to non-food crops. The levels of productivity and yield rates are low. On account of working of these negative factors, most of the hilly portion of the Hill region is deficit in foodgrains production and requires regular reinforcements of food supply from outside. This has created the phenomena of outmigration of working population, dependency of region on outside incomes and inflow of moneyorder remittances. In addition to these, the region's resource inventory shows that considerable industrial and tourist potentials derived from its forests, livestock, agriculture, horticulture, minerals and others await exploitation. Similarly, the region awfully lags behind in respect of the development of infrastructure and other services and amenities.

The road construction programme is yet to make headway. Although literacy levels are high yet the level of educational infrastructure is poor. Power, an important component of infrastructure is little developed and hence the per capita consumption of electricity for various purposes is low. There is also a general lack of medical and other health facilities in the region. The socio-cultural dimensions reflect its distinctive character of unity in diversity. All these characteristics present only a bird's eye view of the region. An indepth study of the district, therefore, finds its place in the subsequent Chapters.

II

In this part, Pauri Garhwal district, the study area, has been introduced in relation to the Hill region and U.P. Its salient features are portrayed to the extent they have a bearing on the development problems of the region.

STUDY AREA

Pauri Garhwal district[21] as a part of the Hill region of Uttar Pradesh has been chosen as a unit of study. In regional scale of analysis appropriate to the Indian situation, the study area is comparable to a micro-region.

"Pauri Garhwal" or "British Garhwal" as a separate district came into existence in 1840 and since then it remained (1815-1960 A.D.) under the administrative control of the Commissioner of Kumaon. Its peripheral situation was perpetuated from the beginning. Pauri Garhwal of the historical past included parts of all the existing seven districts of Dehradun, Saharanpur, Tehri, Uttarkashi, Bijnor, Pauri and Chamoli. In the west, the boundary extended even beyond Dehradun district. The princely states of Thyog, Madhan, Ghoond[22], Rawaingarh portion of Jubbul[23], Ranigarh and its adjoining areas[24], all of which, now form parts of the Himachal Pradesh, were included in Garhwal. In the south, even the portions of Afzalgarh and Najibabad lay in this hill territory. The district lies almost entirely within the Himalayan mountain system. It was one of the largest districts of Uttar Pradesh until one of its sub-division (Chamoli) became a separate border district in 1960.

The Pauri Garhwal district is situated between 29°.10'N. and 30°.15'N. latitudes and 78°.10'E. and 79°.10'E. longitudes. It is bounded by district Chamoli to the north; by district Bijnor to the south; by the districts of Almora and Nainital to the east (the latter only for a short distance near the foot hills) while its north-western boundary is formed by the river Ganga as far as Deoprayag and by the Alaknanda as far as Rudraprayag. The river Ganga separates it from the districts of Dehradun and Tehri Garhwal. The eastern boundary is throughout irregular. The boundary of Tehri Garhwal district coincides with that of the villages assigned to Tehri in 1815. In the south, Kandi road between Garhwal and Bijnor districts linking Ramnagar with Hardwar is the accepted boundary since 1842.

The district has a total geographical area of 5,455 km.[2] and a population of 553,028 according to Census of 1971 dwelling in 3,236 rural settlements and 6 towns (Pauri, Srinagar, Bah Bazar, Kotdwara, Lansdowne and Dogadda). For administrative purposes and planning, the district is divided into 2 tahsils and 14 development blocks. The tahsils are sub-divided into 16 Kanungo circles and 169 Patwari circles for purposes of revenue collection.

The district covers 10.6 per cent of the geographical area and 14.5 per cent of the population of the Hill region of Uttar Pradesh. Further, the district has 15.7 per cent of the working population; 21.5 per cent of the settlements; 13.3 per cent of the forested lands and 14.0 per cent of the cultivated area of the total of the Hill region.

Physical Setting

The district, as could be expected of a Hill region, has a complex physiography and diversified relief features. It consists of a succession of deep gorges, steep hillsides, sharp and irregular ridges and rugged terrain. Its mountain system can best be regarded as a series of spurs from the Tibetan watershed. It has been well-drained by numerous rivers and rivulets, distributed fairly and evenly along northern and southern mountain ranges. Wide variations in rainfall and temperature cause microclimatic conditions. Soils are highly diverisfied and vary from valley to valley according to different ecological conditions.

Resource Potentialities

The district is endowed with considerable potentialities of forest, water, mineral resources awaiting estimation and exploitation. Rainfall, temperature, soil, topography, altitude all have collectively influenced the vegetal cover and type of natural vegetation. Because of high altitudinal range there is vertical zonation of landuse. The forest wealth, rich in quality and abundant in quantity, has annually been accruing to the

State Exchequer a sizeable revenue without much **quid pro quo** to the region. The future course of regional development and specialisation hinges on the utilisation of the potentials of horticulture, livestock, grassland and tourism. To this, the district's natural setting and the location of historical and religious places are bound to play an increasingly important role in the region's economy.

Demographic features

The district under study is characterised by low density of population and low growth rate; progressively increasing literacy rates; sprinkled settlements; high imbalances in sex ratio with a dominance of female population and resultant high female work participation rates and dominance of cultivators, particularly female cultivators. A comparative picture of these is given in Table 2.6.

TABLE 2.6

Salient features of Pauri Garhwal district in relation to Hill region and Uttar Pradesh

S.No.	Characteristics	U.P.	Hill Region	Pauri Garhwal District
1	2	3	4	5
1.	Total Population (in Lakhs) - 1971	883.41	38.21	5.53
2.	Population Growth, decade variation (1961-71)	19.82	21.67	14.65
3.	Population density ($km.^2$)	300	75	102
4.	Urban Population to the total population (1971) %	7.10	14.68	6.30
5.	Rural population in settlements above 500 persons to the total rural population (1971) %	87.90	32.29	16.29
6.	Rural Settlements above 500 population to total number of rural settlements (1971) %	44.70	8.41	3.02
7.	Average population per inhabited settlement (1971)	784	217	171
8.	Scheduled Caste population to the total population (1971) %	21.00	16.05	10.57
9.	Scheduled Tribe population to the total population (1971) %	0.20	3.68	0.10

Table 2.6 (contd.)

1	2	3	4	5
10.	Literates to the total population (1971) %	21.64	31.02	31.53
11.	Male literates to total male population (1971) %	31.76	45.58	50.02
12.	Female literates to the total female population (1971) %	10.70	15.96	15.84
13.	Sex ratio (females per 1,000 males) (1971)	879	966	1,118
14.	Rural Sex ratio (females per 1,000 males) (1971)	889	1,016	1,160
15.	Urban Sex ratio (females per 1,000 males) (1971)	821	719	642
16.	Total workers (in lakhs) (1971)	273.34	16.02	2.51
17.	Workers to the total population (1971) %	30.90	41.93	45.40
18.	Total male workers to the total male population (1971) %	52.20	52.29	47.64
19.	Female workers to the total female population (1971) %	6.70	31.22	43.40

The Settlement Pattern

The physical environment, rugged terrain and inaccessibility account for the occurrence of relatively isolated clusters of settlements in the district. The settlements are widely scattered, small in size and sparsely populated and have a distinct cultural pattern. They are self-contained, endogamous and are internally homogeneous in the absence of interaction with the distant settlements. There is little interaction between the plains and hilly areas. The impact is confined to areas accessible to the main highways. The man-environment relationship is highly localised and is reflected in a variety of ways, such as attitudes, faiths, beliefs, customs, traditions, religion, culture, the ways of life and the values of the people.

Agriculture

In its broad land-use and cropping pattern, the study area shows marked influence of the physical landscape carved out from the interaction of geological structure, landforms, soils and climate. Table 2.6 shows that the economy is basically a subsistence type of economy with agriculture as the mainstay. It is characterised by limited agricultural land potential, scarcity of cultivated land, dominance of dry farming and low proportions covered by irrigation facilities. Irrigation in mountain terrain is an engineering feat of considerable complexity and is carried on by the indigenous system. The levels of agricultural productivity and incomes are cumulatively depressed by the preponderance of small holdings; their fragmentation and sub-division; by the prevalence of a terrace-farming system, prohibitive both in time and energy; by the scattered fields and extensive cultivation and by the pressure of population on land together with high levels of underemployment and unemployment. The problem of low per capita availability of land is compounded further by constantly accelerated soil erosion, primitive and unsophisticated techniques and lack of knowledge and skills of scientific agriculture.

TABLE 2.7
Salient characteristics of the agricultural structure

S.No.	Characteristics	U.P.	Hill Region	Pauri Garhwal District
1.	Total geographical area (km^2)	2,93,413	51,000	5,400
2.	Area under forests to the total geographical area (1969-70) %	16.55	59.00	62.00
3.	Net area irrigated to net area sown (1970-71) %	40.30	21.50	5.10
4.	Gross area irrigated to gross area sown (1970-71) %	35.60	21.70	6.40
5.	Cropping Intensity (1976-77)	133.30	157.10	163.80
6.	Value of gross agricultural production per net hectare sown (in '000 Rs.) (1974-75)	2.80	3.84	4.00

The land-use pattern is distinct and reflects various agronomic, cultural practices and traditional crop system such as mixed and multiple cropping. The crop rotation system has remained unchanged for centuries. Over 90 per cent of the agricultural land is devoted to the production of food crops. Intensive cultivation through irrigation is very insignificant. Soils are varied and characterised by the presence of stones, comparative dryness and poorness. Intensification of cultivation by the application of inputs such as fertilizers and pesticides, is not possible on account of intense soil erosion due to steep gradients and monsoonal downpours.

The institutional factors such as the nature of tenancy, the size of operational holdings, the area under operational holdings are also responsible for determining the levels of productivity in agriculture. As would be revealed from Table 2.8 small holdings predominate. The incidence of tenancy is closely associated with the small-holding cultivation.

TABLE 2.8
Institutional Characteristics

S.No.	Characteristics	U.P.	Hill Region	Pauri Garhwal District
1.	Net area sown to the total area under operational holdings (1970-71) %	92.80	92.70	89.90
2.	Number of holdings below 0.50 hectare to the total holdings (1970-71) %	27.90	39.10	36.10
3.	Area under operational holdings below 0.50 hectare to the total area under operation holdings (1970-71) %	8.70	9.60	11.10
4.	Cultivators to the total workers (1971) %	57.40	72.20	78.00
5.	Agricultural labourers to the total workers (1971) %	11.30	4.11	1.30

The agricultural infrastructure is poorly developed. There is absence of a good network of credit institutions. The existing co-operative banks and co-operative societies cater to the needs of a few. Non-availability of credit, untimely credit, unreasonable rates of interest are the general features. Besides, there is an absence of agencies supplying fertilizers, pesticides, seeds, implements and others. The lack of good marketing, storing and warehousing facilities, throws light on the unorganised marketing system.

Industries

Industrially, the district is very backward. There is not a single intermediate or large scale industry; nor is one planned for the area in the near future. Cottage industries, once prosperous have dwindled by competition. The prevailing social values and institutions immensely inhibit the industrial climate, the entrepreneurship and its constituent ingredients - the capacity and willingness to undertake risks and innovate. Managerial skills are extremely scarce. However, the district has ample scope for developing a large number of agro-based, forest-based, fruit-based, wool-based and livestock-based industries, capable of producing output of substantial value and generating employment to a sizeable extent.

Infrastructure

The district, under study, lacks the basic infrastructural conditions and other services and amenities. It would be observed from Table 2.9 that the district stands favourably better in terms of availability of educational facilities and the level of literacy. However, considering the norms of the Hill region, the existing facilities for transportation and communication; hygiene and health; trade and commerce; and education and power are inadequate. Means of communication are mainly bridle roads, common in the hilly terrain, but for the few main roads that establish links with the plains. These existing highways are also underutilised. The educational facilities are also meagre and lack quality, quantity and spatial distribution. The educational profile of the entire district is so low that there is hardly any local infrastructure, save for relatively high literacy rates, to disseminate the knowledge of scientific materials, which would aid the formulation of a regional plan. The available literature abounds in travel and ethnographic notes. There are not even a few good socio-economic surveys relating to the region.

SOCIO-CULTURAL DIMENSIONS

The area under study is socially stratified into a caste hierarchy of crucial importance. Traditionally, as pointed out earlier, it is divided into two heterogenous groups - the **Bith** and the **Doms**. The **Biths** are divided into Brahmins and Kshatriyas, each in turn is divided internally into **Asal** (Immigrants) and **Khasi** (indigenous). Among Brahmins, for instance **Sarolas** and **Gangaris** are considered to be the **Asal** and **Nanagotri** the **Khasis**. Each of these Brahmins, Kshatriyas and Doms have sprouted out into a number of branches and sub-branches culminating in a caste galaxy.[25] Most of these sub-castes are named after their original settlements such as Dobhal from Dobh, Dangwal from Dang, Nautiyal from Nauti, and Bughana (Bahuguna) from Bughani and so on.[26] Further, the caste hierarchy and caste status differences are actively enforced. The ties of kinship, caste and community are crucial.

TABLE 2.9
Salient features of infrastructure of Pauri Garhwal district in relation to the Hill region and Uttar Pradesh

S.No.	Characteristics	U.P.	Hill Region	Pauri Garhwal District
1	2	3	4	5
1.	Number of villages electrified to the total number (1976-77) %	26.60	14.28	9.14
2.	Length of metalled road per 1,000 km^2 of area (1976-77) (kms)	126.3	64.79	87.32
3.	Literacy rate (1971) %	21.70	31.00	32.00
4.	Number of Junior Basic Schools per lakh of population (1977)	71.40	142.0	178.8
5.	Number of High/Higher Secondary Schools per lakh of population (1977)	4.8	12.2	13.3
6.	Number of Hospitals/dispensaries (allopathic) per lakh of population (1976-77)	2.85	8.95	8.68
7.	Number of beds in hospitals/dispensaries per lakh of population (1976-77)	49.84	121.53	99.67

Variability, viability and internal consistency are the three significant socio-cultural characteristics of the district under study. Family system and family organisation; religion and rituals; customs and traditions; language and dialects; fairs and festivals; folklore and folk dances; habits and the ways of life; dresses and ornamentation; the values and the material culture and others, all manifest a distinctive and unique character of the area.

The character and the racial qualities of the people of the region, such as courage, patriotism, steadfast loyalty, military valour and others are well documented by Traill[27], Ramsay, Atkinson, Walton[28], Jim Corbett, Joshi[29], Pate Ram[30] who knew them well in depth. Their military exploits, in modern times are enshrined in the records of 39th Garhwal Rifles, Lansdowne.[31]

PRESENT TRENDS

The low levels of income, output, investment and employment;

increasing pressure of population; low productivity and dominance of primary sector without corresponding development of tertiary and secondary sectors have converted the study area into a "food-scarcity-prone" area.[32] Its dependency for commodities and services on outside regions has increased considerably during recent years. Inaccessibility hampers functional interactions among people; both within the district and outside the district, keeping thereby the area isolated from the main streams of modernisation. The intra-regional and inter-regional economic and social disparities have increased. The trickling down effects of the so called planned development have not percolated at the grass-root levels. Instead, the backwash effects in terms of outflow of resources - human, natural and financial are tangible and have great implications for posterity. There has also been erosion of moral fibres and cultural values; disturbance of the social fabric and economic exploitation in terms of human and economic resources of the people. In addition, outmigration of the workers has become the characteristic feature of the region and is gaining momentum. This is reflected through increasing imbalance in sex-ratio and high proportions of female cultivators to male cultivators. As a consequence of out-migration, there has been an increasing dependency of the study area on money flow from migrants working outside the region mainly in big cities and towns. Money flow is chiefly by way of moneyorder remittances amounting to Rs. 34 lakhs per month, distributed through 37,000 moneyorders and increasing at the rate of 8.59 per cent per annum. These have significant socio-economic implications.

It is against this background that the present study seeks to highlight the seminal aspects of the regional structure, economy, problems and possibilities of the future pattern of regional development, in conformity with the ecology of the Hill region. The contribution of this area in the regional, national and world culture and growth is yet to be realised by pulling it out from physical preponderance, political neglect, social stagnation and economic backwardness.

NOTES AND REFERENCES

1. It was famous by the name of "Brahmvrat" (Brahmadesh or Brahmashridesh) in ancient times; "Panchaldesh" in Mahabharat times; "Kedarkhand" in Puranic literature; and "Himvant" in Pali literature. Being the holiest part of the country, it is being referred to as "Devbhumi" or "Tapobhumi". Geographers call it "U.P. Himalayas" or "Garhkhum Himalayas" or "Western Himalayas".
2. The descendants of Panwar dynasty who ruled the State

since 1815 were: Sudarshan Shah (1815-1859 A.D.); Bhawani Shah (1859-1871 A.D.); Pratapshah (1871-1886 A.D.); Kirti Shah (1887-1913 A.D.); Narendra Shah (1913-1946 A.D.); and Manvendra Shah (1946-1949 A.D.). For details refer S.P. Dabral: **Uttarkhand Ka Itihas** (in Hindi), Vol. VI.

3. For details, refer Chapter 3.
4. Pascoe, E.H.: **A Manual of the Geology of India and Burma**; Calcutta, 1964, Vol. III, p. 2022.
5. Wadia, D.N.: **Geology of India**, 1949, p. 289.
6. National Council of Applied Economic Research: **Techno-Economic Survey of U.P.**, 1955-56, Chapter VI, pp. 90-97.
7. Franz Kollmannsperger: **Hindustan Times**, dated 26.2.1975.
8. Times of India dated 16.10.1975.
9. Sharma, L.C.: **The Forest Industry in U.P.**, p. 164.
10. The Wild Life Preservation Organisation, U.P. was set up in 1956 to protect the fast diminishing wild life, develop and create wild life preserves and give scientific basis to the management of wild life. At present, there are 7 Wild Life Regions and 2 separate Wild Life Wardens, one each for the Corbett National Park and other for the Sanctuaries. The Hill region has 3 out of 7 Wild Life Regions and 7 out of 11 Sanctuaries of U.P. Pauri Garhwal district has one Wild Life Region and 2 Sanctuaries of Malini and Nandadevi.
11. Chipko Movement (hug the tree) was started by the Sarvodaya leaders of Uttarakhand during 1970-72. It aimed at (i) adequate recognition of traditional rights of the indigenous population in respect of utilisation of the forest resources; (ii) inclusion of village forest units ad administrative and organisational units in Gram Panchayats and higher forests units; (iii) stoppage of the existing contractual system of forest exploitation and (iv) a proper afforestation policy in the region. The movement gained some success and changes were brought about in the forest policy of the Hill region.
12. At the aggregative level of international comparisons, the explanation for differences in female work participation rates lie in some broad non-economic factors such as culture. At a less aggregative level of inter-state comparisons in India, it is not possible to see some strong relationship between economic and demographic factors and female participation. The only relationship between sex ratio and female work participation could be found. Refer,

    Leela Gulati: Female Work Participation - A Study of Inter-State Differences; **Economic and Political Weekly**, January 11, 1975.

Narasimha Reddy, D.: Female Work Participation: A Study of Inter-State Differences; **Economic and Political Weekly;** June 7, 1975.

Sinha, J.N.: Female Work Participation: A Comment; **Economic and Political Weekly,** April 19, 1975.

Leela Gulati: Female Work Participation - A Reply; **Economic and Political Weekly,** August 19, 1975.

13. Pant, S.D.: **Social Economy of the Himalayans;** George Allen and Unwin, London, 1935.
14. Board of Revenue, Uttar Pradesh; Agricultural Census of U.P., 1970-71.
15. The best known of such valleys is the famous Bhuynder Valley of Flowers. It is 16 kilometres in length and 2 to 5 kilometres in width and is enclosed from three sides - the east, the west and the north; at an elevation of 4,000 metres, between the Nar and Gandhmadan Parvat, on the north-east direction of Badrinath. The Valley was discovered first in 1931 by Frank S. Smythe, the famous mountaineer and conqueror of Kamet Peak. He revisited the Valley in 1937 and discovered more than 2,000 varieties of flowers, a mention of which is made in his celebrated book "The Valley of Flowers".
16. "Bugyals" and "Payars" are the natural summer pastures of the mountain shepherds and graziers - the Bhotiyas. At lower elevations, generally upto 4,000 metres, these are locally called "Bugyals" and those beyond "Payars". During the winters, these pastures lie under snow but towards the end of March when snow begins to melt, they are covered with verdure and support a thick carpet of grass and herbage. This grass and herbage is found to be peculiarly nutritious to sheep and a few days grazing on it restores their chilled and famished bodies to their normal condition. It is here that the highest Himalayan habitations are found.
17. Panchbadri: Badrinath, Yogbadri, Dhyanbadri, Bridhbadri and Adbadri.
18. Panchkedar: Kedarnath, Rudranath, Tunganath, Madh-Mahleshwar and Kalpeshwar.
19. Panchprayag: Deoprayag, Rudraprayag, Karnprayag, Nandprayag and Vishnuprayag.
20. Dudhatoli lying at an elevation of over 2,500 metres, is the biggest and the richest grazing area. It is spread over an area of 2,300 square kilometres and accommodates grazing facilities for more than 50,000 heads of cattle at a time. It offers plenty of grasslands growing the small but juicy grasses of "Dudha" and "Toli" in the reserved forests of Khirsu, Dhanpur, Ranigarh, Nalgaon, Pinderwar, Kamolidhar, Khankherkhet, Chhorkhal,

Jakhmolidhar and Santudhar.

21. There has not been any unanimity of opinion either with regard to the origin of the word "Garhwal" or with the period of its nomenclature. Walton believed that it might mean a country of "gadh" - a "gadh" being the local name for a glen - meaning a narrow valley. This conveys the idea of a rugged terrain typical of Garhwal area of Uttar Pradesh. The most prevalent belief is, however, that the name "Garhwal" was a "Bawani" occupied by 52 chiefs each with his own fort. When Ajaypal, the 37th King in the descent of Panwar dynasty, conquered all the 52 forts of the Kedarkhand and became sovereign, the name Garhwal was adopted. This was around 1500 A.D.
22. Dabral, S.P.: **Uttarakhand Ka Itihas** (in Hindi), Veergatha Publications, Dogadda, Garhwal, 1964, Vol. II, p. 27.
23. ibid
24. Raturi, H.K.: **Garhwal Ka Itihas** (in Hindi), Garhwali Press, Dehradun, 1928, p.2.
25. There were 127 Brahmin sub-castes, 124 Kshatriya sub-castes and 27 Dom sub-castes, in the study area in 1950-51 (For details refer Barthwal, Mahidhar Sharma, **Garhwal Mein kaun Kahan,** Naya Hindustan Press, New Delhi, 1951, pp. 32-48. Presently, the number of castes exceeds these.
26. Sarola Brahmin, for instance, spread out from their 12 original settlements viz., Nauti, Maitwana, Khandura, Ratura, Thapli, Chamola, Sema, Lakheri, Samelta, Gairoli, Koti and Dimmar.
27. "The total absence of theft and extreme morality of the people in this province renders any provisions in regard to police unnecessary." - Traill, G.W.: **Statistical Sketch of Kumaon** (1851) quoted in Pate Ram: **Garhwal - Ancient and Modern,** 1937, p. 126.
28. "Their honesty is beyond question. A verbal bargain is seldom repudiated and theft is almost unknown" - Walton, H.G.: **British Garhwal - A Gazetteer, Vol. XXXVI of the District Gazetteer of U.P., Agra and Oudh,** 1911, p. 68.
29. "In dealings they are honest and trustworthy, in pecuniary transaction with one another, the villagers have no recourse to the written engagements." - Pate Ram: op. cit. p. 126.
30. "There was scarcely a more peaceable or honest race in the world" - Joshi, L.D. : **Khas Family Law in the Himalayan Districts of the United Provinces of India,** 1929, p. 23.
31. "Wherever they have been tried they have shown themselves almost equal to Europeans in bravery, and in every other quality of a soldier, may certainly challenge any

position of a native army; for each of these simple mountaineers has hidden away within his inner consciousness that little spark, perhaps dulled by disuse or oppression, which presents the fiercely burning flame of military ardour that burnt in the breast of some old ancestor." - **Historical Records of 39th Garhwal Rifles,** quoted in Joshi, L.D., op.cit. p. 24.

32. In 1825, when the population was small and the cultivated area per head was large, grain was exported to Rohilknand from the southern parganas of the district. Refer. Dhoundiyal, S.P.: **The Economic Life of Garhwal,** An unpublished Ph.D. Thesis, Agra University, Agra, 1945.

THREE

The Resource Base—Physical & Human

In regional studies, an understanding of the different elements that influence the personality of the region, is important. These elements act collectively and the dominant elements generally form a basis of differentiations of the physiographic units. Therefore, in this part of the study, an account of different physiographic elements and their characteristics and distributional patterns is given first, followed by an analysis of resource and settlement structures and finally the different aspects of human resources are presented.

Geological Structure

U.P. Himalayas, despite numerous geological studies[1] is dotted with unsolved problems and remains as one of the most inspiring places for geology on our globe.[2] Auden[3] discussing the tectonic divisions of Garhwal Himalayas, pointed out that Nummulitics are present above Tal series in the outlines of Garhwal Nappes. Upon the Nummulitics and Tal series lies the schistose series which are older. The inner schistose series is composed of two main groups - (i) schistose phyllites, slates, schistose and quartzites; and (ii) banded grey-green slates and mainly purple quartzites.

The rock types in the district differ areally. Overlying the Nummulitics, occur two separate Nappes which are disposed in synclines that are separated for some distance by the anticlinal axis running from just east of Laxmanjhula in the south-east direction, past Jogyana, along the Huinl river. In the Western Amri syncline, the rocks are characteristically green, schistose phyllites with subordinate white schistose quartzites. In the Eastern Bijni syncline, the dominant rocks are purple, green and white quartzites with underlying and subordinate banded green slates. Intruded in these rocks occurs the gneissic granite of Lansdowne. The rock types of the inner schistose series are similar to those underlying the krol series along the Nayar river both in lithology and strike. Underlying the krols from Byasghat to Banghat occur simla-slates with strike varying E.-W. to N.N.E - S.S.W.

Auden observed that the Dudhatoli-Dwarhat-Ranikhet-Almora region represents a syncline or group of synclines which may be the outliers of the Garhwal Nappes. Earlier, however, Middlemiss described a syncline of schists and quartzites intruded by gneissic granite of Dudhatoli. He pointed out that (i) there is an exact similarity between the gneissic granites of Dudhatoli and those of Lansdowne; (ii) it is the only syncline of importance along a line from the plains to the main series; (iii) the abrupt fault-contact of the granite and schistose series of Dudhatoli with the massive limestones is to the east;[4] (iv) the schistose series occurs in the form of syncline with dips inwards towards Dudhatoli, while the rocks surrounding the series, dip away from the mountain; (v) massive limestones outcrop from Manwadevi to Ganpurgarh and have been mineralised; and (vi) overlying the limestones with unconformity, there is a series of acid volcanic rocks which are themselves further to the northwest of basic lavas.

On the south, the Sub-himalayan zone viz., the Siwalik and Bhaber belt of low forest-covered hills, shallow valleys and duns,-displays a great sequence of fresh water deposits of upper tertiary age, aggregating 5,100 metres in thickness and composed in ascending order of lower Siwalik with subordinate shales, middle Siwalik with sand-rock and upper Siwalik with conglomerates.

PHYSIOGRAPHIC UNITS

On account of diversities and variations in landform characteristics, a distinct demarcation of physiographic characteristics is difficult with the help of available records and maps. Nevertheless, the district can broadly be divided into the following physiographic units (Figure 3).

The Bhaber and its uplands

Bhaber comprises of a narrow stretch of plains between the foothills of Siwalik range and the Terai region. It is 5-10 kilometres wide and 95 kilometres long and extends from the Ramganga in the east to the Ganga in the west, with elevation increasing from 300 metres to 600 metres above mean sea level. The Khoh river divides the region between eastern and western Bhaber, termed as Kalagarh Bhaber and Kotdwara Bhaber respectively. The thin layer of rich alluvial soil formed by the

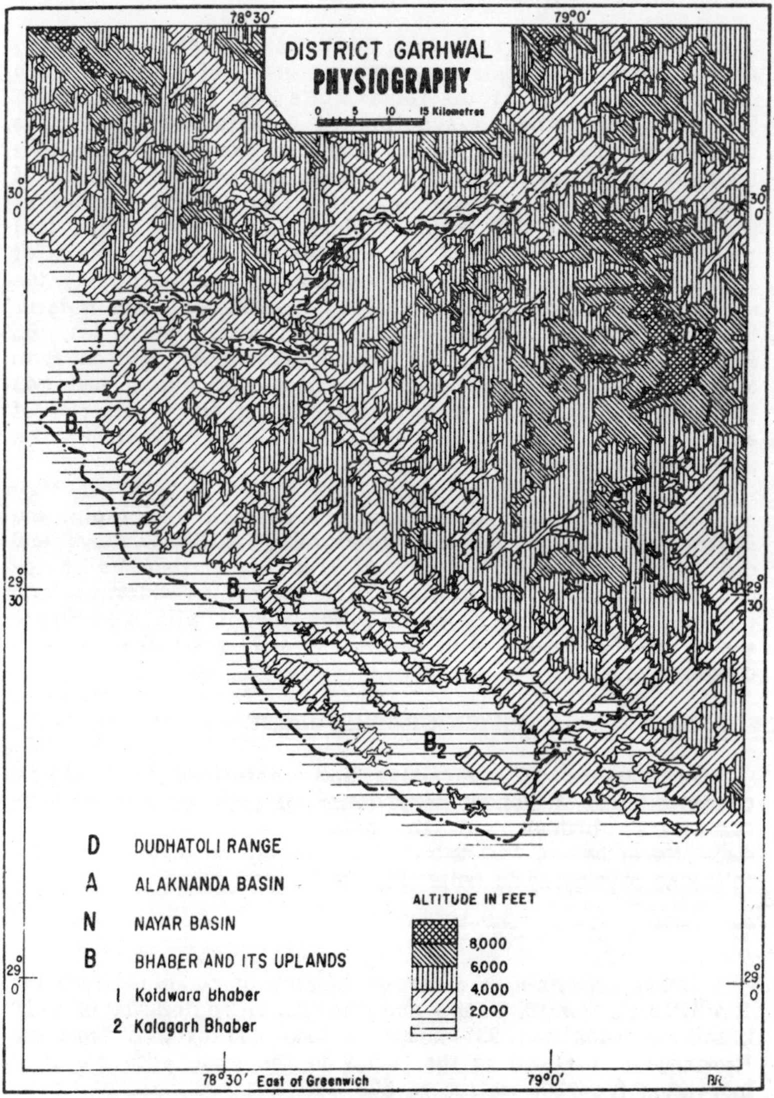
DISTRICT GARHWAL
PHYSIOGRAPHY
0 5 10 15 Kilometres
78°30′
79°0′
30° 0′
29° 30′
29° 0′
B1
N
B2
D DUDHATOLI RANGE
A ALAKNANDA BASIN
N NAYAR BASIN
B BHABER AND ITS UPLANDS
1 Kotdwara Bhaber
2 Kalagarh Bhaber
ALTITUDE IN FEET
8,000
6,000
4,000
2,000
78°30′ East of Greenwich

Fig.3

rivers is suitable for intensive cultivation, specially for paddy and wheat. The uplands ranging between 750 metres to 1,500 metres above mean sea level, are a chain of elongated hill ranges separating the Ganga and its tributaries to the north and Bhaber to the south. Dry farming along terraced slopes is a common feature reflecting land-use adaptation to surface forms of relief.

The Nayar Basin

Nayar is a small tributary of the Ganga consisting of the two branches, the Western and the Eastern, both rising from Dudhatoli range. Both the Nayars have cut the great plateau and have separated the southern spur of the smaller Himalayas from the rest of the Sub-himalayan range. A major part of the district is comprised of the Nayar basin consisting of a chain of hill ranges and the valleys. The hill ranges are characterised by a series of gigantic terraces, their heights generally range between 600 metres to 1,800 metres above mean sea level. The valleys, locally known as **gaddies** are carved out by the small, seasonal streams and comprise of narrow flat lands, bordered by a series of terraces. These areas although patchy are good for cultivation, specially for paddy.

Alaknanda Basin

Although Alaknanda is the biggest river of the district and forms the entire northern and north-western boundary of the district, yet its basin comprises of a small portion of the district. Because of the deep gorges through which the river flows and steepness of the hills, the basin is drained mostly by the small rivulets. Dry farming through terraces, with small patches of irrigated cultivation, is the characteristic feature of the area.

Dudhatoli Range

This range lies at an elevation of over 1,800 metres from the mean sea level, between the Siwalik hills in the south and greater Himalayas in the north. Dudhatoli plateau possesses high summit flat land and relatively gentler slopes with rich cover of grass and grazing land amidst forests capable of sustaining over 50,000 cattle-heads of both the study area and of the adjoining parts of Almora district.

THE MOUNTAIN SYSTEM

Dudhatoli is the most massive range in this part of Sub-himalayas. Its ridge divides the waters which find their way to the plains from those which travel to Hardwar. The southern off-shoot of the ridge divides the waters of Ramganga from either. A chain of spurs branches off from this range on all directions. To the east, lie the spurs of Chorkhal and Khankerkhet; and to the west, the Santhukhal spur. The north-western spur rising from Ad-Badri and ending at Deoprayag, separates the Nayar valley from Alaknanda. The south-western spur of Bharsar separates the valleys of the two Nayars. Binsar spur forms the eastern and southern boundary of the Nayar basin. The Khatli spur continues to the west from Almora border to Rikhnikhal and reaches Chamethakhal where it is called Uttain range. It then passes on to Karaunda (**Kitch-ka-danda**) where the ridge is split into two which enclose Huini valley and separate it, on the one hand, from Nayar and Ganga; on the other hand, from the minor streams flowing direct to the plains. The northern branch continues further until it reaches Kota near the Ganga through Gaind, Bijni and Mala. The main Siwalik spur after being cut at Hardwar by the Ganga branches off into two. Its northerly branch passes through Neelkanth, Pokherkhal and thereafter forms the boundary of the soutern valleys of Huinl, Palain and Mandal rivers, reaching finally to Nainital through Lohachaur. The southerly branch of the Siwalik spur enters Chandighat, passes through Kimsar, Debrana, Amola and after being distorted at many places reaches Kalagarh and finally to Nainital.

Drainage Pattern

Most of the Garhwal area is drained by the Alaknanda and its tributaries (Figure 4). Alaknanda, rising from Alakapuri flank of Satopanth glacier and after meeting its major tributaries, passes through Srinagar and reaches Deoprayag joining Bhagirathi from Tehri Garhwal. Thereafter, receiving Nayar river at Byashat and Huinl river at Phulari near Laxmanjhula, it finally enters Hardwar in the plains. A sizeable part of the district is drained by the Nayar, comprising of two branches - the Western or Dewalgarh river and the Eastern or Chandpur river both rising from Dudhatoli plateau. The Western Nayar, after passing through Chipalghat and Musagali reaches the junction at Batkholu, near Satpuli. The Eastern Nayar, flowing in south-westerly direction through Kainur, Thalisain, Baijro, Domaila reaches the junction. Thereafter, the united stream flows for over 26 kilometres in north-westerly direction to the Ganga at Byasghat. Ramganga and its small tributaries, Mandal and Palain drain the south-eastern part of the district. Ramganga, rising from the Dudhatoli range and flowing in south-easterly direction into Almora, enters Garhwal district in the extreme south and debouches on the plains of Kalagarh. The western part of the district is drained by the Huinl river. Bhaber is drained by Khoh, Malini and Rawasan rivulets. Khoh is the chief of them and is formed of two streams - Langoorgad and Siligad. These rivulets are very small, their volume inconsiderable and their waters lose themselves in sands and shingles after reaching the boulder beds of Bhaber.

Soils

The soils of the district, highly diversified and widely varied, presents an extremely mosaic pattern according to different ecological conditions. It has remained an unsurveyed area constraining thereby the classification of soils. Nevertheless, based upon the attempts made by Negi[5], Dabral[6] and others, the following broad categories of soils emerge. All along the river valleys and in patches throughout the district, alluvial soils are scattered. They are whitish-yellowish-brown, argillaceous and loamy. The clayey soils, rich in silica, aluminium and iron are highly productive, especially for paddy and wheat cultivation. Grey soils, containing large quantity of lime are porous in nature. They are usually adapted for producing pulses. In areas of broad-leaved forests on steep slopes, black soils are found. They are thick, acidic and dark brown in colour and possess a mixture of minerals and high moisture holding capacity. Such soils are fit for potato cultivation. Red-brown soils, extensive in coverage are adapted for the production of diverse crops. They are characterised by high fertility and retentivity of moisture, adequacy of nitrogen and potassium. Lastly, red-soils containing sand, silt and clay, have little or no agricultural value and offer scope for grazing. They are very shallow and marked by rock-out-crop.

Climate

In general, the climatic conditions range from tropical heat to the severe cold of alpine zone. However, micro-climatic conditions dominate due to complicated relief features. The average annual rainfall is 145 centimetres[7] and is characterised by early breaks, showers of local origin accompanied by northerly and westerly winds. The climatic conditions of the Bhaber approximate to those of the sub-mountain districts. There is plenty of rainfall. Temperature varies between 75°F. to 85°F. In the river valleys, the temperature varies between 80°F. to 100°F. During the winters, the valleys are usually shrouded in heavy mist during the night and early forenoon and are followed by severe cold in the evenings and nights. The monsoon rainfall is relatively low as compared to those of the high hills, in the

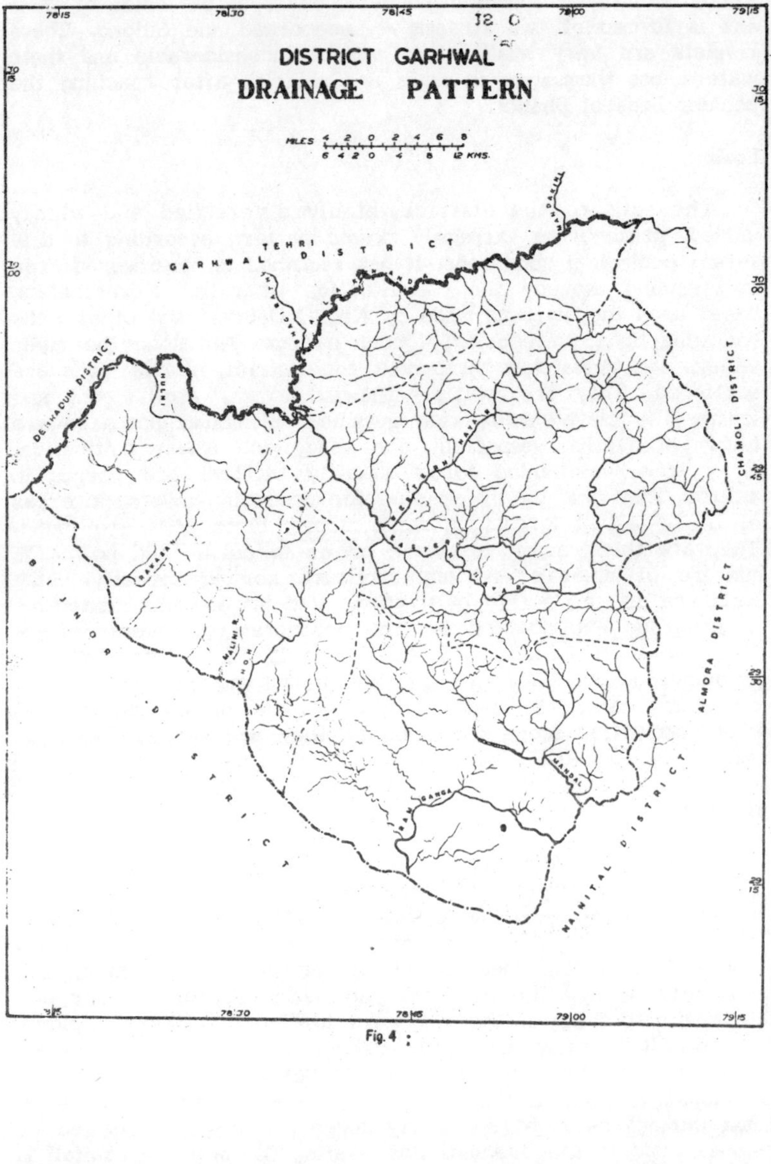
DISTRICT GARHWAL
DRAINAGE PATTERN
MILES 4 2 0 2 4 6 8
6 4 2 0 4 8 12 KMS.
78|15
78|30
78|45
79|00
79|15
TEHRI GARHWAL DISTRICT
DEHRADUN DISTRICT
BIJNOR DISTRICT
CHAMOLI DISTRICT
ALMORA DISTRICT
NAINITAL DISTRICT
MANDAL
RAM GANGA
MALINI R.

Fig. 4

vicinity. In the Mid-himalayan plateau, the mean temperature varies between 50°F. to 70°F. and on the High-himalayan mountains between 30°F. to 38°F.

THE RESOURCE BASE

The structure and the pattern of distribution of physical and human resources provide the spatial framework for the regional studies at different area levels. At the micro-regional scale, an analysis and identification of important topographical units/features would be the basis for the evaluation of land quality, its present use and future capabilities. In this part, therefore, first the natural resources in terms of mineral, water, forest and land resources are being discussed, followed by an analysis of population and settlement structure.

Mineral Resources

The existence of the known minerals and their exploitation in this district has been highlighted by Atkinson,[8] Walton,[9] Sapru,[10] Negi[11] and others.[12] The highly esteemed minerals were iron, copper, lead and gold, the first two richly localised in the Dudhatoli[13] and Dhanpur ranges.

Presently, the known minerals awaiting prospective exploitation (Refer Table 2.1, Chapter 2) are limestone, soapstone, gypsum, dolomite, asbestos, graphite, copper, lead and antimony. Limestone, an important mineral of the area, is almost ubiquitous. It is found in Rishikesh, Manikoth-Neelkanth and in the Lohba-Pinder-Bachhansyun belt. The deposits can be utilised for cement manufacture if the cost of benefication works out to be economical.[14] Substantial deposits of gypsum in Laxmanjhula; copper-ore in Kunet and Dobri and iron-ore from Bharnaun have also been revealed.

Water-Resources

The district is endowed with vast water resource potentialities. The drainage pattern, the run-off of the rivers, the rugged terrain and the sudden change in the levels as between the hills and the plains are the basis for the potential use of water. The hydro-electric potential is distributed fairly, evenly along the northern and soutern mountain ranges. In the north, the Alaknanda and its affluent, the Nayar; and in the south, Ramganga in the east and Huinl river in the west, promise a bright future for the micro-hydel schemes. After the stoppage of the construction of Nayar dam at Marora,[15] near Satpuli in 1948, no sincere effort was made to harness the potentials of either Nayar or of the Alaknanda. The contribution of power-supply from Ramganga Dam at Kalagarh to this district is insignificant. Garhwal-Rishikesh-Chilla power project is the only source of supply of power to it.

Forest Resources

Garhwal district possesses 58 per cent of its total geographical area under forests, out of which 52 per cent is under Reserved Forests and the remaining 6 per cent under Community Forests. Most of the Reserved Forests lie in a broad belt of Bhaber and its uplands stretching from the west to the east and in Dudhatoli range covering the north-eastern part of the district. Considering only the total geographical area reporting for land-utilisation, Community Forests comprise of 14 per cent of the area, distributed throughout the district (Figure 5). The spatial patterns and variations reveal that only 23 patwari circles, lying mostly in Bhaber uplands in the proximity of Reserved Forests, possess over 25 per cent of their respective geographical areas as Community Forests. But along Alaknanda and Nayar valleys, most of the patwari circles (numbering 92) possess less than 5 per cent as Community Forests.

Altitudinal variations in the district have given rise to vertical zonations of the vegetal cover. Such zones can easily be identified. The Sub-tropical zone (below 1,200 metres) consists of a broad belt of Bhaber extending from Ramganga in the east to the Ganga in the west and dots outer ranges of the Himalayas and duns at the foot of the hills. It comprises of the Reserved Forests of Gohri, Laldhang, Kohtri, Palain, Sonanadi, Adnala, Mandal and South Patli Dun ranges. **Sal** (shorea robusta) the most important specie of this zone, is generally found in all valleys specially in Kohtri and Palain ranges. Along the banks of Ramganga and many of the smaller ravines in the forest ranges of Adnala, Mandal, South Patli Dun, **shisham** (Dalbergia sissoo) grows. Bamboos are found in the extensive and accessive forests of Gohri range.

Further north lies the Temperate zone (1,200 - 1,800 metres) containing thickly populated and intensively cultivated areas along the Nayar valley. While **chir** (pinus longifolio) is the dominant tree, other species of importance are **binao** (rhododen dren arborem), **tun** (cedrela toona), **sandan** (enginia dallierglodes), and bhyunl (grewia oppositifolio). The Sub-alpine zone (1,800 - 3,000 metres) covers the vast forests of Dudhatoli range extending over hundreds of square kilometres). The principal trees of this zone are **banj** (querous incaus), **tilonj**

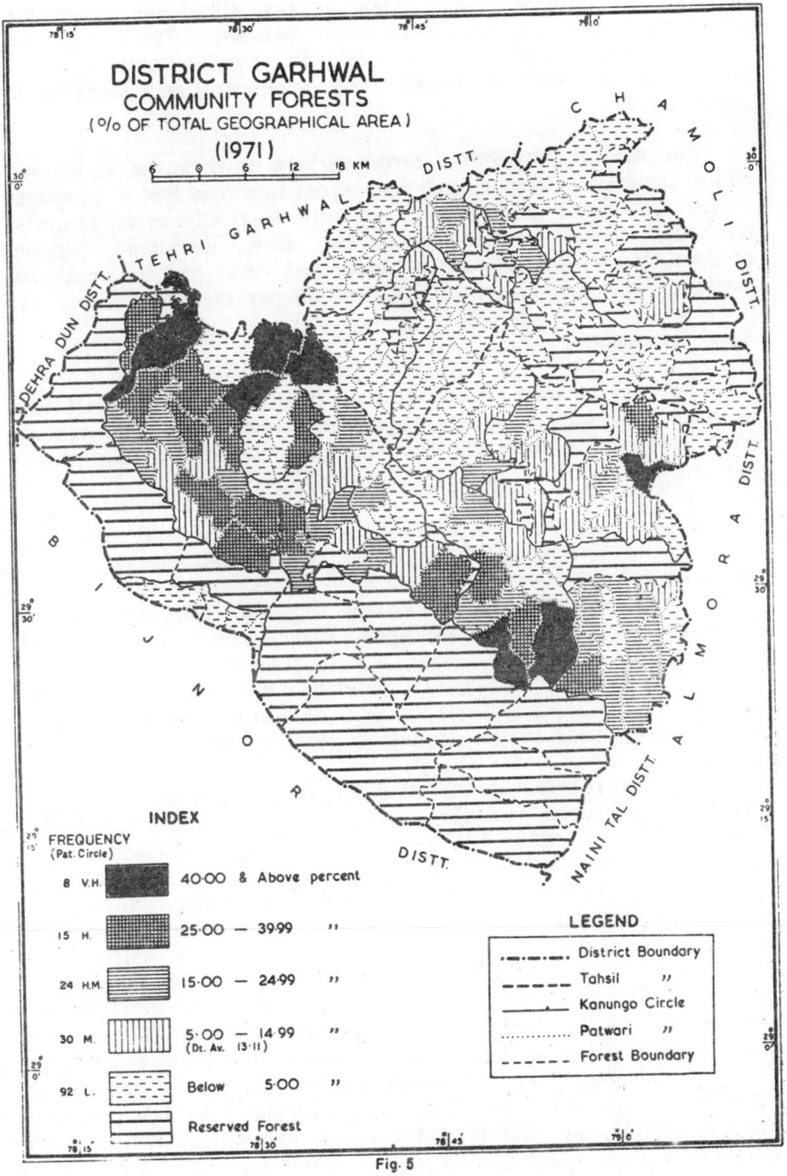

DISTRICT GARHWAL
COMMUNITY FORESTS
(% OF TOTAL GEOGRAPHICAL AREA)
(1971)
6 0 6 12 18 KM
TEHRI GARHWAL DISTT.
CHAMOLI DISTT.
DEHRA DUN DISTT.
BIJNOR DISTT.
ALMORA DISTT.
NAINI TAL DISTT.
INDEX
FREQUENCY
(Pat. Circle)
8 V.H. 40·00 & Above percent
15 H. 25·00 — 39·99 "
24 H.M. 15·00 — 24·99 "
30 M. 5·00 — 14·99 "
(Dt. Av. 13·11)
92 L. Below 5·00 "
Reserved Forest
LEGEND
District Boundary
Tahsil "
Kanungo Circle
Patwari "
Forest Boundary

Fig. 5

(querous diatotes) and **kharsoo** (querous semi caipifolio). Ringal bamboo also flourishes upto 3,000 metres. Himalayan silver fur and spruce known as **raunsala** occur between 2,700 metres and 3,300 metres above mean sea level. The shrubs mainly **kilmora** (berberies asiatica) and **kunja** (rosa moschatta) are plentiful in open space.

The district produces a large variety of both the major and minor products. Timber and fuel constitute the major products while the minor products constitute **katha**, resin, ringals, bamboos, canes, narkuls, baibgrass, lime, limestone, gypsum, boulder, bazri etc. Of these, **katha** and resin are the most important items accruing annually over 60 per cent of the income.

Land Resources

The role of land resources both qualitative and quantitative is vital, especially in a Hill region in terms of their generation of outputs and incomes for the sustenance of existing and potential population.

Table 3.1 brings out the salient features of land resources in Pauri Garhwal district. It would be revealed therefrom that out of a total geogrpahical area of 5.45 lakh hectares, the area under Reserved Forests comprises of 2.88 lakh hectares or 52.84 per cent of the total area. Another 6 per cent (14.11 per cent of the total geographical area reported for land utilisation) is under Community Forests. An analysis of the spatial patterns and variations of this category of land-use have already been made in the preceding pages (Figure 5).

The category "Land not available for Cultivation" comprises of 21.39 per cent of the total reporting area for land-utilisation. Of this "Barren Lands and Lands unfit for Cultivation" occupies 13.66 per cent and the remaining 7.73 per cent is the "Land put to non-agricultural purposes". An analysis of spatial patterns reveals that such lands are the characteristic features, mainly of the northern part of the district. As many as 43 patwari circles, possess over 30 per cent of their geographical area under this category, putting thereby strong constraints on the extension of cultivation. In the southern part of the district however, relatively low percentages of such lands are possessed by a sizeable number of patwari circles. In contrast to these, a majority of patwari circles lying in the central part of the district possess less than 5 per cent of such lands.

The district possesses 23.53 per cent of the reporting area

as culturable waste in the form of permanent pastures, grazing

TABLE 3.1
Salient features of land-resources in Pauri Garhwal District (1970-71)

	Features	Lakh Hect-ares	Per cent to the total
I.	Total Geographical Area	5.45	-
II.	Total Geographical Area under Reserved Forests	2.88	52.84
III.	Total Geographical Area reporting for land-use.	2.57	47.16
	(a) Area under Forests (Community Forests)	0.36	14.11
	(b) Area not avilable for cultivation	0.55	21.39
	(i) Barren and unfit for cultivation.	0.35	13.66
	(ii) Land put to non-agricultural uses	0.20	7.73
	(c) Culturable Waste	0.61	23.53
	(d) Net Area Sown	1.05	40.97

grounds, land under miscellaneous tree crops and groves and fallow lands both old and current. There are wide intra-district variations. Only 39 patwari circles, scattered throughout the district, possess over 35 per cent of their geographical areas as culturable waste. Similarly, a majority of the patwari circles in the Siwalik hills, possesses culturable waste ranging between 25 per cent to 35 per cent. In the north-eastern part, however, there lie extensive tracts of culturable land which are mostly the lower slopes of the hill ranges and land close to the swift flowing streams. The availability of such land is however, a rarity in the Bhaber plains.

On account of mountainous terrain and low level utilisation of water-resource potentials, the land under irrigation is hardly 7 per cent of the net area sown. Intra-regional variations show that as many as 39 patwari circles had less than 1 per cent, 73 patwari circles between 1 per cent to 5 per cent and only 25 patwari circles over 10 per cent of the net area sown under irrigation. The patwari circles of Sukhrao, Motadhak, Saneh and Haldukhata in Bhaber plains however, had 88.08, 73.06, 75.34 and 56.87 per cent of their net area sown under irrigation.

The various types of land-resources discussed provide us clues for increasing both the cultivated area and productivity per hectare. In the study area, however, the limit to cultivation has practically been touched in many of the densely populated areas while in others the pattern of land-utilisation has come much closer to the physical capabilities of land. It is, therefore, imperative to resort to proper land-use planning for optimal productivity as a part of the regional development planning.

POPULATION AND SETTLEMENT STRUCTURE

A study of demographic and settlement structure throws light on the qualitative and quantitative dimensions of the interrelationship between physical and human resources of a region and substantially influence the development process. An attempt has therefore been made to analyse the spatial processes instrumental in accelerating or retarding the development.

Salient Characteristics

Pauri Garhwal district ranks 50th among the 56 districts in U.P. and 4th among the hill districts in respect of size of population (1971 Census).[16] Decadewise variations of population of the district during 1901-71 are presented in Tables 3.2 and 3.3. The district had a population of 2.83 lakhs in 1901 which nearly doubled during the period of 70 years from 1901 to 1971. It recorded highest percentage growth of 14.65 per cent during 1961-71 as compared with 19.82 per cent of U.P. and 24.66 per cent of India. Deviations of exponential growth from actual growth of population were registered mainly during the periods 1911-21 and 1941-51 (Figure 6). It would be observed from Table 3.2 that female population always exceeded the male population during 1901-71.[17] The gap between the two could not be neutralised despite a 4.57 per cent excess growth rate of male population during 1961-71.

The widening gap between the male and female population led to the imbalances in sex-ratio in which females outnumber the males. In general, the sex ratio, both urban and rural, have shown an upward trend since 1901. The number of females per 1,000 males was 1,032 in 1901. The imbalance increased to 1,160 females per 1,000 males in 1971. The urban sex-ratio also shows consistently an upward trend. The number of females for 1,000 males for the years 1951, 1961 and 1971 were 504, 527 and 642 respectively.[18]

The density of population has also increased steadily during the period 1901-71. The density of population of the district

TABLE 3.2

Growth of Population in Pauri Garhwal District (1901 - 1971)

Year	Total Population	Percentage Decade Variation	Male Population	Percentage Decade Variation	Female Population	Percentage Decade Variation
1901	2,83,760	-	1,39,657	-	1,44,103	-
1911	3,16,938	+11.69	1,55,650	+11.45	1,61,288	+11.92
1921	3,20,602	+1.16	1,53,872	-1.14	1,66,730	+3.37
1931	3,52,782	+10.04	1,70,473	+10.78	1,82,309	+9.34
1941	3,97,867	+12.78	1,91,598	+12.39	2,06,269	+13.14
1951	4,22,653	+6.23	1,97,784	+3.23	2,24,869	+9.02
1961	4,82,327	+14.12	2,22,892	+12.69	2,59,435	+15.42
1971	5,53,028	+14.65	2,61,054	+17.12	2,91,974	+12.54

TABLE 3.3
Actual and Exponential Growth of Population in Pauri Garhwal District (1901–1971)

Year	Total Population		Rural Population		Urban Population	
	Actual	Exponential	Actual	Exponential	Actual	Exponential
1901	283,760	283,760	277,726	277,726	6,034	6,034
1911	316,938	312,136	308,260	303,554	8,678	7,747
1921	320,602	343,349	313,362	331,784	7,240	9,947
1931	352,782	377,684	344,963	362,639	7,819	12,772
1941	397,867	415,452	386,923	396,364	10,944	16,400
1951	422,653	456,997	404,710	433,226	17,943	21,057
1961	482,327	502,696	454,829	473,516	27,498	27,037
1971	553,028	552,965	518,181	517,553	34,847	34,715

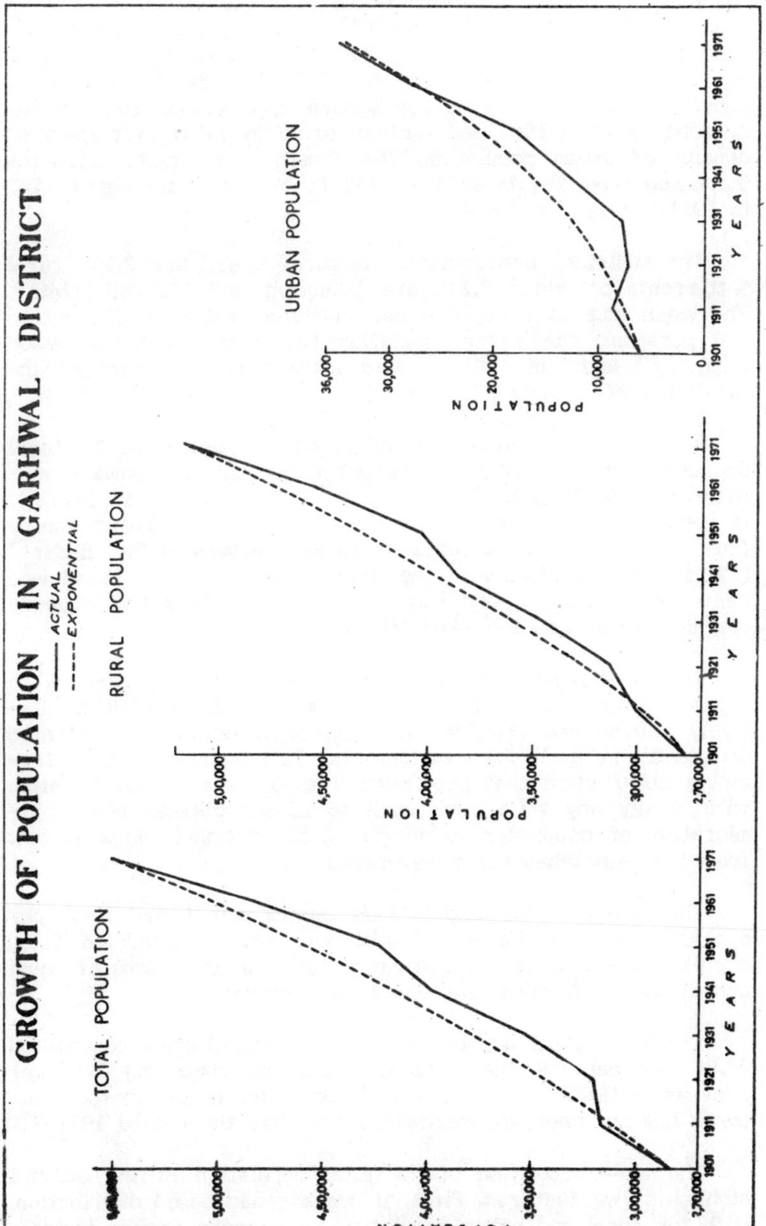
GROWTH OF POPULATION IN GARHWAL DISTRICT
ACTUAL
EXPONENTIAL
TOTAL POPULATION
RURAL POPULATION
URBAN POPULATION
POPULATION
YEARS
1901
1911
1921
1931
1941
1951
1961
1971
2,70,000
3,00,000
3,50,000
4,00,000
4,50,000
5,00,000
0
10,000
20,000
30,000
36,000

Fig.6

(inclusive of Chamoli district) was 33 in 1941; 34 in 1921; 37 in 1931 and 42 in 1941. The overall density of population in the district (excluding the present Chamoli district) increased to 77 in 1951; 88 in 1961 and 101 in 1971. The rural density of population was 70 persons per square kilometre in 1951. It increased to 84 in 1961 and further to 96 in 1971. In respect of density of urban population, the density per square kilometre increased from 289 in 1951 to 445 in 1961 and further to 562 in 1971.

The district, predominantly a rural area, has 3,568 rural settlements of which 3,236 are inhabited and 332 uninhabited. The mean size of population per inhabited village works out to 160 persons. The rural population has considerably increased from 2.77 lakhs in 1901 to 5.18 lakhs (93.6 per cent of the total) in 1971 (Table 3.3).

The urban population constituted 6.4 per cent of total population in 1971. It has increased more than five times from a little over 6,000 persons in 1901 to 34,847 persons in 1971. It is concentrated in only 6 small towns whose population ranges from 11,457 persons in Kotdwara to 580 persons in Bah Bazar 19 (Table 3.4). Kotdwara is the only Class IV town; Lansdowne cantonment, Srinagar and Pauri are Class V towns and Dogadda and Bah Bazar are the Class VI towns.

The total population of 5.53 lakhs is distributed among 3,236 rural and 6 urban settlements. Their spatial distribution is relatively uneven and sprinkled and the population is concentrated dominantly in small-sized settlements. This brings out an interesting observation that population lives in considerable isolation with hardly any shift from small to bigger villages while out-migration of population mainly of males continues as is evident from the high imbalance in sex-ratio.

The district, according to 1971 Census constituted 10.57 per cent as Scheduled Caste and 0.10 per cent as Scheduled Tribe population. The latter concentrated mainly in the towns of Pauri and Srinagar and also in a few rural settlements.

Out of a total population of 5.53 lakhs, Hindus constituted 97.98 per cent of the population and the remaining 2.02 per cent were Muslims, Christians and Sikhs etc. In this composition, there has not been any marked change over the period 1931-71.

The age-composition of the total population of the district highlights two features. First, it has a broad based distribution, both for rural and urban population that tapers rapidly indicat-

TABLE 3.4

Growth of Population of Towns in Pauri Garhwal District (1901–1971)

Year	PAURI TAHSIL						LANSDOWNE TAHSIL					
	Pauri		Srinagar		Bah Bazar*		Lansdowne		Kotdwara		Dogadda	
	Population	% Decade Variation	Population	% Decade Variation	Population	% Decade Variation	Population	% Decade Variation	Population	% Decade Variation	Population	% Decade Variation
1901	-	-	2,091	-	-	-	3,943	-	-	-	-	-
1911	-	-	2,357	+12.72	-	-	6,281	+59.29	-	-	-	-
1921	1,875	-	2,170	-7.93	-	-	5,070	-19.28	-	-	-	-
1931	1,901	+1.38	1,519	-30.00	-	-	4,399	-13.24	-	-	-	-
1941	2,803	+47.97	1,957	+28.83	-	-	6,174	+40.35	-	-	-	-
1951	5,250	+86.63	2,385	+21.87	-	-	4,419	-28.42	4,648	-	1,241	-
1961	7,484	+52.55	3,031	+27.08	535	-	6,381	+44.39	8,148	+75.30	1,919	+54.63
1971	8,878	+18.63	5,566	+83.63	580	+8.41	6,670	+45.29	11,457	+40.61	1,696	-11.62

* This town was added in 1961

ing persistent high fertility rate and outmigration of work force in the higher age-group. Secondly, the percentage of female population continues to be higher in respect of total and rural population but it is persistently much lower in respect of urban population.

The district is marked by high literacy rates. According to 1971 Census, the district ranked fifth among different districts of the state with an overall literacy rate of 31.53 per cent. It also ranked second and seventh in male and female literacy rates of 50.02 per cent and 15.84 per cent respectively. The growth of literacy of the district during 1951-71 has also been remarkable. The percentage of total literates to total population increased from 16.34 per cent in 1951 to 23.37 per cent in 1961 and further to 31.53 per cent in 1971. In the case of male literacy, the percentage increased from 32.00 per cent in 1951 to 43.38 per cent in 1961 and to 50.02 per cent in 1971. The corresponding figures for female literacy were 2.56 per cent in 1951; 6.19 per cent in 1961 and 15.84 per cent in 1971. There has also been an upward trend in rural and urban literacy rates. The total rural literacy increased from 14.67 per cent in 1951 to 21.20 per cent in 1961 and further to 29.56 per cent in 1971. The urban literacy increased from 49.42 per cent in 1951 to 57.29 per cent in 1961 and to 60.11 per cent in 1971.

The work participation rates, spelling out the productive behaviour of the workers in different economic activities, are also high. The overall work participation rate in 1971 was 45.40 per cent. The male work participation rate (47.63 per cent) was relatively higher than that of the female work rate (43.40 per cent). Similarly, the rural work participation rate (46.09 per cent) was higher than the urban work participation rate (35.12 per cent). Such a feature strongly suggests outmigration of male population. As compared to these participation rates, the rates in 1961 were relatively higher because of the adoption of a stricter definition of worker in 1971.

Spatial Patterns and Variations

In this part, an attempt has been made to analyse the spatial patterns and variations of population characteristics such as growth, density, sex-ratio, literacy and work participation and finally of the settlement structure.

Growth and Density of population

A detailed analysis of growth and density of population[20] brings out wide intra-district variations (Figure 7 and 8). The number of patwari circles, having very high positive growth rates increased from 18 in 1951-61 to 20 in 1961-71 while those having negative growth rates increased from 9 in 1951-61 to 11 in 1961-71. However, in the growth-rate range between 5 per cent and 20 per cent lay a majority of the patwari circles. Their number increased from 113 in 1951-61 to 117 in 1961-71 (Figure 7).

An increase in growth-rate leads to an increase in density of population. The frequency of patwari circles progressively increased in the highest range of density of population, of over 250 persons per square kilometre from 17 in 1951 to 28 in 1961; and further to 43 in 1971. In contrast to this, the frequency of patwari circles, in the lowest range of density of less than 100 persons per km^2 progressively declined from 25 in 1951 to 14 in 1961; and further to 9 in 1971. Bhaber region witnessed an overall growth-rate of 45.12 per cent in 1961-71 as against 56.26 per cent in 1951-61. Within the region, Sukhrao (53.75 per cent), Motadhak (78.42 per cent) and Haldukhata (97.92 per cent) recorded very high growth-rates of population. Saneh, having a negative growth-rate of 15.95 per cent in 1951-61 registered a positive growth rate of 76.59 per cent in 1961-71. As a result of growth of population the density of population in the region has progressively increased from 239 persons per km^2 in 1951 to 372 persons per km^2 in 1961 and further to 540 persons per km^2 in 1971.

In the Bhaber uplands, a majority of the patwari circles showed fluctuating growth trends and low density of population. Those lying in the central part of the district registered medium or low growth and density of population. A few patwari circles in the extreme north-east and north-west were marked by progressively increasing growth and density of population due to coming up of nodal centres in them. Among the 94 important rural settlements having a population of over 500 persons each in 1971 the growth-rates varied widely. Out of them 16 patwari circles in the Bhaber plains were marked by high to very high positive growth-rates. In the hilly tracts, 52 settlements registered consistently positive growth-rates; 24 fluctuating growth-rates; and the remaining 2 negative growth-rates.

Sex-ratio

Pauri Garhwal district, as pointed out earlier, has an imbalanced sex-ratio of 1,160 females per 1,000 males.[21] Intra-district variations (Fig.9) are wide. Patwari circles having the highest range of sex-ratio of over 1,400 females per 1,000 males, figured 13 and covered hardly 5.44 per cent of the

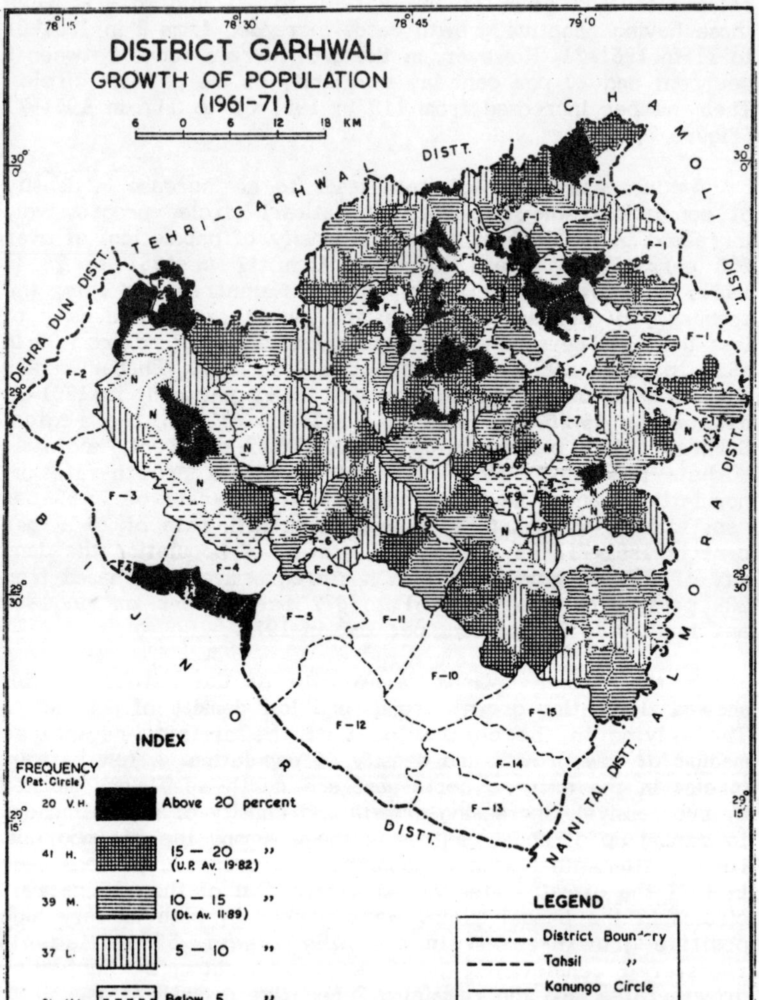
DISTRICT GARHWAL
GROWTH OF POPULATION
(1961-71)
6 0 6 12 18 KM
TEHRI-GARHWAL DISTT.
CHAMOLI DISTT.
DEHRA DUN DISTT.
BIJNOR DISTT.
ALMORA DISTT.
NAINI TAL DISTT.
INDEX
FREQUENCY (Pat. Circle)
20 V.H. Above 20 percent
41 H. 15 — 20 " (U.P. Av. 19·82)
39 M. 10 — 15 " (Dt. Av. 11·89)
37 L. 5 — 10 "
21 V.L. Below 5 "
11 N Negative growth
LEGEND
District Boundary
Tahsil "
Kanungo Circle
Patwari "
Forest Boundary
F-1,2,.... Reserve Forest

Fig. 7

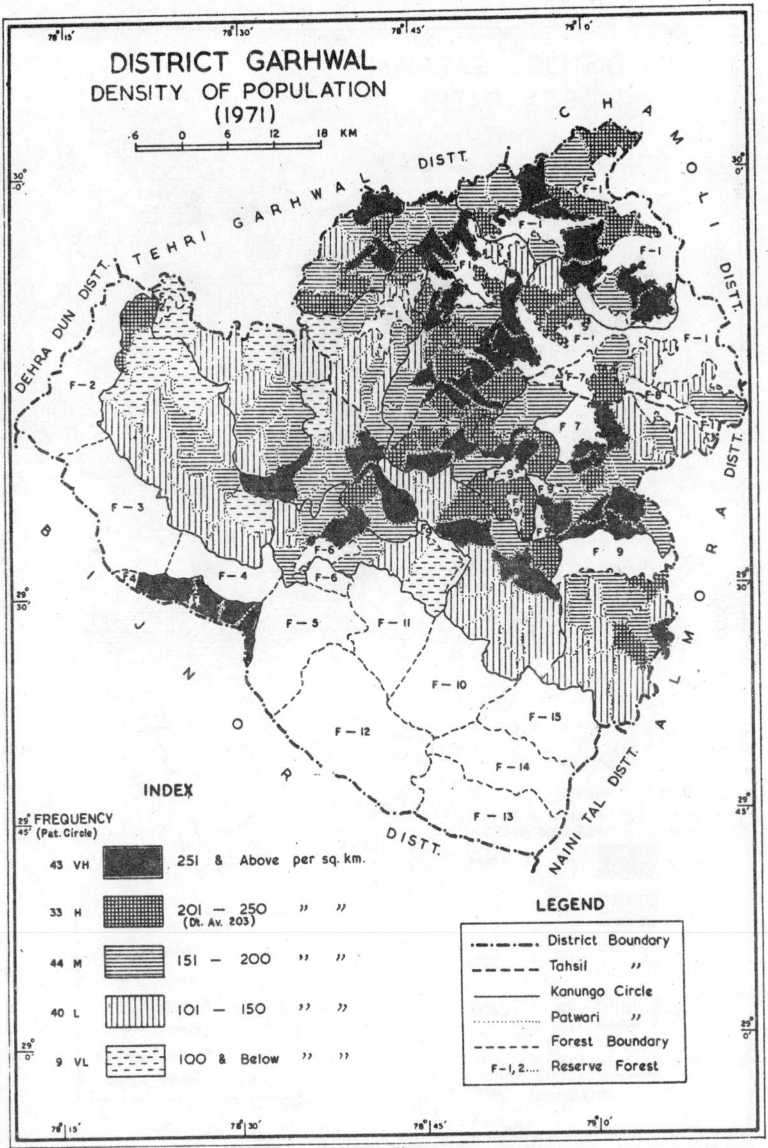

DISTRICT GARHWAL
DENSITY OF POPULATION
(1971)
6 0 6 12 18 KM
TEHRI GARHWAL DISTT.
CHAMOLI DISTT.
ALMORA DISTT.
NAINI TAL DISTT.
BIJNOR DISTT.
DEHRA DUN DISTT.
INDEX
FREQUENCY (Pat. Circle)
43 VH 251 & Above per sq. km.
33 H 201 — 250 " " (Dt. Av. 203)
44 M 151 — 200 " "
40 L 101 — 150 " "
9 VL 100 & Below " "
LEGEND
District Boundary
Tahsil "
Kanungo Circle
Patwari "
Forest Boundary
F-1, 2.... Reserve Forest
78°15′
78°30′
78°45′
79°0′
30°0′
29°45′
29°30′
29°0′

Fig. 8

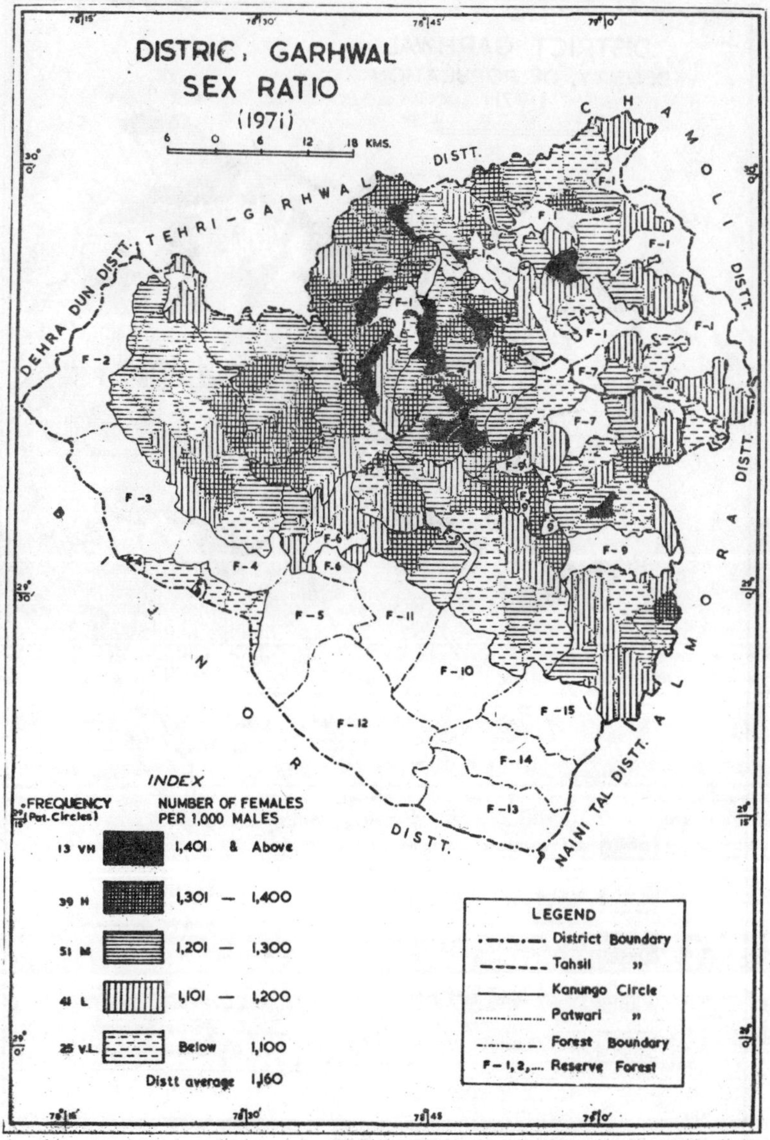
DISTRIC: GARHWAL
SEX RATIO
(1971)
6 0 6 12 18 KMS.
TEHRI-GARHWAL DISTT.
DEHRA DUN DISTT.
CHAMOLI DISTT.
ALMORA DISTT.
NAINI TAL DISTT.
BIJNOR DISTT.
INDEX
FREQUENCY (Pat. Circles)
NUMBER OF FEMALES PER 1,000 MALES
13 VH 1,401 & Above
39 H 1,301 — 1,400
51 M 1,201 — 1,300
41 L 1,101 — 1,200
25 V.L. Below 1,100
Distt average 1,160
LEGEND
District Boundary
Tahsil "
Kanungo Circle
Patwari "
Forest Boundary
F—1, 2,.... Reserve Forest

Fig. 9

population. In contrast to this, Bhaber had an overall sex-ratio of 971 females to 1,000 males. Over 90 patwari circles in the hilly tracts lay in the range of sex-ratio between "1,201 to 1,400" females per 1,000 males and covered 59.03 per cent of population. In the remaining 66 patwari circles the sex-ratios were less than 1,200 females per 1,000 males and covered 45.53 per cent of the population. Sample study carried out in 42 villages confirmed the existence of imbalanced sex-ratio in the district. The range of sex-ratio in those villages varied very widely from 694 females per 1,000 males in Deolad to 1,475 females per 1,000 males in Birgana.

Scheduled Caste Population

The scheduled caste population, as mentioned earlier, constitutes 10.57 per cent of the total population. It is widely dispersed mainly in the rural areas. Spatial pattern (Fig.10) reveals that relatively higher percentage of population is concentrated in upper parts than in the lower parts of the district. Among 169 patwari circles the variations ranged between 0.09 per cent and 25.94 per cent. Patwari circles having over 20 per cent of Scheduled Caste population figured 9 only. Another 33 patwari circles lay in the percentage range between 15 per cent and 20 per cent. But most of the patwari circles numbering 102, had between 5 per cent and 15 per cent as Scheduled Caste population.

Literacy

The district, as stated earlier, is characterised by high literacy rates which varied widely, both temporally and spatially among different patwari circles. In 1971, there were 39 patwari circles having an overall literacy of over 35 per cent as against 2 in 1961 and only 1 in 1951. Similarly, patwari circles in the range between 25 per cent and 35 per cent figured 79 in 1971 as against 38 in 1961 and only 4 in 1951. In the lower ranges, the frequency of patwari circles declined rapidly during 1951-71. In 1971, among 169 patwari circles, the range in respect of total literacy varied from 10.99 per cent in Dhaijuli-III to 67.09 per cent in Saneh (Bhaber) patwari circle. It is observed that the literacy increased relatively faster in those patwari circles which lay in close proximity of towns and had the access of educational and other infrastructural facilities than their counterparts elsewhere.

In 1971, there were 32 patwari circles having an overall male literacy of over 55 per cent as against 8 in 1961 and 2 in 1951. Similarly, in the range between 45 per cent and 55 per

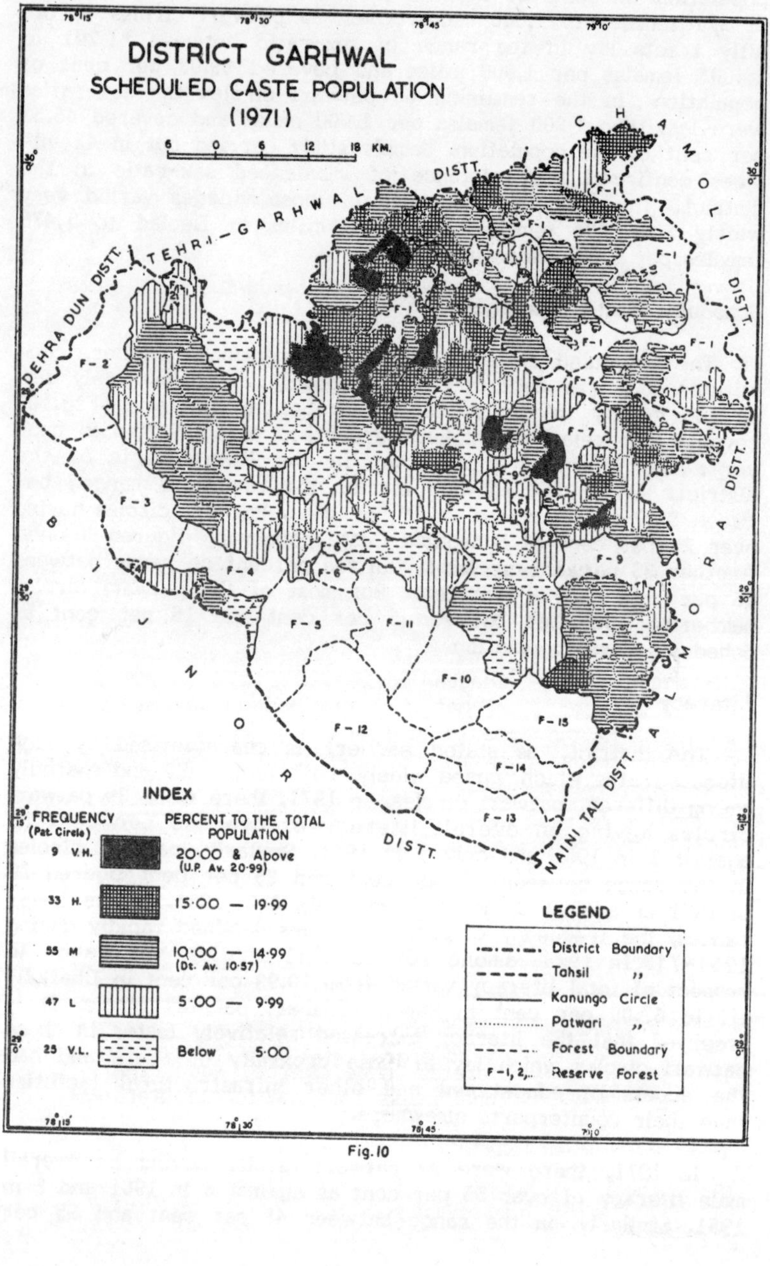
DISTRICT GARHWAL
SCHEDULED CASTE POPULATION
(1971)
6 0 6 12 18 KM.
TEHRI-GARHWAL DISTT.
CHAMOLI DISTT.
DEHRA DUN DISTT.
BIJNOR DISTT.
ALMORA DISTT.
NAINI TAL DISTT.
INDEX
FREQUENCY (Pat. Circle)
PERCENT TO THE TOTAL POPULATION
9 V.H. 20·00 & Above (U.P. Av. 20·99)
33 H. 15·00 — 19·99
55 M 10·00 — 14·99 (Dt. Av. 10·57)
47 L 5·00 — 9·99
25 V.L. Below 5·00
LEGEND
District Boundary
Tahsil ,,
Kanungo Circle
Patwari ,,
Forest Boundary
F-1, 2,.. Reserve Forest

Fig. 10

cent, there were 68 patwari circles as against 62 in 1961 and only 8 in 1951. In the lower ranges the frequency of patwari circles declined rapidly. The variations in respect of overall male literacy in 1971 lay between 22.00 per cent in Dhaijuli-III to 83.96 per cent in Banelsyun I. The regional pattern is similar to that of total literacy.

The spatial patterns in respect of overall literacy also reflect large intra-district variations (Figure 11). In 1971, there existed 34 patwari circles having an overall female literacy of over 20 per cent as against 2 in 1961 and only 1 in 1951. Similarly, in the literacy range between 12 per cent and 20 per cent, there were 75 patwari circles as against 8 in 1961 and none in 1951. There was a major shift in patwari circles from lower ranges to higher ranges of literacy-rates. The growth of female literacy was commendable in 1971, when both the growth and range of variations increased. The percentage variations ranged between 0.96 per cent in Kandarsyun-IV to 32.46 per cent in Katulsyun-II. The regional patterns of female literacy and total literacy synchronise for the year 1971. It would be observed that most of the patwari circles in north-eastern and south-eastern parts of the district possess relatively low literacy rates than their counterparts elsewhere.

A sample study of 42 villages, carried out during 1977-78, also reflects high growth of literacy in the district. The overall literacy in these villages worked out to 38.58 per cent and ranged between 19.81 per cent in Ghansyali to 70.21 per cent in Seela. In the case of male literacy, it averaged 51.57 per cent and ranged between 31.22 per cent in Ghansyali to 83.46 per cent in Lweentha. Similarly, the female literacy averaged 25.77 per cent and variations ranged between 2.83 per cent in Kainur to 61.60 per cent in Seela.

Besides the growth of literacy, the sample study revealed that educational levels are also high (Table 3.5). The educational levels indicate that about 44.23 per cent of the total literates were without any educational level. 34.04 per cent possessed educational level only upto primary or junior level and 16.62 per cent upto high school/intermediate levels. Those who had education beyond undergraduate level constituted 5.11 per cent of the total literates. Male literate population had relatively higher educational levels than the female literates.

Work Participation

One of the outstanding features of the district is the prevalence of high work participation rates. According to 1971

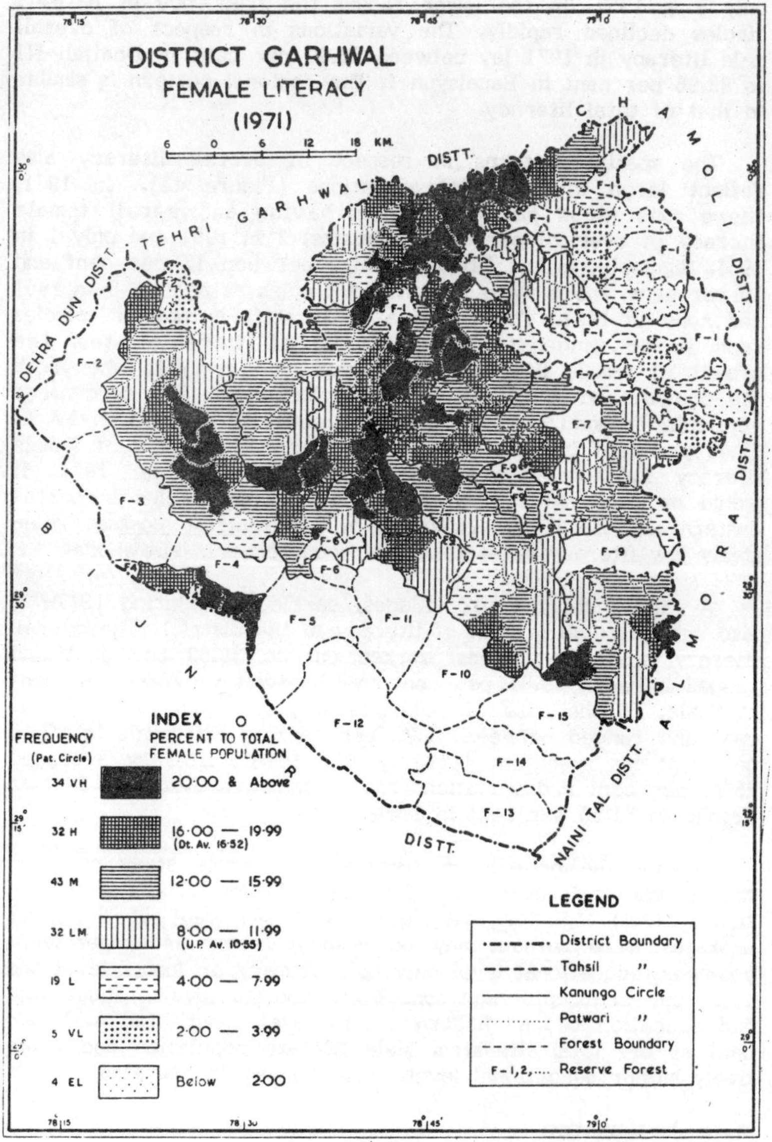
DISTRICT GARHWAL
FEMALE LITERACY
(1971)
6 0 6 12 18 KM.
TEHRI GARHWAL DISTT.
CHAMOLI DISTT.
DEHRA DUN DISTT.
BIJNOR DISTT.
ALMORA DISTT.
NAINI TAL DISTT.
INDEX
FREQUENCY
(Pat. Circle)
PERCENT TO TOTAL
FEMALE POPULATION
34 VH
20·00 & Above
32 H
16·00 — 19·99
(Dt. Av. 16·52)
43 M
12·00 — 15·99
32 LM
8·00 — 11·99
(U.P. Av. 10·55)
19 L
4·00 — 7·99
5 VL
2·00 — 3·99
4 EL
Below 2·00
LEGEND
District Boundary
Tahsil ״
Kanungo Circle
Patwari ״
Forest Boundary
F-1, 2,.... Reserve Forest

Fig. 11

Census, the overall work participation worked out to 45.40 per cent ranged between 16 per cent and 87.73 per cent, among the 169 patwari circles. The male work participation was 52.24 per cent and varied between 26.08 per cent and 70 per cent. The female work participation was 45.31 per cent and ranged between 0.32 per cent and 78.14 per cent among different patwari circles. As many as 68 patwari circles had over 55 per cent as female work participation rates. Between 45 per cent and 55 per cent lay another 38 patwari circles. Those who had female work participation rates below 45 per cent numbered 63. These female work participation rates highlight the great dependency of the region's agricultural economy on its female members, in the absence of male members who migrate outside the region.

TABLE 3.5

Educational levels of literate population in Pauri Garhwal district-Sample Study - 1977-78

Educational levels	Males	Females	Total
1. Without any educational level.	2,273 (39.75)	1,544 (53.02)	3,817 (44.23)
2. Primary and junior level.	1,969 (34.44)	969 (33.28)	2,938 (34.04)
3. High School/Intermediate level.	1,113 (19.46)	321 (11.02)	1,434 (16.62)
4. Degree/Post-graduate level.	332 (5.81)	74 (2.54)	406 (4.70)
5. Technical.	31 (0.54)	4 (0.14)	35 (0.41)
All levels	5,718 (100.00)	2,912 (100.00)	8,630 (100.00)

Note: Figures in the parenthesis indicate percentages to the total.

An analysis of spatial variations reflects distinct patterns for different areas. In the north-eastern parts of the district, female work participation rates are relatively higher whereas in south-eastern parts, male work participation rates are relatively higher. Bhaber region has very low female work participation rates. Interestingly, patwari circles lying along the main highway from Kotdwara to Rudraprayag and beyond, have female work participation rates much higher than the male particpation rates.

SETTLEMENT STRUCTURE

The settlement structure in the hilly region is determined primarily by natural conditions such as physiographic conditions, drainage patterns and altitudinal variations. The small size and sprinkled pattern of the settlements is the consequence of such natural factors. The physiography, drainage and settlement pattern show that the majority of the settlements in the district lie in the altitudinal range between 600 metres to 1,800 metres above mean sea level. The percentage of settlements in the range upto 600 metres is only 11.18 because much of this area is under forests and the topography is rugged, the land being subject to intense gully erosion. Between 600 metres and 1,200 metres, the percentage of settlements is 40.76 and the range between 1,200 metres and 1,800 metres consists of 45.50 per cent of the settlements. At higher altitudes the settlements are rare. The range between 1,800 metres and 2,400 metres has only 2.50 per cent of the total settlements. The most important river basin from this point of view, is that of the Nayar with two of its distributaries, the Western Nayar and the Eastern Nayar. Throughout the valleys of these rivers, particularly along the valley of Eastern Nayar river, the settlements are more in number and the density of population is also relatively high. The Alaknanda, though a mighty river, does not afford much scope for the location of human settlements on account of its ungraded nature and the formation of deep gorges, particularly from Deoprayag to Rishikesh. The settlements in the Ramganga valley are very few as the region through which it flows is for the most part a forested tract. Mandal river, a tributary of the Ramganga river, has larger number of settlements in its valley than any of the river valleys in Bhaber plains.

Distribution of settlements of less than 100 persons

A detailed analysis of the settlement pattern (Table 3.6) shows that in 1971, there were in all 1,381 settlements having a population of less than 100 persons representing 42.67 per cent of the total settlements and 13.84 per cent of the total population. The degree in smallness in size is so extreme that as many as 278 settlements have a population of less than 25 persons. Another 356 settlements have a population range of 25 to 50 persons. Such settlements are distributed spatially throughout the district and their concentration is rarely patchy. The distribution of settlements in this category demonstrated the co-existence of extremes. While the patwari circle of Nandalsyun-I has the distinction of having 100 per cent of its settlement in this category, there were four patwari circles which had none of their settlements in this category. Among the remaining patwari circles, the distribution of settlements ranged between 7.69 per cent and 78.78 per cent. The respective distribution of their population varied between 0.61 per cent to 66.26 per cent.

TABLE 3.6
Distribution of settlements in Pauri Garhwal District-1971

Population size	No. of settlements.	% to the total	Total population	% to the total
Upto 100	1,381	42.67	71,312	13.84
100 - 349	1,617	50.02	3,03,191	58.85
350 - 499	144	4.47	59,163	11.49
500 - 799	78	2.38	47,462	9.22
800 and above	16	0.46	34,061	6.60
All sizes	3,236	100.00	5,15,189	100.00

Distribution of settlements between 100 to 349 persons

This is the most dominant category, comprising of 1,617 settlements or 50.02 per cent of the total settlements and covering 58.85 per cent of the total population. With the exception of one patwari circle, all others show the spatial diffusion of such settlements. Although the percentage of such settlements among different patwari circles varied between 9.69 per cent and 91.65 per cent, a majority of the patwari circles (118 in number) had between 35 per cent and 65 per cent. Patwari circles with very high or very low percentage of their population, in this category, were very few.

Distribution of settlements between 350 and 499 persons

One of the salient features of the settlement structure in the district is that the percentage of settlements above 350 population progressively declines. The present category comprises of only 144 settlements or 4.47 per cent of the total settlements and covering 11.49 per cent of the total population. A large number of these settlements lie in the Nayar basin, covering thereby the areas of relative density and of concentration of population. In contrast to this, a sizeable number of patwari circles in the Bhaber uplands stretching from north-west to south-east of the district, do not possess such settlements.

Distribution of settlements above 500 persons

Based on the features of the topography and settlement sizes, the settlements above a population of 500 persons may be considered as the large-sized settlements. The number of rural settlements above 500 population, according to 1971 Census, is 94; 35 in Pauri tahsil and 59 in Lansdowne tahsil. They, together, constituted 2.84 per cent of the total settlements and 15.82 per cent of the total rural population. Out of these 94 settlements, 78 lie in the population range of 500 to 800 persons; 8 between 800 and 1,000 persons and 6 between 1,000 and 2,000 persons. Gadri is the largest village in the district with a total population of 2,411 persons. Kalagarh, which emerged as a large-sized village during the period of construction of Kalagarh dam is an exceptional village with a population of 16,242 persons. Although these settlements are widely scattered throughout the district, yet a majority of them lie in Kotdwara Bhaber and also in the Nayar basin.

The above analysis of the settlement structure reflects the inherent characteristics of the rural landscape in a hilly area. The dominance of the large number of small sized settlements and their stability and population provide us the basis for the formulation of regional development plan at the district level. It may, however, be pointed out that the norms for the small-sized, medium-sized and large-sized settlements in the Hill region would have to be different in the choice of creating nodal centres for the provision of services and facilities.

NOTES AND REFERENCES

1. For example, H.B. Medlicott (1864), Middlemiss (1885-90), C. L. Griesback (1891), H.D. Oldham (1883-88), Pilgrim & West (1928), J.B. Auden (1937): **Records of Geological Survey of India, Vol.III**; LXVII, LXVIII, XVI; XXIII and LXIX, LXXI respectively.
2. Ganseer, A.: **Geology of Himalayas,** Interscience Publishers, London - A Division of John Wiley and Sons, Ltd., 1964, Chapter VI, p.80.
3. Auden, J.B.: **The Structure of the Himalayas in Garhwal,**

Records of Geological Survey of India, Vol. LXXI, pp.407-433.

4. Auden, J.B. : Traverses in the Himalayas, **Records of the Geological Survey of India,** 1935, Vol.XIX, pp.133-134.
5. Negi, B.S.: Soils of Uttarakhand Division of U.P.: **Geographical Observer,** Vol.5, 1969, pp.75-80.
6. Dabral, M.P.: **Land Utilisation in Garhwal Himalayas;** An unpublished Ph.D. Thesis, Vikram University, Ujjain, 1970, pp.20-21.
7. These data on rainfall etc. are based upon the averages of the rainfall data for the years 1901-1971.
8. Atkinson, E.T.: **Economic Mineralogy of the Hill Districts** of N.W.P., Allahabad, 1882, p.31.
9. Walton, H.G.: **British Garhwal - A Gazetteer,** Vol. XXXVI of the District Gazetteers of U.P., Agra and Oudh, Allahabad, 1910, p.2.
10. Sapru, P.N.: **Industrial Survey Report - Garhwal Division,** Government Press, Allahabad, 1914, p.15.
11. Negi, B.S.: The Mineral Resources of Kumaon and Garhwal, **Geographical Review of India, 1960.**
12. Dabral, S.P. : **Uttarakhand Ka Itihas** (in Hindi), Veergatha Publications, Dogadda, Garhwal, 1976: Vol.VII, p.46.
13. Dabral, S.P. : **Alaknanda Upatyaka** (in Hindi), Veergatha Publications, Dogadda, Garhwal, 1964, p.76.
14. Government of India: National Industries Development Corporation: **Survey of Industrial Programming in the Hill Districts of U.P.** 1969-70, p.2.
15. The construction of a 655 feet high straight gravity concrete dam, at Marora, at an estimated cost of Rs.23.96 crores was envisaged in 1947 to exploit the potentialities of the Nayar Valley for storage of water for irrigation and hydro-electric power generation. The work had, however, to be stopped in 1949, on technical grounds.
16. Registrar General of India: **Census of India, 1971,** Final Population, Part I of 1972, pp.69-73.
17. This was not, however, the characteristic feature of the population during the last century as is evident from the population data for the years 1821, 1853, 1858 and 1865, wherein the males outnumbered the females. For details refer Dabral, S.P.: **Uttarakhand Ka Itihas** (in Hindi), Veerghatha Publications, Dogadda, Garhwal, 1976, Part VII, pp.351-354.
18. The sex-ratios for years 1901-1951 relate to Garhwal district inclusive of Chamoli district and for the rest of the period (1951, 1961 and 1971) relate to Pauri Garhwal district only.
19. Bah Bazar which was included in the list of towns in 1961 possesses a peculiar position. For local

administration, it is a part of Deoprayag Notified Area of the adjoining district of Tehri-Garhwal. The part of the Notified Area lying in Pauri Garhwal district has been deemed to be a separate town for Census purposes.

20. The density of population at the district level conceals the realistic picture and does not convey the magnitude of the problem inherent in intra-district variations. An attempt to cull out the regional patterns based upon the patwari circle units, has therefore, been made. In computing the rural district averages based upon the aggregation of areas of all the patwari circles, the areas under Reserved Forests have been excluded.

21. The average of 1,175 females per 1,000 males was also computed on the basis of the population of 169 patwari circles excluding the population of forest ranges. Forest ranges had together a population of 5,554 persons with a sex-ratio of 333 females per 1,000 males. The overall sex-ratio including the population of forest ranges worked out to 1,160 females per 1,000 males.

FOUR

Structure & Spatial Patterns of the Economy

The resource base, both physical and human, provides the basis on which the edifice of the economy is built. By interaction with the resource base, the working population gets divided among different productive activities, forming thereby the occupational structure of the economy. During the process, a large number of determinants such as the proportion of working population in primary, secondary and tertiary activities, the degree of specialisation, the differences in the levels of incomes and productivity and the consumption patterns of the people influence in moulding the structure of the economy. This chapter, is therefore, aimed at analysing the structure and spatial patterns of the economy in terms of its occupational, agricultural, industrial and infrastructural patterns and variations.

Occupational Patterns

Of the total population of 553,000 in 1971, the number of workers accounted for 251,000 and the remaining 302,000 were non-workers constituting 45.40 per cent and 54.60 per cent respectively. The percentage of workers has come down since 1961[1] accounting for 58.60 per cent of the total population. In 1971, 78.01 per cent of the workers were cultivators and 1.30 per cent agricultural labourers. The percentage of non-agricultural workers was as low as 20.69. As against these, in 1961, cultivators constituted 85.84 per cent of the workers and agricultural labourers 0.48 per cent and the remaining 14 per cent were engaged in non-agricultural activities. In rural areas, in 1971, the proportion of workers constituted 46 per cent; of these cultivators were 81.84 per cent; agricultural labourers 1.33 per cent and the remaining 16.86 per cent were engaged in non-agricultural activities. In 1961, the percentage of workers in rural areas was 59.67 of which cultivators constituted 89.31 per cent.

TABLE 4.1
Occupational Pattern in Pauri Garhwal District - 1961
(Per cent)

Occupational categories	District	Rural	Urban	Forest Ranges
I. Cultivators	85.84	89.31	10.00	19.66
II. Agricultural labourers	0.48	0.48	0.32	-
III. Mining, quarrying, forestry etc.	3.23	3.30	1.59	64.11
IV. Household industry	1.87	1.86	1.91	6.05
V. Manufacturing other than households	0.81	0.53	7.23	4.42
VI. Construction	0.95	0.81	3.88	3.64
VII. Trade and commerce	0.84	0.36	11.99	0.22
VIII. Transport and communication	0.75	0.37	8.95	0.80
IX. Other services	5.23	2.98	54.13	1.10
Total number of workers	283,936 (100.00)	271,397 (100.00)	12,539 (100.00)	12,450 (100.00)
Total workers as percentage of total population	58.86	59.67	45.60	86.18

In the urban areas, the percentage of workers in 1961, was only 45.60 per cent of the total population and the rest were non-workers. Of the workers, only 10.80 per cent were cultivators and 0.32 per cent agricultural labourers. Workers engaged in transport and communications, trade and commerce and manufacturing were 8.05 per cent, 11.90 per cent and 7.23 per cent respectively. In 1971, however, the percentage of workers came down to 35.14. Out of these workers, only 3.10 per cent were cultivators. Those who were engaged in manufacturing, trade and commerce, transport and communications, accounted for 9.62 per cent, 15.77 per cent and 8.68 per cent respectively.

A sizeable population of the district depends on forestry because of a large number of workers engaged in various Forest Ranges throughout the district. As such occupational patterns in the Forest Ranges differed significantly from the general patterns of the district. In these Forest Ranges, workers constituted 86.18 per cent of the total population in 1961. The proportion of workers declined sharply in 1971 and constituted 64.01 per cent of the total population. Of the total workers, 54.77 per cent in 1961 and 64.11 per cent in 1971 were engaged in forestry. And workers engaged in cultivation were only 19.66 per cent and 2.42 per cent in 1961 and 1971 respectively.

TABLE 4.2
Occupational Pattern in Pauri Garhwal District – 1971
(Per cent)

Occupational categories	District	Rural	Urban	Forest Ranges
I. Cultivators	78.01	82.84	3.10	2.42
II. Agricultural labourers	1.30	1.33	0.82	0.45
III. Mining, quarrying, forestry etc.	1.62	1.67	0.62	54.77
IV. Household industry	0.03	0.03	-	0.76
V. Manufacturing other than households	1.49	1.07	9.62	0.73
VI. Construction	0.56	0.45	2.85	1.86
VII. Trade and commerce	1.59	0.86	15.77	2.50
VIII. Transport and communication	0.75	0.35	8.68	2.03
IX. Other services	14.65	11.40	58.54	34.48
Total number of workers	251,093 (100.00)	238,849 (100.00)	12,244 (100.00)	3,555 (100.00)
Total workers as percentage of total population	45.40	46.09	35.14	64.01

There are 6 towns in the district. The percentage of the workers to the total population ranged between 35.33 per cent in Srinagar town to 55.95 per cent in Lansdowne town in 1961. This range varied from 25.11 per cent in Dogadda to 49.01 per cent in Lansdowne in 1971. Lansdowne had over 95 per cent of its workers engaged in the tertiary sector in both years, 1961 and 1971, the highest of all the towns. Most of the workers in this sector were engaged in "Other services" rather than in construction, trade and commerce, or transport and communications. In the secondary sector, Kotdwara led with

17.50 per cent of the total workers in 1971. This percentage has increased from 14.05 in 1961 due to increase in manufacturing activities as well as trade and commerce in the town. In manufacturing, trade and commerce and transport and communications, it has dominated all other towns. The respective percentages of total workers engaged in manufacturing, trade and commerce and transport and communications in this town were 17.50, 25.75 and 20.15 in 1971 as against 13.59, 20.84 and 22.01 in 1961. Pauri, the headquarter of the district, continues to have the highest proportion of workers in the primary sector though the percentage has declined from 34.19 in 1961 to 9.81 in 1971.

An analysis of occupational pattern of important rural settlements having a population of over 500 persons, numbering 94 in 1971, also reveals a high dependence of people on agriculture. In 1951, 64 out of 94 such settlements had over 90 per cent of their population dependent upon agriculture. Another 13 settlements had between 80 per cent and 90 per cent and the remaining 17 settlements had less than 80 per cent. Dependence on the non-agricultural sector was almost insignificant in 1/5th of these settlements. Such settlements had less than 1 per cent of their population dependent upon agriculture. Only a few villages had exceptionally high proportions of their population dependent upon the non-agricultural sector. Settlements in Bhaber plains, had relatively higher percentages of non-agricultural population than their counterparts in the hilly tracts of the district. The important among the latter are Satpuli Talli (89.49 per cent), Jaunk (70.91 per cent), Punar (54.06 per cent), Ujyari (50.98 per cent), Jahari (38.13 per cent) and Kewarsa (37.82 per cent). Punar had the highest percentage of population (12.88 per cent) dependent upon commerce, followed by Satpuli Talli (11.48 per cent). Both these settlements lie on the main transport line from Kotdwara to Badrinath. Satpuli Talli had also the highest percentage (64.20 per cent) of population in "Other services" followed by Jaunk (55.90 per cent), Jahari (32.15 per cent), Ujyari (36.67 per cent), Punar (22.60 per cent) and Kewarsa (21.95 per cent). In "Production other than agriculture" Kalagarh had the highest percentage (30.60 per cent) of population. These patterns of non-agricultural activity at the contact zone between the hills and the plains bring out the possible scope for development of these towns as the functional-economic links in the development strategy.

The occupational patterns of the workers in the large-sized villages for the years 1961 and 1971 reflect a heavy concentration of workers in the primary sector. Cultivators form the major part of the workers and far exceeded the other categories of workers. In 1961, there were over 90 per cent of the workers as cultivators in 58 villages. Another 18 villages lay in the percentage range between 80 per cent and 90 per cent of the workers as cultivators. The remaining villages had less than 80 per cent as cultivators. In 1971, the proportion of cultivators to the total workers came down. The villages which had over 90 per cent of the workers as cultivators numbered 26 only. Those which lay in the percentage range between 80 per cent and 90 per cent numbered 28 and the remaining below 80 per cent. In contrast to the numbers of cultivators, agricultural labourers were not only few in number but also formed part of the labour force in only a few villages. In the Bhaber, villages had relatively lower percentages of cultivators but higher percentages of agricultural labourers to the total workforce than their counterparts in the hilly tracts of the district, both in 1961 and 1971. In the Bhaber, the percentage of agricultural labourers ranged from 1.61 per cent in Ghamandpur to 37.04 per cent, in Shivrajpur in 1971. With the exception of Shivrajpur (37.04 per cent), West Jhandichaur (32.84 per cent) and East Jhandichaur (31.76 per cent), all of the villages had less than 25 per cent of workers as agricultural labourers. Jaunk was the exceptional village where a sizeable percentage (36.91) of workers was engaged in "Mining and quarrying" in 1961. More workers were attracted to this occupation in the succeeding decade with the result that 10 villages had each over 20 per cent of the workers engaged in it in 1971.

The secondary sector is highly undeveloped as is evident from the low proportions of workers engaged. In 1961, Satpuli Talli had the distinction of having engaged highest percentage (21.56 per cent) of workers in the secondary sector among all the large-sized villages. It was followed by Nandpur with a percentage of 10.95. The remaining villages had very low percentages of workers in this sector. Similarly, in 1971, most of the villages had less than 5 per cent of workers engaged in secondary sector with the exception of Sisai (23.75 per cent), Satpuli Talli (17.98 per cent) and Punar (7.42 per cent).

In contrast with the position for the secondary sector, the percentage of workers engaged in the tertiary sector was relatively higher in many of the large-sized villages. In 1961, Satpuli Talli had the highest percentage (67.51 per cent) of the workers in this sector. This was followed by Sitabpur (54.85 per cent), Jaunk (49.12 per cent), Punar (40.97 per cent), Jahari (40.67 per cent) and Kashirampur (32.10 per cent). Most of the remaining villages had less than 20 per cent of the workers in this sector. There was a general increase in percentage in 1971 indicating a shift from primary activities. The pattern reveals that 15 large-sized villages had over 30 per cent of their workers engaged in this sector and the remaining villages had less than this percentage. Satpuli Talli had the highest percentage of workers in Trade and Commerce (22.96 per cent) and Transport (10.36 per cent) in 1961. It continued to lead in 1971 in Manufacturing (17.98 per cent) and Trade and Commerce (43.44 per cent) among all the large villages. In the tertiary sector, "Other services" had engaged relatively more workers. The percentage of workers in this category was highest in Kalagarh village (96.48) followed by Jahari (66.52), Umroli (55.70), Jaunk (54.10) and Kasani (50.83).

A detailed analysis of spatial patterns and variations in occupational structure among the 169 patwari circles of the district was attempted for the years 1961 and 1971 (Figures 12 and 13). It would be observed therefrom that the livelihood pattern is dominated by work in the primary sector reflecting a high level of dependence on agriculture. There are small variations both spatially and temporally in the percentage of workers in the primary sector. The district average for the year 1971 was 84.83 per cent as against 92.98 per cent in 1961. The percentage of workers in primary sector ranged between 73.62 and 99.20 in 1961. The respective range in 1971 varied between 65.14 per cent and 96.19 per cent (Figure 12). Most of the patwari circles having relatively higher proportions of workers in the primary sector lay in the western, south-eastern and north-eastern parts of the district, along-with the fringes of the Forested Ranges. Both the western and north-eastern parts of the district are relatively more backward and pursue more or less primitive agriculture. They are also characterised by inaccessibility and are remote from urban influences. In contrast to these, patwari circles having relatively higher proportions of workers in the non-primary sector lie mostly either in the Bhaber plains, or along the main transport line from Kotdwara to Srinagar and beyond or in the vicinity of urban and other emerging nodal centres (Figure 13). In 1961, there were only 12 patwari circles with over 12 per cent of the workers engaged in the non-primary sector. However, in 1971, with the increase in non-primary activities, the number of patwari circles having over 15 per cent of the workers in the non-primary sector increased to 41. This resulted in the increase of the district average of 7.02 per cent in 1961 to 15.15 per cent in 1971.

Our sample survey[2] conducted in 42 villages during 1977-78 also revealed the patterns and variations similar to those derived from the analysis of the secondary data in the preced-

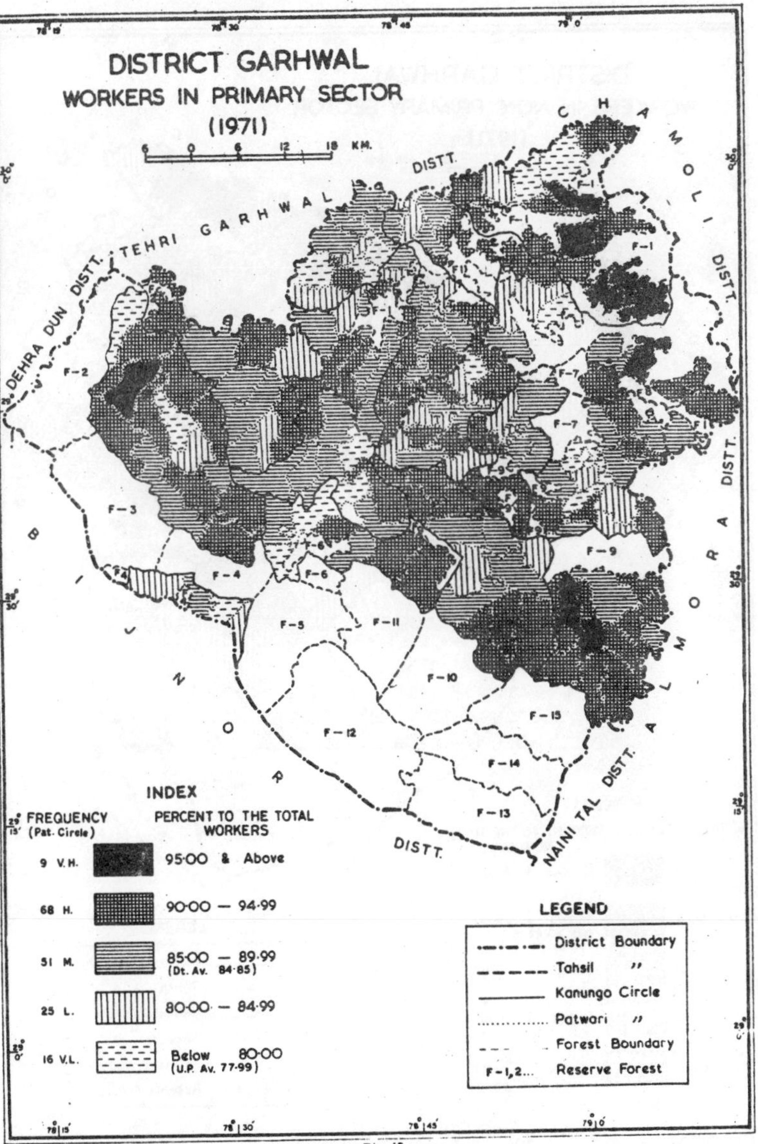
DISTRICT GARHWAL
WORKERS IN PRIMARY SECTOR
(1971)
INDEX
FREQUENCY (Pat. Circle)
PERCENT TO THE TOTAL WORKERS
9 V.H. 95·00 & Above
68 H. 90·00 — 94·99
51 M. 85·00 — 89·99 (Dt. Av. 84·85)
25 L. 80·00 — 84·99
16 V.L. Below 80·00 (U.P. Av. 77·99)
LEGEND
District Boundary
Tahsil "
Kanungo Circle
Patwari "
Forest Boundary
F-1,2... Reserve Forest
TEHRI GARHWAL DISTT.
CHAMOLI DISTT.
ALMORA DISTT.
NAINI TAL DISTT.
BIJNOR DISTT.
DEHRA DUN DISTT.

Fig. 12

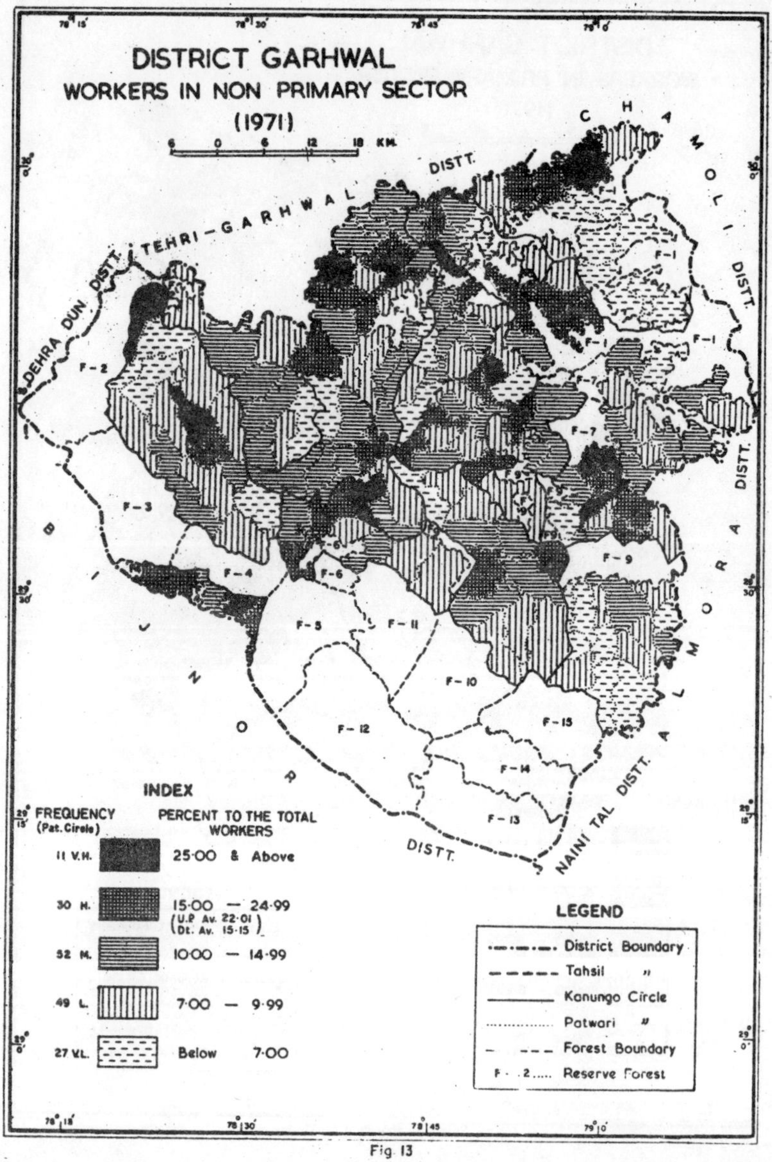
DISTRICT GARHWAL
WORKERS IN NON PRIMARY SECTOR
(1971)
6 0 6 12 18 KM.
TEHRI-GARHWAL DISTT.
CHAMOLI DISTT.
DEHRA DUN DISTT.
BIJNOR DISTT.
ALMORA DISTT.
NAINI TAL DISTT.
INDEX
FREQUENCY (Pat. Circle)
PERCENT TO THE TOTAL WORKERS
11 V.H. 25·00 & Above
30 H. 15·00 — 24·99 (U.P. Av. 22·01) (Dt. Av. 15·15)
52 M. 10·00 — 14·99
49 L. 7·00 — 9·99
27 V.L. Below 7·00
LEGEND
District Boundary
Tahsil "
Kanungo Circle
Patwari "
Forest Boundary
F-2..... Reserve Forest

Fig. 13

ing paragraphs. The total work force in these sample villages was 11,487 or 51.36 per cent of the total population. 67.42 per cent of the workers were engaged in the primary sector, 1.77 per cent in the secondary sector and the remaining 30.81 per cent in the services sector. In the primary sector, cultivators formed the major proportion constituting 61.91 per cent of the total workers. The percentage of agricultural labourers was negligible. Forestry, mining etc. also engaged 4.67 per cent of the workers. In the services sector, trade and commerce and transport and storage accounted for 3.19 per cent and 0.99 per cent of the workers respectively. The major part of work-force in this sector was engaged in "Other services". A further break-up of this category revealed that 6.47 per cent of the workers were engaged in the armed and police forces; 1.28 per cent in teaching; 7.71 per cent in the civil service both central and state; 6.35 per cent in private service and the remaining 3.68 per cent in other occupations.

The age composition of the workers (Table 4.3) in the sample villages also showed that 88.20 per cent of the total workers were found in the age-group between 15 and 60 years. Those who were below 15 and above 60 years of age were 5.37 per cent and 6.43 per cent respectively. Most of them were engaged in agricultural and allied activities.

The foregoing analysis of the livelihood pattern from district level down to the level of important settlements highlights some important features of the economy. The district economy is highly dominated by primary activities, reflecting a high level of dependence on agriculture. Cultivators from a significantly large segment of the primary activities. Agricultural labourers are few and are confined mainly to the Bhaber plains. Forestry is pursued largely by workers in the different Forest Ranges. Secondary activities such as household industry, manufacturing and construction are limited and undeveloped and do not show indications of development either spatially or temporally in terms of growth of income, output and employment. There is, however, a clear shift from agricultural activities to tertiary activities. A sizeable number of workers are engaged in "Other Services". In addition, a few nodal centres both urban and rural, are emerging.

Agriculture

An analysis of the resource base and of occupational structure highlights agriculture as the essential ingredient and the mainstay of the people. It is the most important resource base though it is not the norm of specialisation in long term perspectives of development. It has been the main attractive and dependable source of revenue for the Garhwal Princes, the Gorakhas, the British and the subsequent governments alike. Considering the spatial characteristics of the hill agriculture, the revenue demands had progressively been increasing from time to time.[3] In contrast with the plains, hill agriculture presents peculiarities of its own in terms of the nature and types of cultivation, terrace cultivation, **gul** (leat) irrigation, manuring, crop rotations and number and size of holdings etc. Each one of them constrains the levels of productivity and incomes.

TABLE 4.3

Age composition of workers - Sample Survey - 1977-78

(Per cent)

Occupational Categories	Total No. of workers	Age composition 0-14	15-34	35-59	60 +
I. Cultivators	7,112	6.79	46.39	40.72	6.10
II. Agricultural labourers	97	6.19	56.70	35.05	2.06
III. Mining, forestry etc.	536	5.41	48.32	41.42	4.85
Total Primary Sector (A)	7,745	6.69	46.64	40.70	5.97
IV. Household industry	17	5.88	41.18	29.41	23.53
V. Manufacturing	186	1.08	51.08	41.94	5.90
Total Secondary Sector (B)	203	1.20	48.50	43.11	7.19
VI. Construction	131	0.76	45.80	46.56	6.88
VII. Trade and commerce	366	2.19	53.83	40.98	3.01
VIII. Transport and storage	114	3.51	42.10	50.88	3.51
IX. Other services	2,928	2.83	49.12	39.92	8.13
Total Tertiary Sector (C)	3,539	2.80	49.38	40.40	7.42
Grand Total (A+B+C)	11,487	5.37	47.52	40.68	6.43

Cultivation in the hills is of three types viz., **Katil** cultivation, **upraon** cultivation and **talaon** cultivation; the latter two are more dominant. **Katil** cultivation is the primitive form of hill agriculture and considered as the first stage of terracing. This is comparable to jhumming in north-eastern India. The forest covered with shrubs and bushes is cleared and burnt and the land broken with the hoe. The seeds are then sown broadcast over the ashes which are the only form of manure, the land then hoed or dug to cover the seeds. Irrigation and weeding are not undertaken but a regular rotation of crops usually of inferior types such as **mandua** or ragi (Eleusine coracana), **chua** (Amaranthus frumentaceus), **gohat** (Horsegram or Delichos biflorus), **ogal** (buckwheat), turmeric etc., is followed. After every crop, the land is allowed to lie fallow for 3 or more years. **Katil** cultivation though advantageous from the points of view of increasing the cultivable land and terrace cultivation and destroying agricultural pests etc., is a formidable enemy to forest conservancy, a destroyer of biological and hygienic effects and a constraint on natural reproduction of the forests. **Upraon** cultivation is pursued in upland slopes which are permanently terraced and superior in quality to those of **katil** lands. Their qualities vary according to the available soil nutrients, the evenness of the fields, their proximity to the forests and accessibility of the slopes, nearness to homesteads, transport facilities and their position on sunny or shady aspects of the ridge. However, they are relatively at higher levels without any means of irrigation and are adaptable mostly to dry crops. The kharif crops are **mandua** or ragi (Eleusine coracana), **jhangora** (Oplismenus frumentaceus), **kauni** (Panicum italicum), **bhat** (soyabean), **gohat** (Horsegram or Delichos biflorus), **chua** (Amaranthus frumentaceus) etc., while those of rabi are wheat, barley, mustard etc. Lands irrigated and irrigable, generally at the foot of the hills are known as **talaon** lands. They are characterised by the proximity to the rivers and their tributaries; mild climate; broad level valleys and low lying fields; high fertility and development; existence of permanent irrigational facilities and possession of fine alluvium. Three types of **talaon** lands can easily be identified. The first class lands are known as **seras**. Water supply is perennial and flow gentle; fields are low lying and hot; alluvium consists of the finest clay and double cropping is practised. They are always under cultivation and never allowed to lie fallow. Paddy is the main crop of the kharif season while wheat, barley, mustard are grown in valley bottoms as a rabi crop. **Pancher** lands are the irrigable lands from the intermittent streams on the ordinary hillsides. They are situated at higher levels and possess comparative low productivity. In waterlogged lands like the fens and marshes of the **tarai**, **shimar** cultivation is pursued. These contrasts, in the type of cultivation are an indication of the dominating influence of topography and man's adaptation of agriculture to it.

The steep and rugged mountainous terrain, the scarcity of tracts of level ground; small proportions of cultivable land and the frequent soil-erosion, have all necessitated resort to terracing in the region. Mountain-sides have been cut into handmade fields rising in succession, like gigantic flights of steps, ascending from the banks of streams towards the summits of the hills and known as terraces. The construction of terraces involves enormous labour, time, capital, skill and perseverance. They vary in length, breadth and height according to the form and slope of the ridge on which they are built. The usual width varies between 3 to 6 metres, length between 5 to 25 metres, height between 1.5 metres to 3 metres and the area between 50 to 200 square metres. Terraces 3 to 6 metres wide are common in the **upraon** lands and in some places as many as 500 terraces can be counted in continuous flights. Their repair and maintenance is even more difficult and laborious than their construction as 25 to 40 per cent of the terrace walls break down during the rainy season.[4]

Like the system of terracing, **gul** irrigation is also an arduous task. It requires not only capital, labour and patience but also skills suitable to the local needs and conditions. Excepting the Bhaber region, where irrigation is done through the canals; in the whole of the district irrigation is done by means of small irrigational channels locally called **guls** (leats). They are taken from the numerous streams that feed the larger rivers and are available at the foot of almost every ridge. The length of the **gul** varies according to the height of the land to be irrigated above the bottom of the valleys and the more or less rapid fall in the stream.

Manuring occupies a significant place in hill agriculture due to the poor, shallow and stony texture of soil and its quick impoverishment by the scouring action of the rains. In **katil** cultivation, the burnt ashes are the only form of manure which are spread over the land to give fertiltiy to the soil. In **talaon** lands, silt brought down by leats is considered sufficient to keep them fertile. Manuring is however, needed most in **upraon** lands. Cow and buffalo dung is usually used for manuring. Leaf manure, prepared by the mingling of leaves, dung, urine and litter for some months, is also used. Farmyard manure usually stacked in heaps outside the dwelling houses, is also used as and when required. In the greater part of the district, **goath** system is prevalent. This involves construction of a shed formed by **palla** or **pharkha** - a sort of thatched hurdle about 2.5 metres by 1.5 metres and made up of bamboo, thatch and leaves. Such a shed is called **goath** and is moved from field to field alongwith the cattle, wherever manuring is required.

In agriculture, the system of cultivation, type of crops grown and method of rotation are determined by the nature of the soil, the physical features and the special needs of the cultivators. Owing to mountainous topography and varied cultivation, different crops are grown. In the greater part of the district, however, two harvests of kharif and rabi are raised. The main crops of the former are paddy, **mandua** (Eleusine coracana), **jhangora** (Oplismenus frumentaceus) while wheat, barley and mustard form the main crops of the latter. In the rotation of crops which are elaborate and ingenious, the cultivated area of the village is divided into several parcels or **sars.** Each **sar** is alloted a definite crop rotation. The **sar** growing paddy is called **paddy-sar** or another crop growing **mandua** (Eleusine coracana) is known as **mandua-sar. Mandua-sar** is invariably followed by a fallow season for 3-4 months. In the lands which are too stony and cold or where surface soil is too thin and uneven, **jhangora** and/or **chua** (Amaranthus frumentaceus) is substituted for paddy during kharif and barley for wheat during the rabi. The entire rotation takes 2 years for 3 crops. In the newly reclaimed unterraced land (**katil**) and in the outlying terraces too, one full rotation occupies 5 years. The whole system of rotation[5] of crops in the **upraon** cultivation may be summarised as below.

Upland Terraced Slopes

	Rice-Sar	Mandua-Sar
First Year		
First Kharif	rice, jhangora, kauni, chillies, buckwheat, sesame etc.	Mandua, turmeric, buck-wheat, legumes, chua (Amaranthus) etc.
First Rabi	Wheat, barley or mustard	Fallow
Second Year		
Second Kharif	Mandua	Rice, jhangora, chillies etc.
Second Rabi	Fallow	Wheat, barley etc.

Land Holdings by Size

According to the Agricultural Census of Uttar Pradesh (1970-71), there were 1.01 lakh operational holdings in Pauri Garhwal district in the year 1970-71. It would be clear from

Table 4.4 that a sizeable number of over 36,789 (36 per cent of the total) were less than 0.50 hectare. Another 32.80 per cent were in the range "0.50 - 1.00 hectare". In the higher ranges, the proportions decrease sharply. There were only 23,000 (22.6 per cent) in the range between 1.00 to 2.00 hectares and 8,600 (8.5 per cent) above 2.00 hectares. The total area covered by these operational holdings was approximately 92,000 hectares, of which 33.8 per cent lay in the range between 1.00 and 2.00 hectares followed sharply by the following ranges of over 2.00 hectares with a coverage of 28.6 per cent. Although 68.9 per cent of holdings lay in the range below 1.00 hectare, yet the area covered by them was only 37.6 per cent. An overwhelming majority of the holdings was self-owned and self-operated whereas only 1 per cent of the holdings were such that their operators did not own any part of their holdings and all lands operated by them was either leased in or occupied in an unauthorised manner or both. Again, there were only 72 holdings with an area of 293 hectares which were joint holdings, the remaining being individual holdings.

TABLE 4.4

Number and area of operational holdings in different size-classes in Pauri Garhwal District - 1970-71

(Hectares)

Size-classes	Number	Per cent	Area	Per cent
Below 0.25	15,608	15.3	2,250	2.5
0.25 - 0.50	21,181	20.8	7,891	8.6
0.50 - 1.00	33,457	32.8	24,296	26.5
1.00 - 2.00	23,002	22.6	31,025	33.8
2.00 and above	8,629	8.5	26,335	28.6
All sizes	1,01,877	100.00	91,797	100.00

As could be expected of a hilly terrain, the size of holdings is very small, creating innumerable problems in agricultural operations. The holdings are fragmented to such an extent that an average holding remains uneconomic. In 1970-71, the number of parcels per operational holdings averaged 12 and the average area per parcel was only 0.07 of an hectare. And from Table 4.5 the higher the size-class of holdings, the greater the number of parcels per holdings and the larger the average area per parcel. This is mainly due to the rugged terrain.

A discussion of the salient features of agriculture in the preceding paragraphs shows that a large number of constraints inhibit agricultural productivity. In fact it is a food-deficit region where annually a large part of the food-supply is reinforced from outside. The deficit increases during the periods of poor rains. The requirements for foodgrains vary from place to place with relatively larger demands in the uplands. The problem of food deficiency has been aggravated in recent years by the increasing pressure of population, by the scarcity of cultivated land whose possibilities of extension are remote and also by the progressive depletion of cultivable wastes.

TABLE 4.5

Number of parcels per operational holding and average area per parcel in Pauri Garhwal District - 1970-71

Size-classes (Hectares)	Total holdings		No. of parcels per operational holding	Average area per parcel (Hectares)
	No.	Area		
Below 0.25	15,608	2,250	5.1	0.03
0.25 - 0.50	21,181	7,891	10.2	0.04
0.50 - 1.00	33,457	24,296	10.8	0.07
1.00 - 2.00	23,002	31,025	17.2	0.08
2.00 - 3.00	5,473	13,115	19.5	0.12
3.00 - 4.00	2,072	6,671	20.3	0.15
4.00 - 5.00	649	2,789	23.4	0.18
5.00 - 10.00	398	3,308	22.0	0.36
10.00 and above	37	452	14.4	0.85
All classes	101,877	91,797	12.00	0.07

Crops and Crop-associations

As stated earlier, the main harvests of the district are both kharif and rabi. Important crops of kharif are paddy, **mandua** or ragi (Eleusine coracana), **jhangora** (Oplismenus frumentaceus), **kauni** (Panicum italicum), maize, pulses etc., while wheat, barley, mustard etc. are grown during the rabi season. But the most dominant crops are, however, paddy, wheat and **mandua** or ragi, accounting for over 80 per cent of the gross cropped area in the district. The highest percentage is occupied by paddy (27.98) followed sharply by **mandua** (27.34) and wheat (26.10). The remaining 20 per cent is covered by other crops. Excepting the Bhaber plains, which concentrate mostly on the production of paddy and wheat, the variations in respect of these crops are not very significant. These inferences, based upon the analysis of secondary data pertaining to patwari circles, approximate closely to those based upon the analysis of primary data collected for our sample survey of 218 households in 42 villages. It has been estimated that 77.33 per cent of the gross cropped area is devoted to these three main crops and the rest to the other crops. The percentage variations of these three crops taken together among different land-holding categories are not significant although holdings above one hectare have relatively lower percentages due to greater diversification of crops. Similarly, village-wise percentage variations are not great, in general, although the extreme range was between 42.86 per cent in Kund to 87.38 per cent in Dungripanth. In the light of these findings, a detailed analysis of the spatial patterns and variations of 5 important crops has been attempted.

Paddy

Paddy cultivation in the hills can be considered the best and the most developed form of agriculture. Paddy is grown mostly in **talaon** lands, at the foot of the hills near rivers or their tributaries or other perennial streams where the soil is of fine alluvial deposits. Irrigation is facilitated by the available supply of water and different levels of fields. At some places, ponds and springs give rise to a few patches under paddy. Paddy cultivation under these **talaon** lands or irrigated lands together with the dry farming in **upraon** lands account for over 1/4th (27.98 per cent) of the gross cropped area in the district.

Most of the patwari circles with relatively high proportions of their area under paddy lie in the Bhaber plains and in the central part of the district. As against these, very few patwari circles with high proportions under paddy lie in the east or north-east and particularly along the Alaknanda valley. The variations among 169 patwari circles range between 7.07 per cent and 46.05 per cent depending mainly upon the extent of area under irrigation. As against these, our sample survey, however, revealed that area under paddy was only 24.98 per cent of gross cropped area and varied insignificantly among different land-holding categories. Nevertheless, very small holdings of less than 1/4th of a hectare had less percentage (20.42 per cent) of gross cropped area under paddy. But the percentage variations of the area under paddy in sample villages ranged widely between 3.41 in Kund to 41.21 in Gorakhpur (Bhaber), depending upon the spatial and other characteristics of the villages.

Wheat

Wheat is the most important rabi crop requiring substantial amounts of moisture during both sowing and growing periods. So areas having plentiful spring rains or where the snow falls abundantly during winters are most suited for its cultivation. Neither the moist climate of the valleys nor the areas of excessive rainfall are suitable for its production. The area under wheat in the district is slightly less than that of paddy and accounts for 26.10 per cent of the gross area cropped. The intra-district variations at the patwari circle level are wider and range between 6.91 per cent and 42.43 per cent, depending upon different physiographic, climatic and soil complexes. On the basis of our sample survey, the estimated average of the area under wheat for the district as a whole was 25.83 per cent of the gross cropped area. This was slightly higher but approximating to that worked out on the basis of secondary data for patwari circles. Interestingly enough, in the higher land-holding classes the relative percentages were progressively lower owing perhaps to the diversification of crops. In the sample villages, the range of variations was wider and lay between 11.82 per cent in Kundi to 37.44 per cent in Gorakhpur in the Bhaber plains. The alluvial soil character and availability of irrigational and other infrastructure inputs have enabled such villages to specialise in the production of wheat and paddy not only in the Bhaber plains but also in the uplands.

Mandua (Eleusine Coracana)

Mandua is a staple and important food crop of the kharif season. It can adapt to a poorer soil and to a smaller degree to variations in temperature and rainfall and requires less care. So fields where paddy and wheat are unable to prosper yield a rich **mandua** harvest. It is the crop mostly favoured to the areas of **katil** cultivation and to the inferior uplands, yielding a richer harvest than other crops. Its widespread cultivation is pursued throughout the district excepting the Bhaber plains and accounts for 27.36 per cent of the gross cropped area. Although the areas of concentration are patchy yet many patwari circles in the central, northern and north-eastern parts of the district have relatively high proportions of their respective gross cropped area under it compared with the remaining parts of the district. The district average, on the basis of sample survey, was estimated to be 26.52 per cent of the gross cropped area. The proportions of area in small land-holdings classes are relatively higher than their counterparts in the large land-holding classes. In the land-holding class lying between 0.50 to 1.00 hectare, the percentage of area under **mandua** was 31.68, the highest among all the land-holding classes. In contrast to these land-holding classes, the variations among sample villages were wide enough and ranged around 37 per cent.

Jhangora (Oplismenus frumentaceus)

Jhangora (Oplismenus frumentaceus) and **kauni** (Panicum italicum) are grown in combination with paddy. Whereas paddy occupies the best and the most fertile and irrigated lands, **jhangora** is grown in the relatively infertile, coarser and unirrigated soils. One would often observe that most of the lands on the corners or edges of the better class fields, the inferior terraces and the shady aspects of the fields are generally occupied by **jhangora** or **kauni** or other inferior millets. **Jhangora** accounts for over 10 per cent of the gross cropped area in the district. The intra-district variations are widely ranged around 45 per cent in respect of patwari circles. Most of the patwari circles lying in the western, eastern and the central parts of the district have relatively higher percentages of area under **jhangora** than their counterparts in other parts of the district. The district average for **jhangora** according to our estimates worked out at 9.31 per cent of the gross cropped area. The proportions in the small land-holding classes were relatively higher than those of their counterparts in larger landholding classes. It was the lowest in the land-holding class lying between 0.50 to 1.00 hectare. Among different sample villages the variations lay between 1.13 per cent in Gorakhpur in Bhaber plains to 21.10 per cent in Kund in the hilly tract where jhumming cultivation is still practised.

Barley

Barley is a rabi crop grown in the wheat zone. It is generally grown in areas where winters are severe and soils are coarser and less fertile. It is the hardiest and the most adaptable of all the cereals and does quite well in the damp, hot river valleys as well as in the dry, cold Himalayan altitudes. In the higher elevations, wheat gradually gives way to barley though sometimes both are grown in combination. Barley accounts for 6.59 per cent of the gross cropped area in the district. Intra-district percentage variations are, however, not very pronounced. Only a few patwari circles have over 10 per cent of the gross cropped area, mostly in the northern parts of the district, the southern parts of the district having lower proportions. The percentage of area under barley, as estimated from our sample survey, averaged 6.08 for the district. Among different land-holding categories, the patterns revealed are akin to those of **jhangora** (Oplismenus frumentaceus). The range of variations among different sample villages was from 1.88 per cent in Gorakhpur in Bhaber to 15.42 per cent in Kund in the hilly tract of the district.

Other Crops

The district, in addition to the above important crops produces miscellaneous crops of cereals, pulses, vegetables and others. Important among them are maize, **chua** (Amaranthus frumentaceus), **ogal** (buckwheat); **urd** (rayed kidney beans - Phaseolus radiatus), **bhat** (Soyabean or Glycine soja), **gohat** (horsegram or Delichos biflorus); mustard, rapeseed, sesame; potatoes, onions and other vegetables; chillies, ginger, turmeric, hemp, sugarcane, tobacco, spices, fodder etc. They are mostly grown as mixed crops. Their cultivation and production are, however, extremely variable from village to village depending upon various climatic and physiographic conditions.

Maize, as a kharif crop, though universally cultivated, occupies only 0.59 per cent of the gross cropped area in the district. Our sample survey, however, revealed a percentage of 0.79, higher though not very significantly so. The proportions were higher in higher land-holding classes. Bhaber, has the highest percentage (2.80) of gross cultivated area though in some patchy-tracts of the patwari circles lying in the western part of the district, a relatively higher percentage of gross cropped area is devoted to it. This has been substantiated from our sample survey: both the samples of Kund and Kathur Bara lying in this tract had 13.39 per cent and 2.39 per cent of their respective gross cropped area under it. Besides, **chua** (Amaranthus frumentaceus) and **ogal** (buckwheat) are produced in small areas throughout the district. But, in the patwari circles of Choprakot, Chauthan and Dhaijuli lying in the north-eastern part of the district, relatively higher proportions of gross cropped area is a marked feature of the cropping pattern.

The crops of pulses are highly diversified. The chief among them are **urd** (rayed kidney beans - Phaseolus radiatus), **gohat** (horsegram), **tur**, **bhat** (soyabean), beans (mutter) and pulses (masoor). **Urd** is the most prominent and universal crop and is grown substantially in south-western (in the Udaipur patwari circles) and in central tracts (in Maundarsyun patwari circles along the western Nayar river) of the district. **Gohat** has the characteristic of being grown without any care and is sown thinly. Its sparseness can be noticeable in the infertile and stony areas of **katil** and **upraon** lands. **Bhat** of different varieties is grown in different parts of the district as a mixed crop. It is only recently, that new varieties of soyabean have increasingly been grown. Both **mutter** and **masoor** are rabi crops and are grown alongwith wheat and barley as a mixed crop. The crops of pulses taken together in the district account for 1.05 per cent of the gross cropped area though our sample survey revealed a higher percentage of 3.24 under it and also showed progressively higher proportions in higher land-holding classes. Barring a few villages, the proportional variations were small.

In the district the area under oilseeds as revealed from our survey, accounted for 0.82 per cent of the gross cropped area and varied from 0.16 per cent in the smallest land-holding category of less than 1/4th of a hectare to 2.34 per cent in the highest land-holding category of over 2.00 hectares. Among the oilseeds, mustard is the chief and a little is grown as a mixed crop. In some locations sesame, requiring rich soil and timely and gentle rains, is also grown.

Vegetables of different varieties are produced in limited areas for domestic consumption and to a limited extent for internal barter and for sale. About 1.11 per cent of the gross cropped area in the district, according to our survey, is devoted to the production of vegetables. The percentage area among different land-holding categories varied between 0.16 in smallest land-holding category of less than 1/4th of a hectare to 1.62 in the highest land-holding category of over 2.00 hectares. Among the vegetables the district has, in recent years, started production of potatoes and onions for commercial purposes, especially in the north-eastern tracts of Bharsar and Thalisain as the yields per hectare are comparable to those of the plains.

Apart from the crops discussed in the preceding paragraphs, about 1.32 per cent of the gross cropped area in the district is devoted to the production of miscellaneous crops such as chillies, turmeric, ginger, hemp, sugarcane and tobacco. They are raised for domestic as well as commercial purposes. Both chillies and turmeric flourish best under great heat and therefore are grown side by side. A sizeable quantity of chillies are grown in the patwari circles of Gujru, in the south-eastern tract of the district. Marchula, is the key centre for collecting chillies both for Garhwal and Kumaon and it is from there that they are exported in bulk via Ramnagar. Ginger is mostly grown by the people of the valleys and to a limited extent in the uplands of the Bhaber. Hemp is grown in high slopes having a northern-exposure, in cool and dry ground with ample facilities for manuring. Its use is multi-purpose; the seeds are consumed as condiment; the mature leaves and stems yield **charas** (resinous exudation of hemp); the fibre is woven into a coarse canvas of good strength, locally called **bhangela;** and the wood as torchwood. The north-eastern tract of the district had once specialised in its production but a considerable decline has been marked in recent times. Sugarcane production is one of the important cash crops of the Bhaber region, which is conspicuously absent in the uplands. Besides, crops of tobacco, edible and non-edible oilseeds and fodder are also produced. Tobacco production in the hilly tracts is confined only to domestic consumption.

Crop Combination Regions

A perusal of the characteristics of hill agriculture discussed above shows that the district reflects the varying conditions of altitudes, climate, physiography and soils on the one hand and various agronomic traditions evolved over the centuries such as terracing, manuring, crop rotation, the **gul** system of irrigation etc. on the other. These factors have resulted in sharp intra-district variations in the crops grown. Spatially, different crops are dominant in different tracts. Thus, diversity of crops and mixed farming are the outstanding characteristics of the agriculture. All these factors act as significant constraints in areal differentiation of the cropping pattern within the district.

An attempt to regional differentiation on the basis of percentage of area under each of the five principal crops (viz., paddy, wheat, **mandua** or ragi, **jhangora** and barley) to their respective gross cropped areas in 169 patwari circle units has been made (Figure 14). The methodology adopted in this analysis is the application of the Thomas method[6] - a modified version of the Weaver method[7] and is considered suitable in delineating the areas of different crop combinations in a region like ours, where mixed farming is the predominant type.[8] As a result of its application, four types of crop combination regions have emerged, taking count of variances of each group of combination of crops. The cropping patterns in these crop combination regions, based upon the analysis of secondary data for 169 patwari circles and of the primary data for 218 households in 42 sample villages are summarised in Tables 4.6 and 4.7 respectively. The levels of productivity of important crops in these crop combination regions find a place in Table 4.8. On this basis the salient characteristics of each of the crop combination regions are analysed.[9]

2-Crop Combination Region

The 2-crop combination region comprises of four patwari circles of Motadhak, Sukhrao, Saneh and Haldukhata in the Bhaber plains. They have, in all 75 rural settlements with only 3.22 per cent of the gross cropped area of the district. Yet it has 38.8 per cent of its gross cropped area under paddy and 37.7 per cent under wheat together covering over 75 per cent of the gross cropped area of the Bhaber region. This reflects a high intensity of paddy and wheat cultivation. About 74.5 per cent of the gross cropped area in the sample villages were under these two crops (Table 4.7). The remaining cropped area was devoted to **mandua, jhangora**, pulses, oilseeds, spices, tobacco, sugarcane and vegetables. Productivity levels, as would be observed from Table 4.8, are high especially in irrigated areas. The yields of paddy and wheat in irrigated lands have been estimated as 17.76 quintals and 13.35 quintals per hectare respectively. The corresponding yields in unirrigated areas are 11.44 quintals and 7.59 quintals per hectare. While the yields of **mandua** (6.55 quintals per hectare) and of **jhangora** (5.66 quintals per hectare) are estimated to be the lowest among all the regions, those of barley (8.74 quintals per hectare) and maize (12.33 quintals per hectare) are the highest. Paddy and wheat have increasingly taken the place of **jhangora** and barley respectively. Not only the soils are best suited to both these crops but also food habits have swung against the "coarser cereals": **jhangora** and barley. These high productivity levels of crops especially those of paddy and wheat can be attributed to a variety of reasons. In addition to the abundance of moisture, sufficient rainfall, uniformly warm temperature, adequate irrigation facilities and fine alluvial soil, there is intensive use of land, timely availability and greater utilisation of agricultural inputs such as chemical fertilizers, high yielding varieties of seeds, pesticides and insecticides etc. From Table 4.9 that 83.95 per cent of the net area sown is irrigated in this crop combination region. This has not only facilitated but also accelerated the adoption of high yielding varieties of seeds and the application of chemical fertilizers. About 36.60 per cent of the gross cropped area is under improved seeds and chemical fertilizers. This happens to be the highest proportion among all the crop combination regions. The quantity of fertilizers used per hectare (43.69 kilograms) of gross area sown, is also the highest among all these regions.

3-Crop Combination Region

This crop combination region is the most dominant of all the regions comprising 93 patwari circles, all of them lying in the hilly tracts, throughout the district. About 53.86 per cent of the rural settlements lie in this region. Unlike the 2-crop combination region of the Bhaber, this region, as would be observed from Figure 14 lacks the characteristic of geographical contiguity and hence does not form a single compact block of patwari circles but is rather found in spatially non-contiguous group of patwari circles throughout the district. The region has the best lands available both in the uplands and down in the

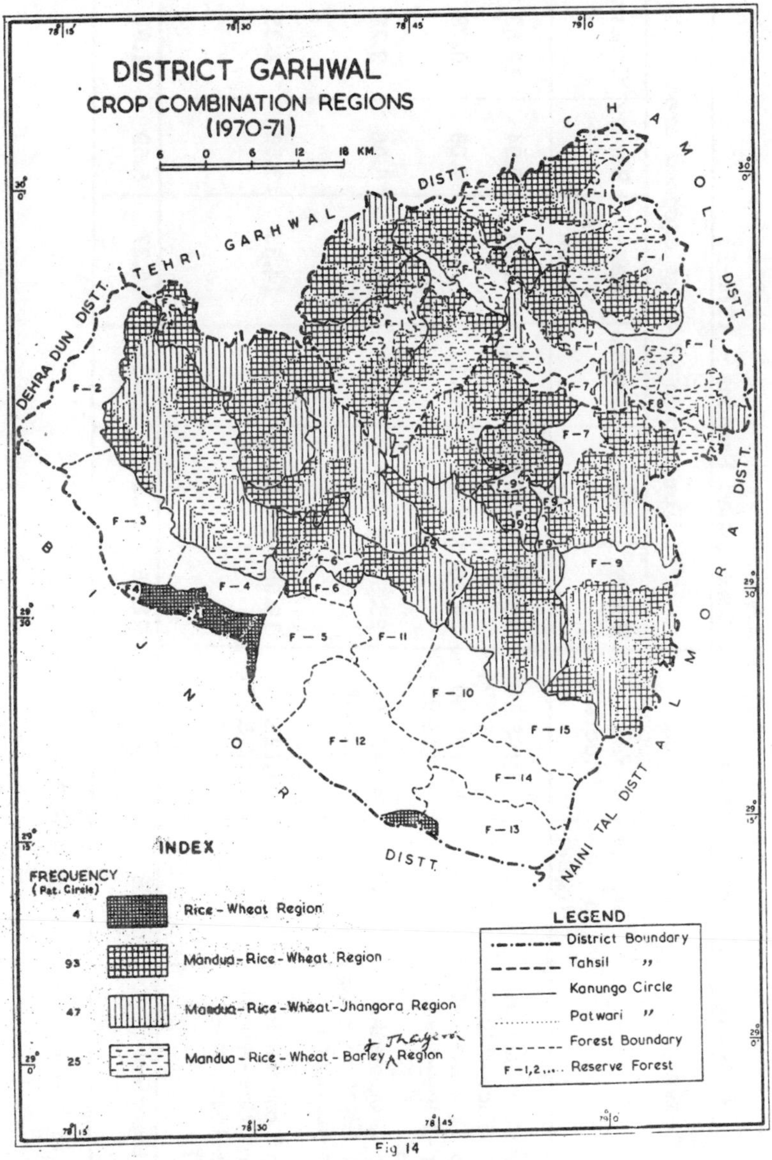
DISTRICT GARHWAL
CROP COMBINATION REGIONS
(1970-71)
6 0 6 12 18 KM.
TEHRI GARHWAL DISTT.
CHAMOLI DISTT.
ALMORA DISTT.
NAINI TAL DISTT
BIJNOR DISTT.
DEHRA DUN DISTT.
F-1
F-2
F-3
F-4
F-5
F-6
F-7
F-8
F-9
F-10
F-11
F-12
F-13
F-14
F-15
INDEX
FREQUENCY (Pat. Circle)
4 Rice - Wheat Region
93 Mandua - Rice - Wheat Region
47 Mandua - Rice - Wheat - Jhangora Region
25 Mandua - Rice - Wheat - Barley Region
LEGEND
District Boundary
Tahsil "
Kanungo Circle
Patwari "
Forest Boundary
F-1,2,... Reserve Forest

Fig 14

TABLE 4.6
Cropping Patterns in different Crop Combination Regions - 1970–71

Cropping Regions	No. of Patwari Circles in the Region	Gross Cropped Area (Hects.)	Percentage of gross cropped area					
			Paddy	Wheat	Mandua	Jhan-gora & Kauni	Barley	Others
I. 2-Crop Combination Region (Rice-Wheat)	4	5,195.14 (3.22)	38.87	37.55	1.42	1.59	2.94	17.63
II. 3-Crop Combination Region (Rice-Wheat-Mandua)	93	83,799.60 (51.85)	28.80	28.80	30.22	7.32	4.08	0.78
III. 4-Crop Combination Region (Rice-Wheat-Mandua-Jhangora/Barley)	47	47,485.02 (29.38)	25.59	23.67	25.48	15.97	6.06	3.23
IV. 5-Crop Combination Region (Rice-Wheat-Mandua-Jhangora-Barley)	25	25,125.10 (15.55)	19.38	18.62	31.82	14.33	13.50	2.35
All Categories	169	161,604.86 (100.00)	27.98	26.10	27.34	10.37	6.59	1.82

Note: Figures in brackets are in percentages.

TABLE 4.7

Cropping Patterns in different Crop-Combination Regions - Sample Villages - 1977-78

Cropping Regions	Gross cropped Area (Hectares)*	Percentage of gross cropped area under									
		Paddy	Wheat	Mandua	Jhangora & Kauni	Barley	Maize	Pulses	Oil-seeds	Vegetables	Others
I. 2-Crop Combination Region (Rice-Wheat)	25.51	38.84	35.68	2.06	2.69	3.09	1.98	7.59	3.16	2.06	2.85
II. 3-Crop Combination Region (Rice-Wheat-Mandua)	134.96	25.72	25.89	28.44	8.12	6.15	0.43	3.32	0.36	0.93	0.64
III. 4-Crop Combination Region (Rice-Wheat-Mandua-Jhangora/Barley)	94.13	21.46	24.46	31.48	11.54	4.78	0.56	2.29	0.90	0.99	1.54
IV. 5-Crop Combination Region (Rice-Wheat-Mandua-Jhangora-Barley)	25.31	20.10	20.73	22.49	14.04	13.56	2.39	1.99	0.64	1.59	2.47
All categories	279.91	24.98	25.83	26.52	9.31	6.08	0.79	3.24	0.82	1.11	1.32

* Data were originally compiled in Nalis - the local method of measurement of land.

TABLE 4.8

Yields per hectare of important crops in various Crop Combination Regions Sample Villages - 1977-78

Crop Combination Regions	YIELDS (Quintals per hectare)							
	Paddy		Wheat					
	Irri-gated	Unirri-gated	Irri-gated	Unirri-gated	Mandua	Jhan-gora & Kauni	Barley	Maize
I. 2-Crop Combination Region	17.76	11.44	13.35	9.59	6.55	5.66	8.74	12.33
II. 3-Crop Combination Region	15.64	10.21	11.35	9.18	8.45	8.54	8.21	8.56
III. 4-Crop Combination Region	15.52	9.95	11.21	9.09	8.26	9.05	8.16	8.78
IV. 5-Crop Combination Region	15.32	9.90	11.00	9.00	8.14	9.15	8.50	10.95
All categories	15.66	10.09	11.42	9.14	8.22	8.59	8.24	9.25

TABLE 4.9

Variations in intensity of cultivation and application of modern inputs in different Crop Combination Regions - Sample Villages - 1977-78

Crop Combination Regions	Gross Area Sown (Hects.)	Net Area Sown (Hects.)	Net Area Irrigated (% of N.A.S.	Area under improved seeds (% of G.A.S.	Area under inorganic fertilizers (% of G.A.S.)	Quantity of fertilizers (per hectare of G.A.S. (kgs)
I. 2-Crop Combination Region	25.75	13.08	83.95	36.60	36.60	43.60
II. 3-Crop Combination Region	137.58	88.90	14.39	6.34	10.91	8.42
III. 4-Crop Combination Region	92.05	60.12	17.86	5.88	9.63	8.42
IV. 5-Crop Combination Region	24.53	16.39	16.38	2.55	4.28	3.96
All categories	279.91	178.49	20.84	8.64	12.27	11.40

valleys, with the **gul** system of irrigation making paddy cultivation possible. It would be observed from Table 4.6 that this region accounts for 51.85 per cent of the gross cropped area of the district. Paddy, wheat and **mandua** are the dominant crops constituting 28.80 per cent, 28.80 per cent and 30.22 per cent of the gross cropped area respectively. These three crops together constitute over 85 per cent of the gross cropped area, though this percentage was somewhat lower when worked out on the basis of our sample survey (Table 4.7). It was, however, revealed that **mandua** constituted the highest percentage (28.44 per cent) of gross cropped area, followed by wheat (25.89 per cent) and paddy (25.72 per cent). The remaining 20 per cent of gross cropped area was devoted to other diverse crops. This is possibly due to the presence of tropical and sub-tropical influences and the absence of physiographic extremes. In this region, the productivity levels of the crops of both paddy and wheat are relatively smaller than those of the Bhaber region owing to the predominance of dry farming and the scarcity of irrigation and other infrastructural facilities. The area under irrigation constitutes only 14.39 per cent of the net area sown. So the area under improved seeds and fertilizers are very limited, constituting 6.34 per cent and 10.91 per cent of gross area sown respectively (Table 4.9). The productivity levels in respect of paddy and wheat, both in irrigated and unirrigated lands are lower than those of the Bhaber region, but are higher than those of other two regions (Table 4.8). While the yields of paddy in irrigated and unirrigated lands are 15.64 quintals and 10.21 quintals per hectare respectively, those of the wheat are 11.35 quintals and 9.18 quintals per hectare respectively. The yield of **mandua** is the highest (8.45 quintals per hectaré) among all the crop combination regions.

4-Crop Combination Region

This crop combination region consists of 47 patwari circles covering in all 29.64 per cent of the total rural settlements of the district. It is not a geographically contiguous region but possesses a relatively larger number of patwari circles in the southern and western parts of the district. Although it covers 29.38 per cent of the gross cropped area of the district, yet it is characterised by a more diversified cropping pattern. From Tables 4.6 and 4.7 the four crops of paddy, wheat, **mandua** and **jhangora** together cover around 90 per cent of the gross cropped area of this region. The respective areas under each of these crops are: paddy (21.46 per cent), wheat (24.46 per cent), **mandua** (31.48 per cent) and **jhangora** (11.54 per cent), all from Table 4.7. The percentage of area under **mandua**, in this region, is the highest among all the crop combination regions. The yields of paddy and wheat per hectare, though low, approximate to the district averages. From Table 4.8 the yields of paddy in irrigated and unirrigated lands are 15.52 quintals and 9.95 quintals per hectare respectively. The corresponding yields of wheat are 11.21 quintals and 9.09 quintals per hectare. The unirrigated areas are, however, suitable for the production of coarser grains such as **mandua** and **jhangora**. The yields of these crops are 8.26 quintals and 9.05 quintals per hectare respectively. The main factors responsible for the low productivity of crops are the dependence of farming on rains, limited irrigated area (17.86 per cent), small area under improved seeds (5.88 per cent) and under chemical fertilizers (9.63 per cent) as well as the very low level of consumption of fertilizers (8.42 kilograms per hectare of gross cropped sown - Table 4.9).

5-Crop Combination Region

This crop combination region consists of 25 patwari circles and covers 14.25 per cent of the total rural settlements in the district. A majority of the patwari circles in the western and north-eastern parts of the district fall in this category and possess a highly diversified cropping pattern. It covers 15.55 per cent of the gross cropped area of the district. Within the region, the five crops of paddy, wheat, **mandua, jhangora** and barley are dominant, which together account for over 95 per cent of the gross cropped area of the region (Table 4.6). The high proportions of area under these crops are also found in the cropping pattern of the sample villages (Table 4.7); 90.92 per cent of the gross cropped area was covered by these main crops and the rest by others. The preponderance of coarse crops is due to lack of irrigation, poor and infertile soils, undulating topography and subsistence farming. Consequently, the yield per hectare is low. The yields per hectare of paddy and wheat in both the irrigated and unirrigated areas are the lowest among all the crop combination regions but the yields of coarse crops are relatively comparable to those of the other crop combination regions (Table 4.8). This is on account of the fact that valuable agricultural lands occur mostly along contour terraces or the gentle slopes; the rest of the lands are inaccessible and the rocky outcrops and steep slopes make cultivation difficult.

Levels of Productivity and Income

The analysis of various crop combination regions of the district brought out the variations in the levels of productivity (Table 4.8) and the extent of utilisation of agricultural inputs in the region (Table 4.9). Sample survey confirmed the finding that the yield per hectare of almost all the crops are low except in irrigated lands which accounted for only 20.84 per cent of the net area sown. The average yields of irrigated and unirrigated paddy are 15.66 and 10.09 quintals per hectare. The corresponding figures for wheat are 11.42 and 9.14 respectively. As compared to these, the yield per hectare of paddy and wheat in Uttar Pradesh were 11.59 and 15.50 quintals (1978-79). The variations in productivity per hectare among different size range of land-holdings are not significant. Yields are low even for coarse grains like **mandua, jhangora** and barley. The average yields of these crops for the district are 8.22, 8.59 and 8.24 quintals per hectare respectively.

The variations in productivity per hectare for different crops among the 42 sample villages were still greater. The average yield of paddy per hectare in irrigated lands varied from 12.58 quintals in Balli in the hilly tract to 17.93 quintals per hectare in Sitabpur (Bhaber) against the district average of 15.66 quintals per hectare. The corresponding range of yields for paddy per hectare in unirrigated lands varied from 7.50 quintals in Kainur to 13.38 quintals in Gadkot, both in the hilly tracts of the district. In respect of wheat, the range of yields in irrigated lands varied between 9.56 quintals per hectare in Kolli in the hilly tract to 13.41 quintals per hectare in Gorakhpur in Bhaber plains. The variations in unirrigated lands was slightly higher and lay between 7.41 quintals per hectare in Kundi to 12.12 quintals per hectare in Matiyalna, again, both in the hilly tracts of the district. In respect of other crops, the variations in yields per hectare were relatively less marked among different sample villages.

The low levels of productivity of different crops are reflected in the low levels of incomes.[10] It is observed that average net annual income per household from agriculture and its allied activities was Rs. 4,431.00 at 1977-78 price level which is 67.64 per cent of the total net income from all sources. Among different size range of land-holdings the variations are between Rs. 1,683.00 and Rs. 10,647.00. These variations were still larger among the different villages and ranged between Rs. 1,916.00 and Rs. 18,745.00. Similarly, per capita income ranges from Rs. 510.00 to Rs. 3,398.00 in different villages and average comes to Rs. 909.00. The variations among different categories of land-holdings were less marked. These figures are comparable with those of the State of U.P. The per capita income of U.P. was estimated to be Rs. 949.00 at current prices (1977-78) as against Rs. 1,210.00 for India as a whole and ranked 12th among all the States of India.[11]

The region's economy is primarily agricultural. As such agriculture and its allied activities contribute a large share to the household's net income from all sources. Out of the net annual income of Rs. 6,550.00 per household in 1977-78, agriculture and its allied activities contributed Rs. 4,431.00 (67.64 per cent) and the remaining Rs. 2,119.00 (32.36 per cent) by other sources. The contribution of kharif crops accounted for 31.78 per cent to the net annual income from all sources, followed by the contributions of livestock (19.74 per cent), rabi crops (14.38 per cent) and vegetables and/or fruits (1.76 per cent). Among the different size range of land-holdings, the respective contributions of kharif crops, rabi crops and of vegetables/ fruits were progressively higher with increase in the size of land-holdings. However, negative correlation existed between the size of land-holdings and percentage contributions to net annual income from all sources. Among the other sources contributing to the net annual income, the important ones are salaries, wages, pension and moneyorder remittances. Moneyorder remittances is progressively becoming a significant source. It contributes 40.70 per cent of the total net annual income from sources other than agriculture and its allied activities. This is followed by contributions from salaries (29.69 per cent), wages (12.03 per cent) and pension (9.63 per cent). Salaries and wages contribute relatively higher percentages in small-sized categories of land-holdings than in the large-sized categories of land-holdings. In comparison to these, relatively higher contributions were made by pensions and moneyorder remittances in the medium-sized categories of land-holdings.

Among the villages the range of variations was larger depending upon the characteristics of the villages. The contribution of kharif crops to the household's net income from all sources was 31.78 per cent and ranged from 13.84 per cent in Chopriyun in the hilly tract to 52.98 per cent in Gorakhpur in the Bhaber plains. The variations were relatively less marked in the case of rabi crops and lay between 6.08 per cent in Naithana in the hilly tract to 30.41 per cent in Gorakhpur in the Bhaber plains as against the district average of 14.38 per cent. A similar range of variations existed in the contribution of livestock. Vegetables/fruits contributed the least and varied from 7.51 per cent in Naithana to 34.40 per cent in Kundi, again, both in the hilly tracts of the district, against an household's average of 1.76 per cent.

A large majority of the households in the sample villages supplement their incomes from agriculture and its allied activities by the incomes from other sources. As such the percentage contributions to their total annual net incomes varies widely depending upon the occupational structure of the households. However, moneyorder remittances among 'other sources', is increasingly becoming a significant source of income. Among different villages, contribution to an household's total net annual income from sources other than agriculture and its allied activities ranged from 5.24 per cent in Punar to 100 per cent in Kasani against the district average of 40.70 per cent.

Despite low levels of productivity of different crops in the district, the sample survey revealed that there are areas where specialisation in the production of some specific crops such as of pulses, vegetables and fruits can be achieved as a long-term strategy. The yield per hectare of potatoes, onions and groundnuts in Thalisain and Chakisain in the north-eastern parts of the district had been found to be quite encouraging, and compares with that of the plains. Similarly, Bharsar area in the north-eastern part of the district has been found quite suitable for the production of apples and vegetables. The yield per hectare of apples, potatoes and cabbages is sufficiently high and has paved the way for commercial production on a small scale.[12] The experiments conducted on the production of new and high yielding varieties of soyabean have also been successful. This is evident from the study of sample villages that people respond favourably to the adoption of high yielding varieties. Besides, there are the areas which can specialise in the production of potatoes, onions, cabbages; garlic, ginger, turmeric and a variety of pulses; apples, papayas, walnuts and others.

The low levels of productivity in the district can be attributed to a large number of factors such as variations in climatic conditions, soil-differentiations, availability of irrigational facilities and the extent of utilisation of agricultural inputs etc. The sample survey revealed that the net irrigated area for the district was 20.84 per cent of the net area sown in 1977-78. The extent of utilisation of the improved seeds and fertilizers in the district was also extremely low. The district averages for areas under improved seeds and fertilizers accounted for 8.64 per cent and 12.27 per cent of the gross area sown respectively. Similarly, the quantity of fertilizers used was only 11.40 kilograms per hectare of gross area sown. Among different size-range of land-holdings the percentage variations in respect of the areas under improved seeds and fertilizers and the quantity of fertilizers used were not much.

The variations were, however, marked very widely among the different sample villages. 10 out of 42 samples had no irrigational facilities in them. The variations in respect of net irrigated area among the remaining 32 samples were extremely wide and ranged from 0.49 per cent in Ghansyali in the hilly tract to 93.97 per cent in Gorakhpur in the Bhaber plains. In respect of the area under improved seeds and fertilizers, the variations were relatively less marked. Area under improved seeds varied from 0.65 per cent in Ghansyali to 76.50 per cent in Thanger, both in the hilly tracts of the district. Similarly, the area under fertilizers varied from 0.65 per cent in Ghansyali to 39.56 per cent in Dungripanth. The quantity of fertilizer used was relatively very small in most of the sample villages.

The low levels of productivity and incomes in agriculture can also be attributed to the increasing operating expenses such as the purchase of seeds, manures and fertilizers, repairs and maintenance of terraces and hiring of labour for different agricultural operations. Hitherto, most of the agricultural operations used to be carried out by the household labour itself and the operating expenses used to be met mostly from the domestic production. But with the outmigration of labour force and its resultant inflow of moneyorder remittances, these expenses have increasingly been met from outside income. The phenomenon of outmigration of working population creates the scarcity in labour force, which in turn, lowers the agricultural productivity and causes deficiency in food production. In general, seeds hitherto used to be kept from domestic production during harvesting season are either not kept or if at all kept, they are usually consumed due partly to the food deficits and partly to the guaranteed prospective income from moneyorder remittances. As such the requirements of seeds have increasingly been met from open market at relatively higher prices. Similarly, there has been a paucity in domestic animals due to shortage in labour force causing thereby the shortage among others, of indigenous manures. This has led to an increase in expenditure on manures and fertilizers. Repairs and maintenance in a majority of cases are no more done by the household labour but by the hired labour from outside.

The increasing operating expenses as discussed in the preceding paragraph would have been still on higher scores, had most of the agricultural operations not been undertaken by the households comprising mainly of the females, themselves. It has been estimated that the average annual operating expenses per household for the district as a whole amounted to Rs. 449.00 or nearly 13 per cent of the annual gross income of Rs. 3,479.00 from agriculture. Of the gross annual operating expenses of Rs. 449.00 per household the gross annual expenses on seeds, labour and manure and fertilizers accounted for 44.23 per cent, 29.76 per cent and 9.39 per cent respectively. The percentage variations were less marked among the different size of land-holdings although they were relatively more marked among the sample villages.

Field enquiries revealed that the productivity of crops in most of the villages lying in the vicinity of the forested lands of the district is adversely affected by the progressively increasing menace of wild animals (bears, deer, wild pigs, monkeys and porcupines). Their interference has been extensive and destruction of crops rampant. It has been observed that people in some sample villages have even given up the cultivation of land in the vicinity of jungles due to constant interference from wild animals. In some others, a round-the-clock vigilance has to be kept for months by beating of the drums in order to protect the standing crops. Further, with the enforcement of Wild Life Preservation Act and consequent imposition of restrictions on killing of wild life, the areas of their interference has extended deep into the areas of cultivation approximately upto 15 kilometres from the areas of their protection.

It has been observed from our sample survey that many villages experience the scarcity of work-force especially of the young and energetic male workers due to outmigration of working population. As such the remaining work force, comprising mainly of the females, plays its role in the decision making process of the agrarian organisational structure. A majority of them were not found to be innovative and progressive and lacked initiative and drive in applying scientific methods and techniques with a view to increasing the levels of productivity in agriculture. Often, they cling to their rigid attitudes towards traditional pattern of cropping methods and agricultural practices. They have also developed an attitude of dependency upon the officials of the government machinery. The officials also have not identified themselves with the masses and cultivated a spirit of self-help, faith and confidence in them. The untimely availability and the improper application of agricultural inputs in many cases, have been instrumental in reducinq the yields per hectare. In other cases, the land has become unfit for cultivation due to improper use of chemical fertilizers. Consequently this has adversely affected the agricultural productivity.

The phenomenon of outmigration of working population as pointed out earlier, has created scarcity of labour work force, particularly of the males. This is also reflected in the relatively higher labour charges. In the sample villages, ploughing of land which is mainly the work of the males presents an acute problem. The labour is either not available on time or charges are exorbitant and obligatory. Ploughing on contractual basis averages Rs. 500.00 per hectare. The daily wages for labour range between Rs. 12.00 to Rs. 15.00 without meals or Rs. 5.00 to Rs. 7.00 plus one breakfast and one meal. Crop sharing involves one third to one half of yields to the owner of land, depending upon the quantity and the level of production in the land. Terracing is an ingenious job and therefore comparatively higher rates averaging Rs. 4.50 per square metre are charged. Besides, other operating expenses are also incurred influencing the levels of productivity and income.

The above analysis of the levels of productivity and income has amply demonstrated that the income from agriculture and its allied activities, at present, is quite inadequate to maintain its existing population. The district has, therefore, to rely upon to a great extent on the outside incomes. Notwithstanding such a constraint, there exist potential areas for specialisation in the production of some specific crops and as such the prospects of commercialisation as a viable proposition cannot be underestimated. Lack of irrigational facilities, inadequate use of agricultural inputs, increasing operating expenses and others are not such constraints as cannot be overcome. What is, however, pivotal is the problem of outmigration of working force around which other problems revolve.

Consumption Pattern

The low levels of productivity and incomes as analysed in the preceding pages is reflected in the expenditure patterns of the consumers. An overwhelming majority of outmigrants leave behind wives and the aged at home; their subsistence and maintenance inevitably necessitate frequent remittances of incomes from outside. As such the remittances are mainly utilised for the purchase of consumers' goods rather than for production purposes. This is evident from the following analysis of the consumption pattern based on our sample survey.

It has been pointed out earlier that the average annual net income from all sources of an household worked out to Rs. 6,550.00. This income was found to be insufficient for the maintenance of the family and as such had to be supplemented by borrowing. It was found that borrowing was resorted to by 23.39 per cent of the total number of households surveyed, varying from 38.64 per cent in the size range of land-holdings of less than 0.25 hectare to 14.63 per cent in the size range between 1.00 to 2.00 hectares of land-holding class. Annual borrowing per household averaged to Rs. 291.00 which was relatively higher in the households having small-sized land-holdings than in those having large-sized land-holdings. Among the different sample villages, annual borrowing per household ranged widely and lay between Rs. 71.00 in Kathur Bara to Rs. 2,064.00 in Gorakhpur (Bhaber) depending upon the economic power and requirements of the households in the villages. The annual savings per household were inconsiderable. They too were mainly confined to the households accruing income from sources other than agriculture and its allied activities.

As compared with the net annual income per household discussed in the preceding paragraph, the total annual expenditure per household at 1977-78 price level worked out to Rs. 6,217.00 or approximately Rs. 518.00 per month. The variations in expenditure per household among different size-range of holdings ranged from Rs. 3,440.00 to Rs. 11,108.00. The variations were, however, much wider among the different sample villages and lay between Rs. 4,101.00 in Matiyalna in the hilly tract and Rs. 18,921.00 at Gorakhpur in the Bhaber plains.

Of the total annual expenditure of Rs. 6,217.00, the expenditure on food items constituted 69.20 per cent, the expenditure on non-food items 20.79 per cent and the remaining 10.02 per cent on items of miscellaneous character such as marriages and other religious functions etc. A sizeable portion of the total expenditure on food items is incurred on cereals and pulses (48.40 per cent) of which rice and wheat are the dominant ones. The expenditure on items such as ghee, dalda, oil, milk and other milk products accounted for another 35.46 per cent of the total expenditure. Besides, sugar and gur (0.23 per cent), tea (4.21 per cent), tobacco and cigarettes (2.24 per cent) were the other food items of importance. The percentage of expenditure on food items per household in small-sized land-holdings was relatively greater than in the large-sized land-holdings. But among different villages the variations ranged from 54.94 per cent in Lacchi-Saingaon to as high as 81.72 per cent in Kundi depending upon the levels of productivity and incomes.

The expenditure on non-food items constituted 20.79 per cent of the total expenditure on different items of consumption. Clothing is the most important among non-food items. It covered 37.52 per cent of the total expenditure on non-food items. This was followed by expenditure on education (19.96 per cent), items of toilets (9.57 per cent), footwear (8.16 per cent), fuel and lighting (7.27 per cent), conveyance (6.62 per cent) and medicine (5.90 per cent). The percentage variations of expenditure per household on non-food items were similar to those of the food items and marked more widely among different villages than among different size-range of holdings. The percentage of expenditure on non-food items per household, in contrast to those of food items, increased with the increase in the size-range of land-holdings.

The foregoing analysis of the consumption pattern indicates that bulk of the incomes of the people either generated through agriculture and its allied activities or received through outside remittances is absorbed in meeting the consumption expenditure, leaving thereby little room for savings to accumulate. Simultaneously, the margin of savings of the working force outside the region is also reduced due to disruption in family organisation and resultant maintenance of two and sometimes three establishments. The productive capacity of the region does not increase as the levels of savings and investments are not influenced and process of capital formation does not take place. As such, the demand for both agricultural and non-agricultural goods is met through the small traders and retailers, who in turn depend heavily on the big businessmen and wholesalers controlling their commercial transactions from the terminals of Ramnagar, Kotdwara and Rishikesh. Thus, the large inflows of remittances is absorbed in the form of consumption expenditure contributing very little to the betterment of the regional economy.

Infrastructure Facilities and Amenities

A well developed infrastructure together with a strong functional organisation constitutes the base for economic development of an area. The difference between an economically developed region and a backward region does not rest merely on the availability of resources. A region with abundant resources may well remain backward unless its resources have suitable channels for exploitation. A good network of transport and communication with availability of abundant power and water-resources and provision of other services and amenities, at reasonable terms, would make the region susceptible to economic development than an area lacking in these facilities. The existence of infrastructural and other facilities contribute towards economies in initial capital investments on economic and social overheads and consequent reduction in costs, accelerating thereby the tempo of economic development in the region. This part of the chapter deals first with the existing infrastructure facilities followed by a discussion on other services and amenities.

Roads

The terrain is hilly and rugged and extremely difficult involving difficulty in the movement of raw materials and finished products. The existing road network is far short of the needs of the region and poses problems in spatial interactions both in terms of flow of goods and services. Until the beginning of road development in forties in the region, the region was connected by the bridle paths which formed the important means of communications. Their significance, is however, rapidly declining owing to the development of motor-roads in the area in recent years.

Bridle Roads

The existing bridle paths in the region are more or less the same which have been used since long. Among them the important ones are mentioned here. The central and the western parts of Garhwal are oriented to Kotdwara station, the terminus of a branch of the former Oudh and Rohilkhand Railway and now of the Northern Railway from Najibabad, opened in 1897. Lansdowne was connected with Kotdwara in 1909. Until the interior of the region was linked, Dogadda, situated at the junction of the Khoh and Silligad rivulets was for all practical purposes, the terminus. This town (Dogadda) is stagnant in terms of population growth and declining in its trading activities. The cart road between Kotdwara and Dogadda was the first stage on the long journey to the interior from Khoh river to Dadamandi. Thereafter, it ascends the Langur range, crosses at Dwarikhal and reaches Banghat on the river Nayar after a descent of 10 kilometres. From Banghat, a branch road follows the line of the Nayar westward upto Byasghat, the junction of the Nayar and the river Ganga. The main line continues to the north and reaches Pauri via Adwani. From Pauri, two bridle paths were in use for onward travel. Persons carrying their load, usually followed along the ridge past Khirsu, Bainswara and to the Chatwapipal (now in Chamoli district). But those hiring ponies, sheep and goats, usually descended to the Ganga valley at Srinagar and following the course of river as far as Rudraprayag and thereafter either along with the Mandakini river or along with Alaknanda river, depending upon the destination one was to follow. The second important bridle path leaves cart road at Fatehpur about 3 kilometres from Dogadda and crossing the Langur range, descends to Nayar valley at Ukhlet. Thereafter, it has two branches following two Nayars. The valley of Western Nayar river brings the road to Mason. Pauri is 19 kilometres away from Mason to the north-west. After Mason at Chipalghat, the main Pauri-Almora bridle path is crossed and after that the road continues to follow the valley upto Dudhatoli watershed and beyond to Chandpurgarhi. The second branch follows the Eastern Nayar river.

The third important bridle path connects Afzalgarh (Bijnor district) to this district, crossing Ramganga at Dhikala with Banjadevi in Patty Painon. Formerly, the hill trade was largely done with bi-weekly bazar at Kalagarh on this path. The bridle path then connects Banjadevi with Rikhnikhal and reaches the Eastern Nayar river at Churani, thereafter connects Pokhra in Patty Talain where it ends.

In 1907, the Moradabad-Ramnagar branch of former Rohilkhand and Kumaon Railway and now of Northern Railway was opened, thereby linking Ramnagar with the eastern patties of the Pauri Garhwal district. Upto Marchula, bridle-wheeled traffic was possible. But from Marchula, a tolerable bridle path follows the Deogadh, Sald Mahadev, Kuchyar, Bironkhal and Baijro. From Baijro, the road bifurcates into two branches connecting it with Kainur and Bungidhar. The Bungidhar branch of the bridle path continues over a shoulder of Dudhatoli to Lohba.

The patties west of the Pauri-Dogadda road and south of the Nayar river had the choice of three routes to the plains. The first, by a path along the Langur range to Dwarikhal; the second between Byasghat and Chaukighat and the third between Byasghat and Laxmanjhula and thereafter via Rishikesh to Hardwar. The last one has been the most important pilgrims' route, following Alaknanda river on the left and reaching Laxmanjhula at a distance of 56 kilometres.

Pauri is connected with Almora by two bridle roads. The first follows the Khirsu ridge upto Mandakhal, then to Musagali. Thereafter, it goes to Saknyana over the watershed to Kainur on the Eastern Nayar and finally to Bungidhar where it leaves the district, reaching Almora. The second path proceeds to the Jwalpa, Pokhra, Baijro and continues in the Almora district.

Deoprayag in Tehri Garhwal district is connected with Pauri by bridle path. Another path connects Pauri to Byasghat. Apart from this, a cross road runs from Srinagar through Khirsu to Musagali and another leads from Khirsu to Chantikhal.

An analysis of this type of communication system depicts the extent of spatial interactions among the people living in a large number of small and sprinkled settlements. Such a poor communication sytem has, in fact, been due to region's physiography and the pattern of settlements. The physiographic structure determined the directions of the bridle paths, mostly from north to south, along the river valleys rather than from east to west. Consequently, the interactions among the people, over the space, also followed from north to south. Similarly, the pattern of settlement structure dominated by the small-sized settlements of less than a population of 500 persons constrained much of the interactions. In order to bridge the communication gaps and speed up the interactions among the people, the road construction programme has been pursued which is mostly on the lines which bridle paths had thrown open in the past.

The accessibility to roads in the district has been very poor, in the past, because of the terrain. The main roads link north-south connecting the railheads of Rishikesh, Kotdwara and Ramnagar in the plains with the interior centres of tourist and religious importance. The road construction programme in the district accelerated only after the strategic importance of the district was recognised owing to the Chinese aggression in 1962. The speeding up of the programme followed in the seventies with the result that the intra-district linkages developed and inaccessibility conditions reduced.

The district is linked by three important roads which start from railheads of Rishikesh, Kotdwara and Ramnagar. The Rishikesh-Srinagar road, 108 kilometres in length, lies in the Tehri Garhwal district, on the right of the river Alaknanda. It handles the major tourist traffic and also the pilgrims going to the shrines of Kedarnath and Badrinath. The most important road in the district is, however, the one that starts from Kotdwara and links the areas along the central axis of the district. The length of the main road in the district is 186 kilometres linking Kotdwara with Dogadda, Satpuli, Patisain, Bubakhal, Pauri, Srinagar, Rudraprayag and Gholtir, where the boundary of Chamoli district starts. The third road that links the district, starts from Ramnagar and connects Mohan, Marchula, Dhumakot, Bironkhal and Baijro. The total length of the road in the district is 60 kilometres and serves the eastern patties. A branch road, 10 kilometres in length connects Dhumakot with Nainidanda.

The main highway from Kotdwara to Rudraprayag is linked by connecting roads both from the east and the west and serves the district. The following Table 4.10 and Figure 15 illustrate the spatial linkages developed during the recent years.

In addition, some connecting roads have since been completed and others are under completion. This has led to link the hitherto isolated nodal points. Thalisain has been connected with Nautha, Damdewal and Baijro by extending the existing roads. Similarly, Chipalghat has been connected with Chakisain; Patisain with Pabau via Khirku; and Srinagar with Bughani and Khirsu. Very shortly, others would be linked: Banjadevi with Nainidanda via Haldukhal; Silogi with Rishikesh via Singtalli Bridge; and Bhareth with Hardwar via Dwili. A number of other connecting roads are also under way and would reduce the inaccessibility in the interior region of the district.

TABLE 4.10

Motorable Roads in Pauri Garhwal district - 1975

S.No.	Name of the road	Length in kms.
1.	Kotdwara - Rudraprayag road	186
2.	Kotdwara - Kalagarh road	77
3.	Kotdwara - Kalalghati - Lal Dhang - Chila - Hardwar road	61
4.	Chila - Gohri - Bidasani - Kandara road	27
5.	Dogadda - Paukhal - Bhrigukhal - Kandi - Bhareth road	75
6.	Dogadda - Sendhikhal - Rathwadhap - Banjadevi road	49
7.	Fatehpur (Dogadda) - Lansdowne road	22
8.	Deriakhal (Lansdowne) - Rikhnikhal - Banjadevi road	49
9.	Lansdowne - Gumkhal road	10
10.	Gumkhal - Dwarikhal - Silogi road	45
11.	Satpuli - Rithakhal - Pokhra - Vedikhal - Baijro road	94
12.	Satpuli - Banghat - Marora - Byasghat road	18
13.	Satpuli - Ekeswar - Naugaonkhal road	33
14.	Banghat - Naithana - Adwani - Kandoliya - Pauri road	44
15.	Patisain - Naugaonkhal - Chaubatakhal - Damdewal road	38
16.	Bubakhal - Pabau - Chipalghat - Nautha road	38
17.	Bubakhal - Khirsu - Farkhandakhal road	16
18.	Pauri - Kholachauri - Deoprayag road	30
19.	Ramnagar - Mohan - Dhumakot - Bironkhal - Baijro road	60
20.	Dhumakot - Nainidanda road	10
21.	Rishikesh - Deoprayag - Srinagar road	108

A review of the road construction programme as detailed in the preceding pages, however, reveals that inaccessibility conditions are still prevalent in many parts of the district. This is especially so in the patties of Dhangu in the west and the patties of Choprakot, Chauthan and Dhaijuli in north-east of the district. The costs of transportation are, therefore, high and sometimes abnormal and are reflected variously, particularly in

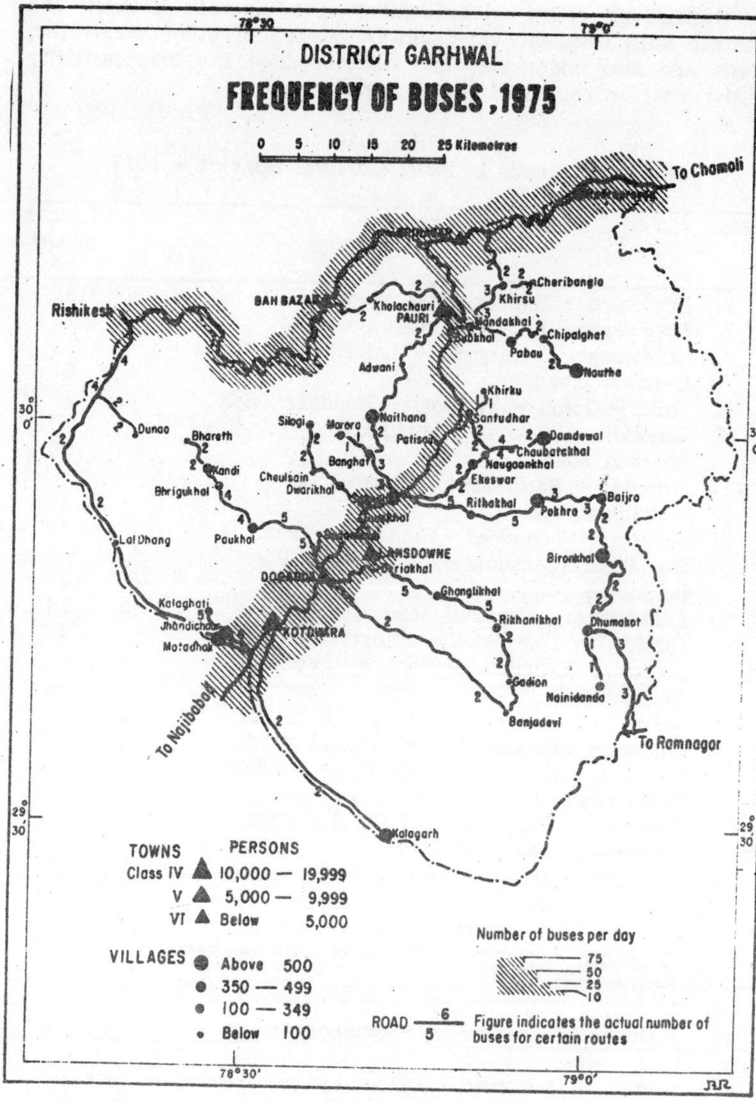
DISTRICT GARHWAL
FREQUENCY OF BUSES, 1975
0 5 10 15 20 25 Kilometres
78°30
79°0'
30° 0'
29° 30'
To Chamoli
Rishikesh
BAH BAZAR
Kholachauri
PAURI
Cheribangla
Khirsu
Mandakhal
Chipalghat
Pabau
Nauthe
Adwani
Khirku
Santudhar
Naithana
Silogi
Marora
Patisain
Damdewal
Chaubatakhal
Naugaonkhal
Dunao
Bhareth
Kandi
Banghat
Cheulsain
Dwarikhal
Bhrigukhal
Ekeswar
Rithakhal
Pokhra
Baijro
Paukhal
Lal Dhang
Bironkhal
Ghanglikhal
Rikhanikhal
Kalaghati
Jhandichaur
Motadhak
KOTDWARA
Dhumakot
Gadion
Nainidanda
Banjadevi
To Najibabad
To Ramnagar
Kalagarh
TOWNS
PERSONS
Class IV 10,000 — 19,999
V 5,000 — 9,999
VI Below 5,000
VILLAGES
Above 500
350 — 499
100 — 349
Below 100
Number of buses per day
75
50
25
10
ROAD 6 5
Figure indicates the actual number of buses for certain routes
78°30'
79°0'

Fig. 15

the costs of foodgrains and other consumers' goods purchased from the railheads of Ramnagar, Kotdwara and Rishikesh. It has been observed that the cost of transporting one quintal of foodgrains by a mule averages Rs. 1.50 per kilometre. For instance, the costs range between Rs. 40.00 and Rs. 50.00 from the nearest motor head of Baijro to Bungidhar and to other villages beyond in the patty of Chauthan lying to the north-east of the district. Similarly, the cost amounted to Rs. 25.00 from Chipalghat, the nearest motor head, to Chakisain through bridle path. The charges are still higher in the villages beyond Chakisain (such as Risti and Saunth) and range from Rs. 45.00 to Rs. 55.00 per quintal. These costs are however, in addition to the existing toll taxes and freight charges levied upto the nearest motor-heads. They are levied at the rate of 5.5 paise per quintal per kilometre for pucca roads and 6.5 paise per quintal per kilometre for kutcha roads. Thus a quintal of foodgrains costing Rs. 200.00 at Ramnagar, Kotdwara and Rishikesh costs between Rs. 250.00 to Rs. 270.00 in the remote and inaccessible areas.

These costs, however, increase further during the rainy season when the roads are blocked by the landslides and the bridges are washed away or destroyed, cutting off thereby the main communication lines. Field observations show that the construction of new bridges and bridle paths in some areas have awfully been neglected. The absence of a bridge, for instance, on a small rivulet at Raitpur near Gadkot sample village, 6 kilometres from Satpuli leads to a virtual closure of the primary school for 3 months annually during the rainy season. Similarly, the absence of a bridge on the entire course of Huinl river not only enhances the transport costs but also takes away a toll of human and animal lives every year. Trekking along the Bachhansyun rivulet in its course of 25 kilometres, from its upper reaches near Dobri to Khankara, is extremely difficult and enormously risky. Besides, there has been an utter neglect of the repairs and maintenance of the existing bridges and roads. The Khatligad bridge near Bironkhal; Kulasu bridge near Kandiya sample village on the Eastern Nayar river; and the Bakhlana and Syngtalli bridges near Byasghat and Rishikesh, both on river Alaknanda respectively, bear testimony to the extent of negligence.

The above analysis brings out clearly the relationship between the existing inaccessibility conditions and the transport costs. The interactions among the people in the region, depend largely on the accessibility conditions facilitated by the development of road transport. A perusal of Figure 15 also shows that the frequency of buses is the highest on the route leading from Kotdwara to Rudraprayag. Next in frequency is the route from Rishikesh to Srinagar. The areas close to these routes are the ones which have the greatest interactions among the people due to urban influences. The farther the areas from these routes, the lesser is the interactions among the people. These are also the areas of highest intensity of moneyorder remittances due to outmigration of working population, a detailed account of which is given in the following Chapter.

Power

Power is one of the essential ingredients of infrastructural development of a region. It is vital not only for domestic consumption but also for the development of industries and others. In the context of a hill area, electric power has to be viewed from high costs of generation and distribution. In the absence of coal in the area, its transportation from other parts of the country is both costly and difficult and therefore, steam generation is also difficult. Similarly, due to fairly scattered population and difficult terrain conditions, the transmission costs of electricity are also high. The choice is, therefore, left to the establishment of small generating units to be located in close proximity of the consuming centres. Since the district possesses vast hydro-resource potentials because of a network of rivers having good waterfalls, the best alternative would perhaps be through micro-hydro-power generation for the production of cheap power.

Hydro-electric power in the district is supplied by different transmission lines: 37.5 Kw. line linking Kotdwara with Dogadda and Lansdowne and another 11 Kw. line linking Deoprayag with Pauri and Srinagar. With the completion of Ramganga Power Project at Kalagarh, the district has been sharing the benefit of 198 Mw. of electricity, though the bulk of the power generated is transmitted to the U.P. plains. The Genthicheera Hydel Scheme with a capacity of 200 Kws. of electricity and Deoprayag Hydel Scheme with a capacity of 100 Kws. have been producing electricty for the district. Besides, a number of micro-hydel schemes and transmission and distribution works are under different stages of formulation, execution and implementation in the district for providing power for domestic and industrial purposes.

With the increase in supply of power the implementation of electrification programme in the district has been gaining momentum. All the 6 towns of the district are electrified. Kotdwara, Dogadda, Pauri and Bah Bazar had been electrified by the end of the year 1958-59. Lansdowne alongwith Jaharikhal were electrified in 1961-62; Laxmanjhula in 1962-63; Srinagar in 1963-64 and Rudraprayag in 1964-65. The Rural Electrification Corporation took up the task of electrification of rural areas. By the end of 1970-71, 18 villages, constituting a barely 0.59 per cent of the total number of villages in the district, had been electrified. This number increased to 276 or 0.85 per cent of the total number of villages in 1975-76. During the next three years, the electrification programme was implemented rapidly. The number of villages electrified by the end of the year 1977-78 had increased to 415 and constituted 12.82 per cent of the total number of villages. This percentage was, however low as compared to the figures for the Hill region (18.50 per cent) and U.P. (31.12 per cent) as a whole. Likewise, the per capita consumption of electricity was also relatively much low (7.6 Kwh.) as compared with those of the Hill region (75.5 Kwh.) and U.P. (86.4 Kwh.) during 1976-77.

Health

The district in the past lacked medical and other health facilities. In 1965-66, there were 39 hospitals/dispensaries with a capacity of 276 beds only. These health facilities were available in small towns only. By 1977-78, the number of hospitals and beds had increased to 84 and 695 respectively. Considering the norms of the hill areas, these facilities would be quite inadequate. Most of these facilities are located in distant places from the villages. The rural folk, in over 96 per cent of the villages are compelled to travel over 5 kilometres for getting these facilities. This percentage is relatively higher when compared with those of the Hill region (83.37 per cent) and U.P. (72.40 per cent) as a whole. The inaccessibility conditions and the topographic features therefore, call for an imperativeness for providing more facilities in the district.

It is revealed from our sample survey that the district lacks good hospitals/dispensaries. There is, very often, a dearth of well qualified doctors, particularly those of the specialists. In the absence of medicines, hospital equipments and other essentials, owing to the limited grants given by the government, the patients have either to linger on or are compelled to go out of the district for their medical treatment. The condition of Ayurvedic hospitals/disapensaries is still worse as is observed from Katghar Hospital in Dhangu Patty and Bungidhar hospital in Chauthan Patty in the north-eastern part of the district. The incidence of tuberculosis, stomachpain, anaemia, leucorrhoea was found to be relatively high among the patients. This is mainly due to the poor dieting and drinking habits of the people.

Education

Despite a number of factors constraining the educational development in the district, the region has a high male, female and total literacy when compared with other districts of the Hill region or with other districts in U.P. According to 1981 Census (provisional estimates) the district has an overall literacy of 41.90 per cent as against 27.40 per cent of U.P. and 36.17 per cent of India. The male literacy of 58.19 per cent is relatively much higher than those of U.P. (38.90 per cent) and India (46.74 per cent). The corresponding figures for female literacy for the district, U.P. and India are 27.12 per cent, 14.42 per cent and 24.88 per cent respectively. A detailed analysis of the intra-district variations has already been made in Chapter III (Figure 11) while dealing with the demographic characteristics.

A study of educational development shows that the number of primary, middle and high/higher secondary schools increased by 13.07 per cent, 35.23 per cent and over 300 per cent respectively during the period 1950-51 to 1970-71. The enrolment of students in primary classes has increased by 100 per cent from 1950-51. The increase in the enrolment in the middle schools was 3.5 times that of 1950-51 and double that of 1960-61. The increase in enrolment in high school/higher secondary schools was only twice that of 1950-51. Enrolment in the case of girls was comparatively higher at all levels than those of the boys. The increase in educational facilities has led to a reduction in distance of schools from villages.

In spite of the educational facilities available our field observations in the samples of Kainur, Gadri, Kolli and Kundi villages revealed that education of children, especially of girls is neglected. In the relatively more isolated, inaccessible and underdeveloped parts of the district, such a phenomenon could be witnessed, particularly among the people belonging to the lower strata in the caste hierarchy. Instances were not lacking when parents preferred sending children to the armed forces for getting livelihood to giving them education beyond primary or middle standard. There were still others who after obtaining their undergraduate level of education or below were neither employed for lack of employment opportunities nor were they getting any university education due partly to the inaccessibility of institutions of higher learning and partly to the low levels of income and productivity.

Banking and Postal facilities

The development of a region depends also upon the extent

of availability of banking and postal facilities. The banking sector in the district comprises of the State Bank of India, Punjab National Bank, Punjab & Sindh Bank and District Central Co-operative Bank. By the end of 1970, the State Bank of India had already established 4 branches in the urban centres of Pauri, Kotdwara, Lansdowne and Kalagarh and one sub-office in the rural area of Swarg Ashram under Rishikesh branch. On the recommendations of Lead Bank Survey[13] conducted in 1970, 2 new offices were opened in the prospective rural growth centres of Rudraprayag and Satpuli in 1972. Later in 1975, facilities were also extended at the Srinagar town. The Punjab National Bank is established at Kotdwara, Dogadda and Srinagar while Punjab and Sindh Bank at Srinagar. The District Central Co-operative Bank is relatively well developed and better managed. Its head office is located at Kotdwara and has 4 branches in the urban centres of Kotdwara, Srinagar, Pauri and Lansdowne and 9 branches in the rural centres of Nainidanda, Dhumakot, Satpuli, Bhrigukhal, Kandi, Rikhnikhal and Pabau. Besides, the Land Development Bank is also operating in the district with its office at Pauri.

The average population served by a commercial bank in the district worked out to over 82,000 persons. This figure is comparable with those of U.P. (91,000) and India (52,000). But the per capita deposits were low and figured Rs.23.20 only as against Rs.41.10 for U.P. and Rs.85.40 for India as a whole. Similarly, the average deposits per office were also relatively low and accounted for Rs.2 million only in contrast to Rs.5.16 million for U.P. and Rs.5.85 million for India as a whole. However, in terms of the deposits per account, the State Bank of India stood favourably high with Rs.1,993.00 per account as against Rs.727.00 for the District Central Co-operative Bank, Rs.561.00 for Primary Agricultural Credit Society and Rs.306.00 for District Co-operative Development Federation.

Besides, the district has a network of postal services. There were 329 post offices as on 1st April, 1973. Of these, there were 2 higher Selection Grade Postoffices of Pauri and Lansdowne; 53 Sub-Post offices of different grades; and 274 Branch Post offices.[14] The number of post offices providing savings bank facilities is 296. All towns are directly served by the post offices whereas the number of villages directly served by post offices is 289. The district has 13 Public Call Offices and 33 Telegraph Offices. All urban areas have Post and Telegraph Offices. Apart from the banks, co-operative societies and post offices the district adminstration is the only other institutionalised finanical agency in the district. It happens to be one of the best recognised and the most sought after agency for the provisions of credit. The district administration operates its credit through its decentralised administrative units comprising of 2 tahsils, 3 sub-tahsils and 14 development blocks.

Of all the financial institutions, post offices are the most important mobilisers of savings. The amounts of per capita deposits lodged with the post offices are smaller than those with commercial or co-operative banks. But their aggregate deposits far outstrip those of commercial and co-operative banks taken together. This is primarily due to the reason that post-offices have a large and well spread network of offices all over the district. They are easily approachable by their customers existing and potential and their employees have a close liaison with the local people since they mostly belong to the areas where they serve. Owing to these reasons, the total deposits with the post offices accounted to Rs.26.60 millions in over 53,900 accounts, thereby bringing out per account deposits to Rs.494.29 only. Post offices are important because of the moneyorder remittances on which the Hill region's economy by and large depends.

Credit operations by the commercial banks in the district were highly circumscribed during the fiftees. These operations were geared up slowly during the late sixtees and gained momentum during the seventies. The per captia advances by the commercial banks worked out to Rs.2.60 as against Rs.13.20 for U.P. and Rs.60.30 for India as a whole. Similarly, the average credit per office was low and amounted to Rs.225,000 in contrast to Rs.1,650,000 for U.P. and Rs.4,13,000 for India as a whole. Upto the year 1968, the State Bank of India among all the commercial banks had the monopoly in the field of credit provision. But later, the Punjab National Bank took the lead in the provision of credit to the district economy. The credit for the lead attained by the Punjab National Bank is exclusively due to the large-scale liberal financing of medium-term loans by its branch at Kotdwara, to the transport operators for the purchase of automobiles carrying goods and/or passengers.

Co-operative institutions are playing their pivotal role in the provision of short and medium-term credit to the agricultural sector. Efforts are also been made to finance long-term requirements of the cultivators. The District Central Co-operative Bank is the central agency for providing such credits through its member co-operative societies.

Apart from the financial institutions, the various offices of the district administration are advancing loans for various purposes. High priority is being accorded to the development of transport and communications; agriculture and allied activities; irrigation and power. Besides, loans are also advanced for the purpose of orchards, soil conservation, construction of irrigation channels and reservoirs; taccavi loans for the purchase of fertilizers, seeds etc. are also offered.

Marketing Facilities

It is observed that the region lacks even the basic marketing facilities both in terms of quantity and quality. The existence of merely 68 grocers' shops, 61 tea shops and 27 cloth shops and a few others of miscellaneous character in 42 sample villages corroborates our viewpoint. Both the shops and the small-scale industrial establishments are located mainly either in the largesized settlements or on the road-sides of the spatially diffused emerging growth-centres. Shops dealing with utensils were few and far between and figured 6 only in the sample villages. Occupations like tailoring, earthenware and pottery-making, blacksmithy, carpentry and haircutting are pursued by the lower caste Hindus as their traditional and hereditary professions. While tailoring and earthenware-making are predominantly rural ones; the remaining ones are becoming progressively the urban. Similarly, the needs of the people for medicines and other health-care requirements are fulfilled chiefly by the urban centres as would be visualised from the fact that there existed only 5 chemists shops in the sample villages. The small-scale establishments such as flour mills (**atta-chakkies**), oil-presses and others were also few and far between. People operated handdriven **chakkies** in over 50 per cent of the samples and in the rest of the samples, water-driven and power-driven **chakkies** were in vogue. With the increase in power supply, the power- driven **chakkies** are fast replacing the traditional hand-driven and water-driven **chakkies** in the region. Likewise, the requirements of agricultural inputs such as fertilizers, seeds, insecticides and pesticides are mainly met either directly by the block officials at their headquarters or through village level workers in addition to the services rendered by the existing 6 seeds and fertilizers depots and 7 co-operative stores in the sample villages.

Lack of marketing facilities is reflected in the existing inter-dependence of villages in carrying out their day to day barter and monetary transactions of varied agricultural products in different areas particularly in the remote and inaccessible parts of the district. Although due to micro-level variations in climatic and other conditions, different regions and within regions different villages specialise in the production of different agricultural commodities; yet their level of production is small and is confined to certain areas only. As such most of the transactions in them are also limited in scale, localised in character and are confined to vegetables and to some extent to pulses and cereals. Potatoes and onions constitute the dominant items of transactions among vegetables. Others of lesser importance are turmeric, garlic, ginger, chillies, radish and pumpkin. Paddy, wheat and **chua** (Amaranthus frumentaceus), are the main items of transactions among cereals but they are transacted only on a very limited scale in some areas. Among the pulses, blackgram, lentils, soyabean and **gohat** (Horsegram or Dolichos biflorus) account for relatively larger shares of transactions. Lack of marketing facilities in the region has however, in recent years induced retailers and wholesalers from outside the district to undertake barter transactions in agricultural commodities by the manufactured goods. Such transactions fetch them abnormal profits and on some to the tune of over 500 per cent. This has resulted in draining out the resources and exploitation of the region by the outsiders.

Drinking water and other facilities

One of the objectives of the Sixth Five Year Plan (1978-83) under the Minimum Needs Programme was to provide all scarcity and problem villages the facility of drinking water. In 1971, only 10.16 per cent of the villages in the district had sources of water-supply outside the villages as compared with 22.80 per cent in the Hill region and 3.41 per cent in U.P. as a whole. Our sample survey, however, revealed that a majority of the sample villages did not have sources of water within the villages. Thus the supply of drinking water is a significant problem which becomes acute during the summers when water supply at sources usually recedes. It was also observed that drinking-water has to be supplied by means of trucks and mules in some villages, while in some other it was sold at Rs.2.00 per cannister. The scarcity of drinking-water supply in the villages may be attributable partly to the absence of water sources and partly to the non-exploitation of the existing water sources. Both the deforestation and road construction works have adversely affected the water supply at many places. In others, the water supply has completely been stopped by blocking the small streams and rivulets. Added to these are the negligence and apathetic attitudes of the officials of Local Self-government Engineering Department in the matter of repairs and maintenance of the existing system of drinking water-supply.

Besides the lack of drinking water facilities, the most felt needs of the people in the villages, in order of their preference, are for the provision of irrigational facilities; accessibility to transport and the protection of crops from the destruction by the wild animals. Among the medical facilities, the most felt need observed is for the establishment of maternity and child welfare centres especially in the interior of the district. Scarcity of fuelwood, grass and fodder and timberwood are the other problems for which the locals in some areas have to struggle hard for procuring them by trekking daily long distances and sometimes places beyond 20 kilometres. The timberwood is generally obtained from the nearest marketing centres in town areas such as Ramnagar, Kotdwara, Rishikesh, Byaschatti etc. In addition to these needs, the inaccessibility of educational institutions particularly the higher level ones; lack of bridle paths, roads and bridges; excessive growth of lantana grass (**kuri**) in the cultivated areas; the destruction of crops by insects especially by the local one called **kurumula**; scarcity of cultivated land; absence of marketing facilities and the dearth of male work-force due to outmigration have been found to be the significant constraints in the sample villages.

Extent of inaccessibility of the services and amenities

The foregoing analysis has in detail, thrown sufficient light on the existing availability of services and amenities in the district. It has been observed that lack of transportation and communication has been the main bottleneck in making the services and amenities accessible. The extent of inaccessibility conditions prevailing in the district can be visualised from our analysis of the sample villages **vide** Table 4.11.

With the exceptions of primary schools and Branch Post offices, a majority of the facilities were found relatively more inaccessible in the sample villages. Over 90 per cent of the samples had primary schools within the villages. The correponding percentage for Branch Post offices was relatively lower (43 per cent). But another 40 per cent of the sample villages had this facility within a distance of less than 5 kilometres. It would be observed from the Table 4.11 that district headquarter lay at a mean distance of over 70 kilometres from our sample villages. This was followed by the locations of degree colleges (38.10 kilometres), tahsil headquarter (37.14 kilometres) and hospital (20.48 kilometres). The remaining facilities lay at the mean distances below these. The coefficient of variations for most of the facilities was over 65 per cent indicating thereby higher degrees of inaccessibility conditions in the district.

Levels of Functional Organisation

Our analysis has amply demonstrated that the district under

TABLE 4.11
Extent of inaccessibility of the services and amenities in Pauri Garhwal district Sample Survey - 1977-78

Services and amenities	Mean Dista-nce	Standard Deviation	Coefficient of Variations
1. District Headquarter	70.83	35.02	49.40
2. Tahsil Headquarter	37.14	16.20	43.62
3. Block Headquarter	19.05	10.48	55.02
4. Kanungo Circle Headquarter	17.38	12.30	70.70
5. Patwari Circle Headquarter/ Police Station	4.10	2.91	70.97
6. Middle School	2.43	2.09	81.48
7. High School/Inter College	5.50	3.08	56.00
8. Degree College	38.10	27.75	72.83
9. Banks	18.57	12.68	68.28
0. Sub Post-office	8.93	6.10	68.31
.1. Hospital	20.48	11.70	57.13
2. Dispensary	4.23	3.20	75.65
.3. Maternity and Child Welfare Centre	7.38	5.02	68.02
.4. Health Centre	13.93	10.07	72.22
5. Family Planning Centre	14.35	9.63	67.11
6. Veterinary Hospital	16.43	11.80	71.82
.7. Stockman Centre	6.69	4.48	66.94

study possesses a low level of functional organisation. Not only are the services and amenities inaccessible owing to the lack of transportation and communication facilities but their spatial locations are also found to be both inadequate and ubiquitous. This is due partly to the existence of small sized settlements in this mountainous terrain and partly to the utter neglect in providing the services and amenities.

The low level of functional organisation is reflected in the existing functional gaps possessed both by the urban and rural settlements. Of the 6 small urban centres, Pauri, the headquarter of the district had the largest number of functions figuring 38. This was followed by Kotdwara (31), Srinagar (20), Lansdowne (13) and Dogadda (12). Bah Bazar on account of its peculiar location had only 3 functions and shared other functions with the Deoprayag town lying across the Alaknanda river. In addition, 1,152 rural settlements out of a total of 3,236 settlements in the district possessed in all 1,474 functions of various kinds. Most of them lay in the small-sized settlements especially in the size range of population lying between 100-349 persons comprising of 50.02 per cent of the total settlements of the district.[15] This would be evident from the functionwise break-up of settlements in different size-range of population given in Table 4.12.

It was also observed that the spatial pattern of functions is a dispersed one and hardly shows concentration of functions in the settlements. This is especially so in the patwari circles lying in western, north-eastern and south-eastern parts of the district. Patwari circles in the central part of the district have settlements with relatively more functions in them. Out of a total of 169 patwari circles, 118 had in them such settlements as had two or more functions. The remaining 51 patwari circles had in them such settlements as possessing barely one function. Patwari circles with settlements bearing large number of functions were few and far between. For instance, Jahari in Kaudiya II, Kalagarh in Saneh and Punar in Dhanpur II patwari circles had only 9, 8 and 7 functions respectively.

Major functions and the number of settlements having these functions together with the weightages[16] considered for getting the composite functional scores for the 169 patwari circles and 6 urban centres are given in Table 4.13. It has been observed that the composite functional scores in a majority of patwari circles were very low although the range varied widely with a mean score of 290.19 and the median value of 94.57. The functional scores were relatively very high (over 1,000) in respect of the patwari circles of Kaudiya II, Choprakot II and Dhanpur

II due to the increasing functions in the emerging nodal centres of Jaharikhal, Thalisain and Rudraprayag respectively. Besides, as is expected of them, all the urban centres with the exception of Bah Bazar had relatively high functional scores.

A two dimensional graph with logarithms of population in the abscissa and those of comopsite functional scores in the ordinate (Figure 16) distinctly reveals the higher ranking order of the urban centres in respect of both the size and functions. But it does not reveal a clear ranking order of the patwari circles. The plausible explanations for such a paradox are two-fold: first, the variations in the size of population are too small to have a similar level of functions in each of the patwari circles. The bulk of the patwari circles, numbering 145, lie in the population range of 2,001 to 4,000 persons. Of the rest, 13 patwari circles have a population of less than 2,000 persons and 11 patwari circles more than 4,000 persons. Secondly, the contributions of large-sized villages to the composite functional scores of their respective patwari circles were relatively insignificant. This is contrary to the generally accepted relationship between the size of population and the number of functions. The reason is obvious. Even the most of the large-sized villages do not possess the requisite level of functions and hence contributions insignificant to the composite functional scores of their respective patwari circles.

Variations in the Levels of Functions

Based upon the composite functional scores, an attempt has also been made to cull out the patterns and variations in the levels of functions in respect of 169 patwari circles (Figure 17). The urban centres, as was expected of them, possessed extremely high composite scores. Apart from these urban centres, the functional scores of 5 patwari circles were very high. This was a reflection of the relatively larger nodal centre with large number and higher order functions in them. They are: Punar (Rudraprayag) in Dhanpur II, Thalisain in Choprakot II, and Pabau in Ghurdorsyun III patwari circles in the north east; and Jaharikhal in Kaudia II and Pokhra in Talain II patwari circles in the central part of the district. Rudraprayag lies on the main road from Kotdwara to Badrinath. It has since been declared as a class VI (Town Agglomeration) town in 1981 Census. Pabau is the headquarter of the Development Block and links by road the settlements in the areas and beyond to the north. Thalisain too is a Block headquarter and is linked by motorable roads from three sides. Its prospects to emerge as nodal centre have become brighter by the progressively increasing functions in it. With the establishment of a degree college,

TABLE 4.12

Functionwise break-up of rural settlements in different size-range of population in Pauri Garhwal district - 1971

Functionwise break-up of settlements	Size - Range of Population					
	Less than 100 persons	100 - 349 persons	350 - 499 persons	500 - 999 persons	1,000 + persons	All Ranges
Settlements with 1 function	206 (14.92)	589 (36.43)	107 (74.31)	34 (39.53)	2 (25.00)	938 (28.99)
Settlements with 2 functions	12 (0.87)	91 (5.63)	18 (12.50)	26 (30.23)	1 (12.50)	148 (4.57)
Settlements with 3 functions	7 (0.51)	22 (1.36)	5 (3.47)	5 (5.82)	1 (12.50)	40 (1.24)
Settlements with 4 functions	2 (0.14)	7 (0.43)	2 (1.39)	7 (8.14)	1 (12.50)	19 (0.59)
Settlements with 5 functions	-	2 (0.12)	2 (1.39)	-	-	4 (0.12)
Settlements with 6 functions	-	-	-	-	-	-
Settlements with 7 functions	-	-	-	-	1 (12.50)	1 (0.03)
Settlements with 8 functions	-	-	-	-	1 (12.50)	1 (0.03)
Settlements with 9 functions	-	-	-	-	1 (12.50)	1 (0.03)
Total Number of settlements with function(s)	227 (16.44)	711 (43.97)	134 (93.06)	72 (83.72)	8 (100.00)	1,152 (35.60)
Total Number of settlements	1381 (100.00)	1617 (100.00)	144 (100.00)	86 (100.00)	8 (100.00)	3,236 (100.00)

TABLE 4.13
Major Functions and Weightages - 1971

Functions	Number of functions	Number of settlements having	Weightages
I. Education			
(i) Primary School	926	896	3.61
(ii) Middle School	119	116	27.90
(iii) High School/Higher Secondary/Intermediate Colleges	65	59	54.85
(iv) Colleges/Polytechnics	8	5	647.20
II. Postal/communications			
(i) Post office	256	256	12.64
(ii) Post office with telephone	38	33	98.06
(iii) Post and Telegraph office	13	13	248.92
(iv) Head/Sub-Post office	53	45	71.91
III. Medical & Health			
(i) Dispensary	3	2	1618.00
(ii) Health Centre/T.B. Clinic/Nursing Hospital	2	2	1618.00
(iii) Family Planning/M.C.W.	26	24	134.83
(iv) Hospital	50	44	73.55
IV. Banking			
Banks	32	21	154.10
V. Administrative			
(i) District Headquarter	1	1	3236.00
(ii) Tahsil/Sub-tahsil H.Q.	5	5	647.20
(iii) Block H.Q.	14	14	231.14

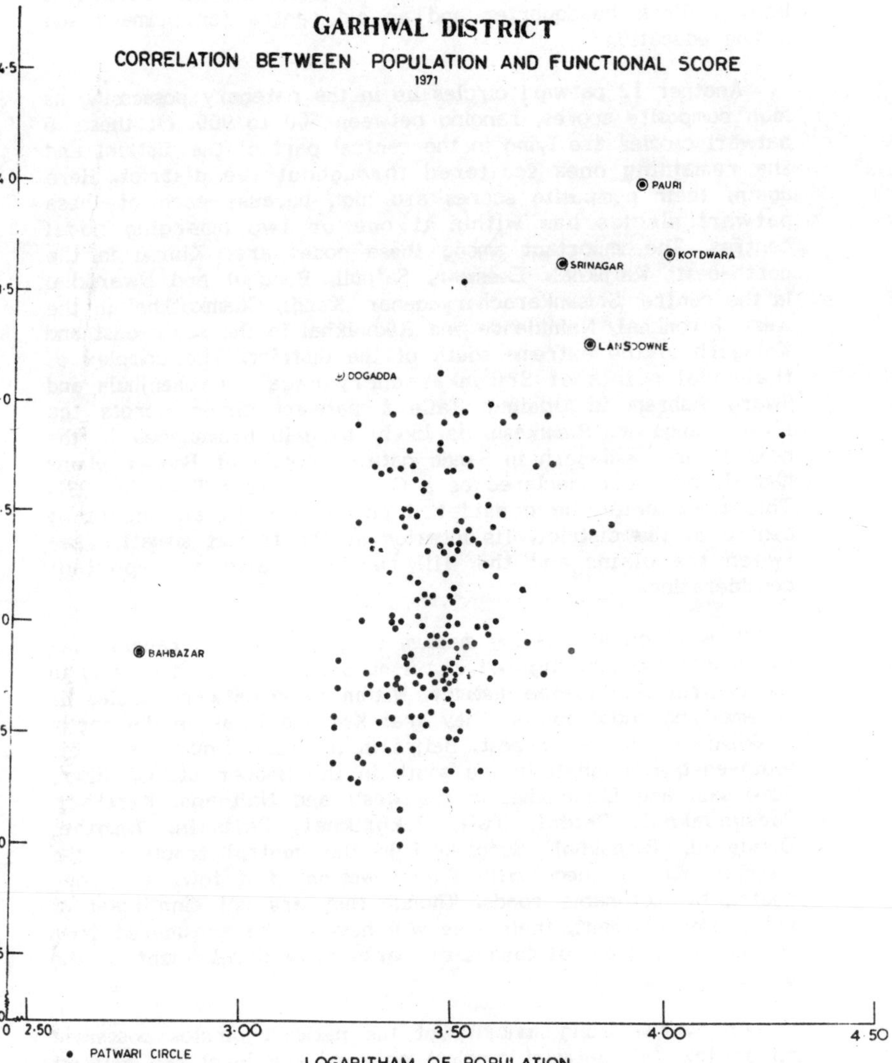
GARHWAL DISTRICT
CORRELATION BETWEEN POPULATION AND FUNCTIONAL SCORE
1971
LOGARITHAM OF COMPOSITE FUNCTIONAL SCORE
LOGARITHAM OF POPULATION
PAURI
KOTDWARA
SRINAGAR
LANSDOWNE
DOGADDA
BAHBAZAR
PATWARI CIRCLE
URBAN CENTRE
0.0
0.5
1.0
1.5
2.0
2.5
3.0
3.5
4.0
4.5
0
2.50
3.00
3.50
4.00
4.50

Fig.-16

Jaharikhal is rapidly coming up as a nodal centre in the close proximity of Lansdowne town a military cantonment. Pokhra is both a Block headquarter and an old centre for primary and middle education.

Another 12 patwari circles lie in the category possessing as high composite scores, ranging between 600 to 900. Of these, 6 patwari circles are lying in the central part of the district and the remaining ones scattered throughout the district. Here again, their composite scores are high because each of these patwari circles has within it one or two emerging nodal centres. The important among these nodes are: Khirsu in the north-east; Kaljikhal, Ekeswar, Satpuli, Banghat and Dwarikhal in the centre; Srisankaracharyanagar, Kandi, Chamkotkhal in the west; Bironkhal, Nainidanda and Rikhnikhal in the south-east and Kalagarh in the extreme south of the district. The complex of the nodal points of Srisankaracharyanagar, Laxmanjhula and Swarg Ashram in Udaipur Talla I patwari circle across the river Ganga at Rishikesh, is likely to gain prominence in the near future. Kalagarh in Saneh patwari circle of Bhaber plains has already been declared as a Class IV Census Town in 1981. This town could be considered potentially as an important centre of the district. Its location at the transit situation between the plains and the Hill region is also an important consideration.

Patwari circles having medium composite scores ranging between 300 and 600, figured 21. A majority of them are lying in the central part of the district. Within these patwari circles lie 15 emerging nodal points. They are: Kot and Lwali in the north; Chakisain in the north-east; Baijro in the east; Dhumakot in the south-east; Kalalghati in the south in the Bhaber plains; Silogi, Sumersain and Bhrigukhal in the west; and Naithana, Kanskhet, Parsundakhal, Paidul, Toli, Pokhrikhet, Patisain, Amotha, Damdewal, Rithakhal, Sanglakoti in the central tracts of the district. All of them, with the exception of a few, are connected by motorable roads. Though they are not significant at the present moment, their role will have to be considered from the point of view of long-term perspective development of the district.

An overwhelming majority of the patwari circles possessed either low (43 patwari circles) or very low level (88 patwari circles) composite functional scores. They are widely distributed and occur as contiguous tracts with very little evidence of spatial organisation.

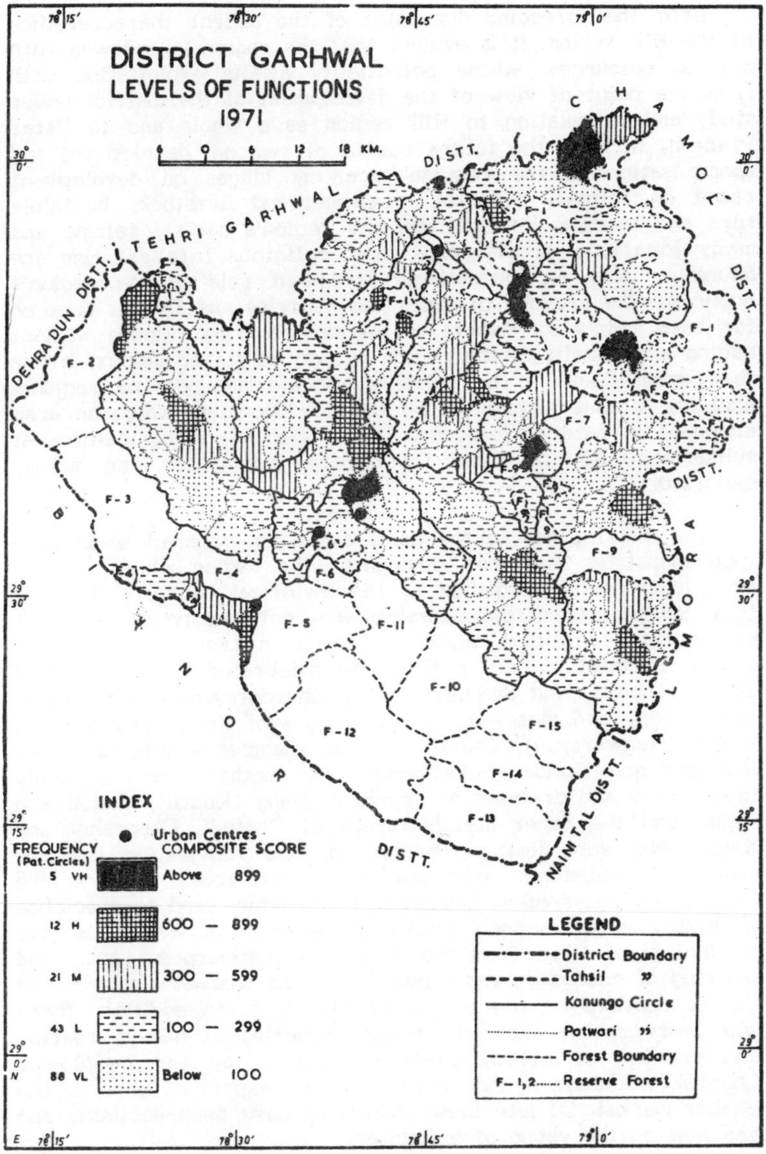

DISTRICT GARHWAL
LEVELS OF FUNCTIONS
1971
6 0 6 12 18 KM.
78°15′
78°30′
78°45′
79°0′
30° 0′
29° 30′
29° 15′
29° 0′
TEHRI GARHWAL DISTT.
CHAMOLI DISTT.
DEHRA DUN DISTT.
BIJNOR
MORADABAD DISTT.
NAINITAL DISTT.
ALMORA DISTT.
F-1
F-2
F-3
F-4
F-5
F-6
F-7
F-8
F-9
F-10
F-11
F-12
F-13
F-14
F-15
INDEX
Urban Centres
FREQUENCY (Pat. Circles)
COMPOSITE SCORE
5 VH Above 899
12 H 600 — 899
21 M 300 — 599
43 L 100 — 299
88 VL Below 100
LEGEND
District Boundary
Tahsil "
Kanungo Circle
Patwari "
Forest Boundary
F— 1, 2....... Reserve Forest

Fig 17

Industrial Structure and Potentialities of Pauri Garhwal District

From the foregoing discussion of the salient characteristics of the Hill region, it is evident that the region is endowed with natural resources, whose potentiality awaits exploitation both from the point of view of the development of the district under study and in relation to Hill region as a whole and to Uttar Pradesh. In fact, the future course of regional development and specialisation of the regional economy hinges on development based on forests, minerals, grassland and livestock, horticulture and tourism. For tourism, the region's natural setting and many locations of historical and religious interest also are bound to play an increasingly important role in the region's economy. The produce of mines and quarries and forests have so far been mainly for export to the neighbouring regions without adding any benefit to the region by way of its processing within the region itself.[17] The relative backwardness of the regional economy is thus highlighted by the conditions, in which an area abundant in natural resources has to depend on agriculture at subsistence level, while its natural resources are mainly exported.

The district had in the past, a number of small scale cottage industries scattered throughout the region which used to meet local needs. A glance at the historical background shows that indigenous entrepreneurship was not lacking but that it subsequently declined, under competition from factory-made goods. To mention only a few: the celebrated coppersmiths of Simlhat (Lohba) and Simkhet (Pattey Ghurdorsyun) and Srinagar; the pottery and glassware manufacturers of Kanda (Aswalsyun), Ujyari (Gagwarsyun), Kainur; the glass-bangles manufacturers of Srinagar and Phalda (Patwalsyun); the leather workers mainly the tanners and dressers of Srinagar, Dang (Khatli), Gadoli and Simla; and the paper manufacturers of Dhaijuli, Choprakot and Kandarsyun were famous. Besides, in some villages, in Kandarsyun Patty millstones were cut out of the rocks found in the bed of Dhaijuli rivulet. The village Chandpur, used to specialise in making wooden vessels from a single block of wood. Also the production of fibre from the hemp - a multipurpose plant; and weaving of coarse canvas known locally as **bhangelas** was one of the occupations of the people of Chandpur. In addition, there was basketmaking and net-making; gathering of honey; rearing and trading of sheep, goats and cattle by the people of Choprakot, Chauthan and Dewalgarh; and export of ghee to the Bhaber market. Of late these industries have been declining and are now on the verge of extinction.

The Present Structure and Pattern of Industrial Development

The present structure of industries in the district despite vast potentialities is virtually in its early stage of development. The district does not possess any large scale industrial unit nor is one planned presently.

In 1950-51, there was only one registered factory in the entire district. By 1960-61 the number of registered factories increased to 3. The number further increased to 5 by 1965-66 but remained constant till 1970-71. By the end of 1975-76, the number increased to 8. The employment in these factories was 277 persons in 1960-61, 467 in 1965-66 and 744 in 1975-76. The industrial estates, one at Kotdwara and the other at Srinagar were built with 12 sheds. But they have not generated any industrial climate mainly because they are not based on the region's resources, nor do they act as link industries to the existing ones. There exists only one Industrial Tranining Institute at Srinagar.

The small-scale industrial units, numbering 70 in 1975-76 employed 642 persons only. These industrial units with the exception of two, one at Satpuli and the other at Nautiyalgaon, are concentrated in the small towns of Kotdwara, Pauri and Srinagar. Kotdwara town possesses the maximum number, 57 in all, of industrial units followed by Pauri with 9 units and Srinagar with 2 units. These units are engaged variously. Out of the total, 22 units are forest-based. Industrial units based on agriculture and horticulture number only 13. The largest number of units are the engineering units which are mainly servicing and repairing units. Besides, 7 other industrial units are producing goods of various kinds. The details of these units are given in Table 4.14. The number of cottage industries is about 2,000 with an investment of about Rs.15 lakhs. This sector has about 45,000 self-employed workers. Most of these units are engaged in making woollen knitwear from wool locally available.

It would be observed from the foregoing analysis that the regional industrial structure commensurate with the resources of the area and the region's role in the rest of the economy of U.P. is still to emerge.

Industrial Potentialities of the District

The scope for the development of industries in this region cannot be underestimated. They may be based on the local raw materials and may enhance the level of employment and income generation. Such industries can initially be developed only at a

TABLE 4.14

Small-scale Industrial Units in Pauri Garhwal District-1976

Name of the Industrial units	Place(s) of Establishment	No. of Units	Total Employment
I. **Forest Based Industrial Units**			
(1) Resin, Turpentine and varnishes	Kotdwara	4	39
(2) Wood Furniture	Kotdwara	4	94
(3) Cardboard Packing Boxes	Kotdwara	3	24
(4) Wood Sawing	Kotdwara	3	22
(5) Washing Soap	Kotdwara	4	24
(6) Lead Pencils	Kotdwara	1	18
(7) Wax Candles	Kotdwara	1	2
(8) Medicines	Kotdwara	2	89
II. **Agro-based Industrial Units**			
(1) Rice Mills	Pauri	2	3
	Kotdwara	1	1
(2) Processing of fruits and agricultural products	Kotdwara	3	53
(3) Agricultural implements	Pauri	1	6
(4) Atta Chakkies	Pauri	1	3
	Kotdwara	1	5
	Nautiyalgaon	1	2
(5) Tobacco and Hukka	Kotdwara	3	118
III. **Engineering Industrial Units**			
(1) General Engineering goods	Kotdwara	5	27
	Srinagar	1	36
(2) Printing	Kotdwara	4	22
	Pauri	1	36
	Srinagar	1	6
(3) Servicing and repairing	Kotdwara	7	52
	Pauri	3	17
(4) Electrical goods	Kotdwara	3	9
(5) Plastic goods	Kotdwara	3	12
IV. **Miscellaneous**			
	Kotdwara	5	14
	Pauri	1	4
	Satpuli	1	4
TOTAL		70	742

small scale because of the economic conditions prevailing, namely the restricted demand, lack of capital and entrepreneurship and low per capita income.

The Government of India and the State Government, however, have realised the need for developing the village and cottage industries in view of their role in the rural sector of the economy. The Planning Commission in its report on the Second Five Year Plan observed, "village and cottage industries in their different aspects are an integral and continuing element in the economic structure and in the national planning."[18] The emphasis on small scale industries continues in the subsequent Five Year Plans and in the economic and social policy declarations from time to time.

Owing to their very nature such industries provide good potential for employment at relatively low capital investments, with short gestation periods, simpler techniques of production, wider dispersal possibilities, mobilisation of entrepreneurial motivation etc. The entire industrial sector potentialities may be grouped into the following categories:

I. Forest Based Industrial Potentialities;
II. Livestock Based Industrial Potentialities;
III. Agriculture Based Industrial Potentialities;
IV. Mineral Based Industrial Potentialities;
V. Miscellaneous Industrial Potentialities; and
VI. The Tourist Industry and its Potentialities.

Considering the regional characteristics and pattern of population distribution, small-scale industries based on local produce ought to gain priority because of the possibilities for dispersed development. These have to be integrated with the facilities for marketing and social welfare which are lacking at the moment. Likewise, there is need for integrating plans for tourism. It may also be mentioned that any large-scale industry, whether or not based on the natural resources, would tend to create 'islands' of development with very little impact on the surrounding area, at least initially. Added to this is the problem of degradation of natural environment which follows large-scale exploitation of the natural resources with little regard to physical land-use planning. The local culture, which is evolved through very close interrelationship, between the people and environment, also needs to be sustained and further integrated in the course of development. It is in this context that the micro-regional study has its special significance as a prelude to plans for the development of the region.

I. Forest Based Industrial Potentialities

The forest resources, have been discussed in Chapter three. The development possibilities based on forestry are listed below:

(1) **Paper Industry**: The district under study, owing to abundant forest resources possesses considerable potentiatlities for the development of a 'paper industry'. It can produce paper, newsprint and pulp in some quantity as major constituents of the raw materials such as bamboo, coniferous wood and **sabai** grass are available. Bamboo and coniferous wood constitutes 68.7 per cent and sabai grass 5.8 per cent of the raw material component of the paper industry. It should be possible to establish a paper mill, with a capacity of 20 tonnes a day at Satpuli, a central place connected by roads from all sides and situated at the confluence of Western and Eastern Nayar rivers. Carrying pine timber by means of water transport through these rivers and the availability of water supply would be additional advantages accruing from such a set up.

(2) **Rope-making from grasses and other fibres**: Different kinds of raw materials for the manufacture of ropes are available in plenty all over the district. These are **bhaber, malu, bichhu, bhimal, bhang, rambans.** Local people make use of these materials mostly for home consumption with very little for exchange in the commercial markets. Bhaber grass grows wild all over the tarai areas of Kotdwara and Kalagarh. This grass is used for the manufacture of ropes and paper. The rope manufactured with this grass is used for cot strings and also for bundling bamboos and wood. **Bhimal** tree though scattered, grows throughout the district. Its small branches are cut generally after the winter, the leaves are used as fodder, the wood as torches for lighting purposes and the fibre for making ropes and floor matting. **Malu** is a reddish coloured creeper and has great potentialities in the manufacture of ropes. **Rambans** grows wild over the hilly region; the fibre is strong and works very well in water and its fibre is used in making fishing nets. **Bichhu** grass fibres are very strong and very good types of rope can be manufactured. The fibres of **bhang** are considered very strong and fine in texture and are used for producing cloth, hats, hold-alls etc. The fibres can be dyed into several colours and utilised for the manufacture of carpets and **bhangelas.** Mat making from **padera** grass is another source to be utilised for the industrial purpose.

(3) **Ringal, Bamboo and Cane work**: Ringal is a type of cane similar to bamboo in appearance and can be used in making baskets and mats of different types. Different types of cane can

be used for making baskets, tiffin boxes, chairs and various other articles. **Simúl** trees grow scattered all over the hills. There are great possibilities of expanding the industry.

(4) **Resin and Turpentine**: Oleo resin is the raw material used in the manufacture of resin and turpentine. Resin is used in various industries like the paper industry in the sizing of paper, in the soap industry etc., while turpentine is used in paints, varnishes and printing inks. There is a considerable potentiality of such industry. Already resin is being collected and distributed to the government factory for the manufacture of resin and turpentine at Bareilly.

(5) **Wood and its products**: A number of products can be manufactured from wood. Walking sticks and batons can be manufactured out of **ash, kail** and **oak** trees. The whole industry of stick and racket-making and wood-carving has great potentialities of further development in view of large supplies of the raw material. Pen-holders, pencils and beam-scales can be manufactured. The wood of **deodar** for pen-holders and pencils and mango for beam scales would be feasible. Coarse wrapping paper can be manufactured with the help of forest products. Conifers can be used for the newsprint paper industry as already noted.

(6) **Oil Extraction Industry**: A few variety of seeds should be experimentally used for oil extraction and might then provide a profitable industry. The seeds of **chillu, banj** and **pine** seeds can be utilised for industrial purposes. **Chillu** yields oil for massaging and cooking purposes. Banj oil is used in the manufacture of soap.

(7) **Sericulture Industry**: Sericulture encompasses a large number of activities such as cultivation of mulberry/oak trees, rearing silk worms, reeling silk and silk weaving. At each stage, it provides considerable employment opportunities. Silk fibre is the utlimate product in this process and can be put to a variety of uses. Mulberry silk worms feed on mulberry leaves while tasser silk worms are reared on oak leaves. At present, sericulture activity is confined to Bilkhet in Kaljikhal block and Khirsu in Khirsu block. The future development of this industry depends on a phased programme for the expansion of area under mulberry/oak trees, enhancement of the supply of silkworm eggs and increasing emphasis on marketing of cocoons and reeling of silk.

(8) **Saw Mills**: These can be an important industry in the district. For continuous and planned operation of a saw mill, it

is imperative that it is sure of a perennial supply of timber and for this the district is ideally well matched.

(9) **Shuttlecocks and Cricket bats:** There is ample scope for an industry producing shuttlecocks and cricket bats despite the fact that feather shuttlecocks are going out of fashion.

(10) **Grey Cardboard Plant:** Since waste paper, grasses, wheat and rice stalk are the major raw materials and are available in plenty, there exists the possibility of such an industry.

II. Livestock Based Industrial Potentialites

The Dudhatoli area in this district is mainly suitable for a grassland and livestock economy. In recent times, the availability of livestock and poultry birds has been reduced owing to lack of knowledge about feeding, breeding and management of livestock which results in undernourishment and malnutrition of animals. The following industries have potentialities of development:

(1) **Tannery for hides and skins:** The population of livestock is mainly concentrated in this district. The livestock will be sufficient to supply raw hides and skins for a plant producing leather. The processed hides can be transported down to the plains where the demand is sufficient to take care of the offtake of such units. The contact points between the hills and the plains could well be the main points for inter-regional commerce and for the development of the Hill region's economy. Such an industry would generate employment to a sizeable population of the district. Different types of tanning materials are available in different parts of the region. **San** makes the leather hard and reddish in colour. **Dhaura** and bakali give softness to the leather and give yellow colour. **Mahua** gives hardness to the leather. **Anwala** mostly found in tarai areas, gives softness to the leather and leather produced by it remains white in colour. Likewise, other tanning materials **viz., kaphal, oak-bark, reh, myrabolan** are other tanning materials which could be utilised.

(2) **Milk and Egg Powder Plant:** There is considerable demand for milk and egg powder in the hill areas. At present, these are brought from outside the region in order to meet the demand of military personnel, stationed at border districts. Therefore, such a plant together with a pasteurisation and milk products plant and poultry farms can be established. They would be instrumental in enhancing the existing low levels of income.

The pattern of dairy development recently undertaken in the Himachal Pradesh could be adopted for this region, on a scale consonant with and keeping in view the demand for the adjoining areas, based on the market surveys.

(3) **Footwear and Leather goods:** Because of the recurring nature of demand for footwear and leather goods, establishment of a suitable footwear industry in this region would be highly advantageous. A small mechanised footwear industry may be planned and located in the district.

(4) **Wool Industry** : The existence of large number of sheep in the region and the efforts on the part of the Animal Husbandry Department of Uttar Pradesh to open Sheep Breeding Centres would open new dimensions for the development of this, often a neglected field. The utilisation of available wool would make use of the talent available in the village. The existing units, however, are not performing well owing to the lack of organisational skill on the part of the woollen trades.

(5) **Bone-meal and digester:** If bones are also collected, a bone digester can be set up for home-made manure which may help the local people. The local people are, at present, using compost manures of leaves of trees and phosphate-rich bone manures would complement these.

III. Agriculture Based Industrial Potentialities

A number of industries can be developed provided a sustained effort is made. Some of them are mentioned below :

(1) **Fruit Processing and Canning:** The region produces large quantity of fruits, particularly in the Bharsar lying in the north-eastern part of the district. These are not even transported owing to the lack of transport. Therefore, there is no incentive for horticulture though in parts of the Hill region, this industry could be the major activity and means of livelihood. Further, fruits grown in the region are processed elsewhere, with the result that the region loses substantial revenue. Fruit canning and production centres can be established. Efforts can be directed to bringing more land under orchards in different parts of the region suitable for this purpose. It may be mentioned, that in Bharsar about 196 hectares of land are being developed, as an orchard belt. These experimental areas should become the main areas of innovation for the spread of horticulture and associated industrial development.

(2) **Bee-keeping**: There is a real possibility of increasing this industry in the region, particularly in view of the abundance of flora, which bees can harvest throughout the year. The different types of flora which can be available in different parts of the Hill region remain in the flowering state in one or the other season. This industry is now, however, receiving serious attention and encouragement.

(3) **Oilseed Milling**: Mustard and linseed are the chief oilseeds produced in the Bhaber region and so an industry for oilseed milling can be established.

(4) **Rice Milling and Rice Bran Oil**: With increase in the production of paddy, this industry could be developed. Large quantities of the finer varieties of rice are produced in the Bhaber. In addition to traditional huller type and sheller type, modern rice mills could be established. Again, establishment of minirice mills with a capacity ranging between 200 to 250 kilograms an hour to 3 tonnes an hour could be an useful proposition.

(5) **Cattle and Poultry Feeds**: Cattle and poultry feeds are manufactured out of the waste products after milling of cereals, pulses, oil etc. Saw dust also forms the basic raw material for cattle and poultry feeds. With the establishment of rice, oil and sawing units in the region, these raw materials will become available in the region in plenty. This industry has to be planned in an integrated manner with food processing industries and of grassland areas.

IV. Mineral Based Industrial Potentialities:

Availability of the minerals and their prospective exploration are discussed in Chapter III. However, it is relevant to note here that some important industries are likely to emerge. Some of them may be mentioned here:

(1) **Cement** : In view of the contemplated programme of the government, with respect to the construction of roads, dams and other building activities, the requirements of cement to cater to the needs would be considerable. At present, no cement producing facilities exist in the district. Since adequate quantities of raw material (limestone and gypsum) are available, the possibility of a cement plant cannot be ruled out.

(2) **Domestic Electric Appliances**: Owing to the envisaged growth and development of electricity in the hill districts, it is expected that electric power will increasingly be available for

domestic purposes. This would stimulate demand for domestic electric appliances. Similarly, the feasibility should be explored of establishing a small-scale electric furnace for the manufacture of ferrosilicon and other special iron alloys in the area in view of the magnesite chlorite schists reserves at Mohankhal area of the district.

(3) **Mosaic Floor Tiles:** Mosaic floor tiles are used for attractive and decorative floorings as well as for wall-paving. The major raw material for the manufacture of mosaic floor tiles is marble chips of which accessible reserves ought to be explored as a matter of urgency.

V. Miscellaneous Industrial Potentialities

There are a number of other industries which can be developed. A few of them are mentioned below:

(1) **Automobile Repair Plant:** The establishment of such a plant is based on the fact that the existing fleet of vehicles plying in the hill districts and the likely increase in its number in the next few years consequent upon the completion of the network of roads in the district is likely to increase. And, wear and tear are heavy and likely to remain so even when surfaces are better, it is only because of steep slopes.

(2) **Jobbing Workshops for Agricultural Implements:** Considerable number of agricultural implements would be necessary to effectively achieve the targets of agricultural production. Therefore, the need for establishing jobbing workshops for agricultural implements would be imperative. Agriculture in a Hill region does require a distinct type of implements in comparison with those used in the plains. Hence, the entire fabrication of implements, used in the Hill region needs to be planned, on the basis of regional conditions like in Japan.

(3) **Can Making Manufacture:** As discussed earlier, the food processing and canning industries have potential in the district. This would give rise to the requirements of tin cans and cases. A can-making plant is feasible in the circumstances.

(4) **Cold Storage Plant:** In view of the abundant availability of fruits, eggs and poultry, consequent upon the development of this sector, there is a good scope for establishing suitable cold storage facilities. This would benefit the cultivators, the orchard owners and the poultry farmers.

(5) **Medicine Manufacturing:** There is ample scope for the

manufacture of allopathic and ayurvedic medicine from herbs. Cultivation of rare medicinal herbs on a commercial basis is possible. A variety of valuable medicinal herbs and plants of importance for oil extraction and perfume manufacturing are found in the region under study.

Industrial development in the district is handicapped by inadequate transport, power, finance and other infrastructural facilities. Topographical and geophysical conditions constrain the speedy development of infrastructure. Nor are the human, social and political factors less important impediments. Amongst the human factors are listed the dearth of properly trained and motivated people at the entrepreneurial, managerial, technical and skilled workers levels. The competitiveness of the government in many cases has retarded the growth of many private enterprises in the region. The apathetic attitude, red-tapism, procrastination and the indifference of the State Government towards orchardists in respect of marketing, storage, transport has caused them to incur losses in lakhs of rupees. No progress was made towards setting up of resource-based and demand-based industries recommended by the National Industries Development Corporation. Also, the Central Government's attitude towards this region, during the first Four Five Year Plans has been one of negative where positive discrimination is called for and was dominated by the 'politics' of 'regional pulls'.

The above analysis of the considerable potentialities of industrial development shows that the problem needs a thorough probing and prospective exploration, so that the formulation of suitable policies, criteria and strategies for achieving the social ends of the people and the professed aim of all the Five Year Plans as noted earlier becomes possible.

The evaluation of the industrial potential as attempted above serves to build up some picture of what would be an optimal pattern of regional industrial development. The existing structure of industry and its pattern of distribution, however, is only a very weak link for specializing of the region's economy. The localities and areas where cottage industries have been functioning and the areas potentially suited for their development would serve as a basis in working out a generalised pattern of development. The major natural resources like limestones for cement, and their exploitation, await the formulation of regional development plans for different regions of Uttar Pradesh. It is within this framework that the small scale industries, infrastructure and facilities required by the people have to be located in selected areas/locations. Land-use planning and development of small-scale industries seem to be a priority for stabilization of the population which under the acute pressure on limited cultivable land has perforce to migrate. These would largely influence the spatial pattern of development of this district and in general the Hill region as a whole.

VI. The Tourist Industry and Its Potentialities

A synoptic account of the tourist potentialities in the Hill region as a whole has already been made in Chapter II. Pauri Garhwal district, as a part of the Hill region, presents similar features, with minor variations. It abounds in natural endowments: natural beauty and salubrious climate; religious sites and historical places; fauna and flora catering to the diverse interests of the tourists. The altitudinal ranges varying upto 3,000 metres and geographical conditions make this possible.

There are a number of temples of Vaishnav, Shaiv and other sects in the district reflecting man-environment relationship. One would hardly find any settlement which does not possess its own temple. Some of the important temples which attract an estimated 5,000 people or more are : Mahadev Temple, **Ekeswar**; Tarasar Temple, **Tarasar**; Bindeswari (Binsar) Temple, **Chauthan**; Shiva Temple, **Mundneshwar**; Jwalpadevi Temple, Jwalpa; Kuinkaleswar Mahadev Temple, **Pauri**; Kamleswar Mahadev Temple, **Srinagar**; Kamleswar Mahadev Temple, **Lansdowne**; Rajrajeshwari Temple, **Dewalgarh**; Sri Raghunath Temple, **Deoprayag**; Rudranath Temple, **Rudraprayag**; Byas Temple, **Byasghat**; Sidhbali Temple, **Kotdwara**; Mahadev Temple, **Sald Mahadev**; Bhubneshwari Mata and Neelkanth Mahadev Temples, **Neelkanth**; Bileswar Mahadev Temple, **Kimgadigad**; Banjadevi Temple, **Banjadevi** and Kalidevi Temple, **Rathwadhab**. These and a host of other religious places are potential centres of tourist attraction.

A number of historical sites and religious places can also be of valuable tourist attractions. The historical sites of Srinagar, Dewalgarh, Ranihat, Deoprayag, Tarasar, Lansdowne, Binsar, Sald Mahadev and Kotdwara, to mention a few, are well known and arouse historical curiosity. They speak of archaeological findings, architectural skills and sculptural excellence of bygone times. Added to these are the innumerable places of interest for the tourists.

In addition to natural beauty and bracing climate, nature has also provided the district enormous variety of fauna and flora, a description of these has already been made in Chapter II. The fauna of the district is however, well preserved in the

Corbett National Park and Malini Sanctuary to which annually a number of tourists visits.

The tourist industry not only in the district but also in the Hill region as a whole, is at the moment, hadicapped by numerous bottlenecks. Lack of a suitable planning and development strategy, weak organisational structure, absence of appropriate financial and credit institutions, the apathetic attitude of the State Government and stray and uncoordinated efforts of its agencies, have been responsible for the neglect of this industry in the past. Other problems which are corroding the industry at present are the non-availability of good accommodation, inadequacy of transport, lack of water supply, poor roads, inadequate medical facilities, absence of amenities alongwith the roads and poor catering. In addition, the insufficient development of recreational and entertainment facilities and utter neglect of communication media have been responsible for retarding the development of tourism in this Hill region.

The tourist industry has a vast economic potential. Given a dispersed development, one can visualise a substantial impact on the region's economy both direct and indirect. Directly, the economy can be geared up through the construction of hotels, boarding houses, restaurants, cinema houses; clubs, shops, paying guest suites and development of transport and communication. Indirectly, subsidiary occupations like poultry farming, dairying, growing fruits and vegetables; the establishment of cottage and handicrafts industry and manufacture of souvenirs etc. Basic infrastructure will have to be provided in the form of electricity, water supply, medical, public health facilities, communication and wayside amenities. Financial arrangements through a network of financial and credit institutions will have to be made. All these efforts would lead to multiplier effects in terms of income, employment and capital formation in the region.

The foregoing analysis of the structure and spatial variations of the economy shows that it is highly dominated by primary activities. The secondary and tertiary activities are least developed and do not show indications of development either spatially or temporally in terms of growth of income, output and employment. Agriculture is the most essential ingredient and mainstay of the people despite the fact that agriculture in the hills presents peculiarities of its own in terms of the nature and type of cultivation, terracing, gul system of irrigation, manuring, crop rotations, uneconomic and small size of holdings etc. All these characteristics act as significant constraints in areal differentiations of the cropping pattern leading to diversification and interculturing of crops. Food crops are mainly grown and as such a small proportion of land is devoted for the cultivation of non-food/commercial crops. The yield per hectare of almost all the crops is low except in irrigated lands. The main factors responsible for the low yield of crops are, among others, the lack of irrigational facilities, inadequate use of agricultural inputs, lack of modernisation and increasing operational expenses. The operational expenses are mainly due to the scarcity of labour force owing to outmigration. The low level of productivity in agriculture is reflected in the low level of income of the people which is quite inadequate to maintain the existing size of population. The district has, therefore, to rely upon to a large extent, on incomes from sources other than agriculture and allied activities, especially on outside incomes which flow into the district through different modes, chiefly by way of moneyorder remittances. The bulk of the income of the people whether generated through agriculture and allied activities or received through outside remittances, is absorbed in purchasing the consumer goods, both agricultural and non-agricultural but mainly the food items. In fact, annually a large part of food is imported from other regions to meet the deficit. The low level of agricultural structure is compounded further by the low level of infrastructural development in terms of roads, power, education, medical and other health facilities, banking and other credit institutions. The existing inaccessibility conditions due to lack of transport and communication pose problems of spatial linkages and interactions both in terms of goods and services. Besides, the level of functional organisation is very weak. The spatial pattern of distribution of various facilities and amenities is of dispersed type even at their low level of availability. This is reflected in the existing functional gaps occuring both by the urban and rural settlements. The level of industrial development of the district is also low. Its potentials are yet to be harnessed. The future course of industrial development, in fact, hinges basically on forests, minerals, grassland and livestock, horticulture and tourism. For tourism, which has a large economic potential, the district's natural setting and many locations of historical and religious importance are bound to play an increasingly important role in the economy. They are, at present, located at random in places such as Kotdwara, Lansdowne, Srinagar and Pauri. Thus, the regional industrial structure commensurate with the resource structure and the region's role in relation to both the Hill region and Uttar Pradesh as a whole is still to emerge.

NOTES AND REFERENCES

1. This is primarily due to the revised definition adopted in

1971. The Census of India, 1971, defines a worker as "a person whose main activity is participation in any economically productive work by his physical or mental activity. A man or woman who is engaged primarily in household duties such as cooking for own household... should not be treated as a worker for the main activity." Thus, if a person engaged in "economically productive work" but only as his secondary activity, he/she is not considered as a worker. In the definition of Census of 1961, even secondary economic activity qualified a person to be considered as a worker.

2. For details refer Chapter one.

3. Increase in revenue demands since 1815 can be viewed from the following statement:

Revenue Settle-ments	Year of Settle-ment	Period of Settle-ment	Name of the Settlement Authority	Revenue demand per annum
I.	1815	1815	Traill	Rs. 35,990.00
II.	1816	1816	-do-	Rs. 41,782.00
III.	1817	1817-20	-do-	Rs. 45,548.00
IV.	1820	1820-23	-do-	Rs. 54,995.00
V.	1823	1823-28	-do-	Rs. 64,900.00
VI.	1828	1828-33	-do-	Rs. 67,725.00
VII.	1833	1833-38	-do-	Rs. 69,254.00
VIII.	1840	1840-60	Batten	Rs. 68,682.00
IX.	1860	1860-90	Beckett	Rs. 96,311.00
X.	1896	1896-1926	Pauw	Rs. 1,66,727.00
XI.	1926	1926-66	Ibbotson	Rs. 2,55,161.00
XII.	1966	1966-	Govt. of U.P.	Over Rs.3 lakhs

4. Pant, S.D.: **Social Economy of the Himalayans**; George Allen and Unwin Ltd., London; 1935, p. 93.
5. Pant, S.D.: **Ibid**, p. 138.
6. Yeates, Maurice H.: **An Introduction to Quantitative Analysis in Economic Geography;** McGraw Hill. New York, 1968, pp. 33-40.
7. Weaver, John C.: "Crop Combination Regions in the Middle East", **The Geographical Review,** 1954; Vol.44, pp. 175-200; and also
Weaver, John, C.: "Crop Combination Regions for 1919 and 1929 in Middle West", **The Geographical Review,** 1954; Vol.44, pp. 560-572.
8. Weaver's method involves an application of the definition

of statistical variance. It has been defined as

$$\sigma^2 = \frac{\sum d^2}{n} = \frac{\sum (x_i - x)^2}{n}$$

The mean X in the above definition is often termed as "expected value" in an array of numbers. Weaver substituted the expected theoretical percentage for the expected value. The variance can therefore, be calculated for each group and the group that exhibits the minimum variance is the combination that classified the region. However, this method does not cover all the agricultural activities and as a technique for universal application, it fails in this respect in the regions where mixed farming is practised. The Thomas method is an extension of Weaver method and covers the whole spectrum of agricultural activities. Thus, it is designed to make use of all the data available for calculation of the variances for each crop combination.

9. The regionwise details of the samples are as follows:

Crop Combination Region	No. of villages surveyed	No. of households surveyed	Names of the villages
2-Crop Combination Region	2	13	Gorakhpur and Sitapur
3-Crop Combination Region	22	115	Lweentha, Deolad, Lachhi-Saingaon, Dumlot Málla, Birgana, Matiyalna, Gadri, Sainji, Chamrara, Kolli, Dungripanth, Marora, Kundi, Sundergadna, Naithana, Punar, Kola, Barswar, Amaldu, Kathur-Bara, Kasani and Umethgaon
4-Crop Combination Region	13	67	Ghansyali, Riksal, Kainur, Kandiya, Gadkot, Janasu, Kund, Seela, Dwari, Balli, Ghangli, Juledi, and Thanger
5-Crop Combination Region	5	23	Aingar, Chopriyun, Nagar, Kalna-Dewalgarh, and Balli

10. The estimates of income are based on the survey of 218 households in 42 sample villages. For details refer Chapter-I.
11. Government of Uttar Pradesh, Economic & Statistical Division (1980); **Statistical Diary,** p. 47.
12. Bharsar has recently been developed by the Government of U.P. as an orchard cum fruits and vegetables nursery, at an estimated cost of Rs. 1.18 lakhs; in an area of 196 hectares lying at altitudes ranging between 1,850 to 2,350 metres from mean sea level. The apple orchard is the biggest in Asia and grows 32 varieties of apples of which 12 are exportable. Potatoes grown here are one of the best and yield per hectare comparable to those of the plains.
13. State Bank of India, New Delhi: **Lead Bank Scheme Survey Report on Garhwal District, U.P.,** 1971.
14. For details refer Chapter V.
15. For details refer Chapter III.
16. In the present study 5 major functions were considered for the purposes of ranking the patwari circles and the urban centres. Considering the importance of frequency of availability of a particular function, weightages (W) given to each of the variables of these functions were calculated according to their frequency of distribution with the help of the following formula*

$$\text{Weightage (W)} = \frac{(Fi)}{N} n$$

Where Fi is the number of settlements;

N is the total number of settlements where a particular function is available;

n is the unit of i

* Sharma, A.N.; **Spatial Approach for District Planning,** Concept Publishing Co., New Delhi, 1981.

The composite functional score of a patwari circle was thus obtained by summing up the functional scores of the settlements within a patwari circle.

17. National Industries Development Corporation: **Survey of Industrial Programming in Hill Districts of U.P.,** 1969-70, p.2.
18. Planning Commission, Government of India: **Second Five Year Plan,** 1956, p. 429.

FIVE

Impact of Population Migration and Moneyorder Remittances on the Economy of the Region.

Population movement is inherent in the very process of development-socio-cultural and economic. Scholars working in the field of demography, human geography, sociology, economics and planning have approached the problem differently though the complementarity of each discipline's viewpoint is at once revealed. The area or space element constitutes the common framework through which the cause and effect of population movement is understood and evaluated in terms of its impact on the areas involved. The factors that induce population migration have been varied. However, the objective of outmigration has primarily been to seek better economic opportunities with a view to increasing an individual's income, leading to material advancement and enhanced social esteem. Migration is both seasonal and permanent over varied distances and its effects are both good and bad. We have instances of the vicious circle of poverty → outmigration → poverty in the case of under-developed regions of India. Likewise, there are instances wherein outmigration has brought about prosperity by way of flow of funds, technology and cultural contacts. Whatever the effects: good or bad, in general the phenomenon of migration occurs and always tends to increase with increase in industrialisation and economic development of the country. The process of economic development brings about large scale mobility and shifts in population (rural-urban, rural-rural, urban-rural and urban-urban) which vary sometimes widely among different regions within the country. Low levels of output and income on the one side and low levels of saving, investment and capital formation on the other side, increase the dependence of the regions not only on outside incomes from the outmigrants but also on outside consumption goods. These outside incomes flow through various channels but chiefly by way of moneyorder remittances. An attempt has been made in this Chapter to highlight the nature, magnitude, directions and patterns of outmigration of working population, followed by a detailed study of the spatial patterns and variations in moneyorder remittances into the district. Their impact on the existing and future structure of the economy of the region forms the concluding part.

The Extent and Patterns of Migration

Pauri Garhwal District is one of the few districts of the state of Uttar Pradesh which gains practically no population from outside. Instead, there has been a growing tendency of outmigration of people due to low levels of productivity and income. The district, according to 1971 Census had a population of 553,000 of which 47.20 per cent was male and 52.80 per cent female. The rural population constituted 93.78 per cent and the remaining 6.22 per cent was urban. Of the total population of 553,000 nearly 39.76 per cent was migrant population. Migration of female population was relatively much higher than that of male population and accounted for 74.38 per cent of the total migration of population. Among the different categories of migration, the intra-district migration was the highest and comprised of 78.06 per cent of the total migrant population. As compared to this, the inter-district migration was only 17.18 per cent. The extent of migration to the various states of the country beyond the state of enumeration from the district under study constituted 3.53 per cent. The remaining 1.23 per cent was accounted for by the migrant population living abroad.

Intra-District Migration

The intra-district migration relates to the short distance movement of the people, mainly due to search for making a living on primary occupation or marriage migration, migration of labourers at the time of harvesting or migration for education etc. Out of a total migrant population of 220,000 (1971 Census) the extent of intra-district migration was to the tune of 172,000 or 78.06 per cent of the total. This was the highest among different categories of migrant population. The major segment of this was constituted by female migrants (83.88 per cent) of the total intra-district migrants. Of the total migrant population of 172,000 the extent of migrant workers was 115,000 or approximately 66.95 per cent of the total. The percentage of female workers far exceeded that of the male workers. It would be observed from Table 5.1 that an overwhelming majority, mainly of the females, was engaged as cultivators (87.47 per cent). Those who worked as agricultural labourers constituted 1.23 per cent of the total migrant workers engaged in different activities. Due to dominance of primary activities, the number of workers engaged in the secondary and tertiary activities was relatively very small. However, a large majority of the workers, mainly the males, were engaged in tertiary activities, mostly in household and other miscellaneous work.

Inter-District Migration

The inter-district migration relates to the migration of the people outside the district but within Uttar Pradesh. This movement is due to the push factor which operates under condition of low land productivity, scarcity of cultivable land and absence of any other occupation. These migrants as corroborated by the field enquiry are also mostly unskilled and low paid workers who are mostly employed for household and other miscellaneous work. The inter-district migration in 1971 constituted 17.18 per cent of the total migrants. Out of the total migrants of 37,755 persons in this category about 54.15 per cent of them were migrant workers. The percentage of male workers (79.88 per cent) far exceeded that of the female workers (21.12 per cent). It would be observed from Table 5.1 that 27.08 per cent of the total workers were engaged in primary activities, 4.52 per cent in secondary activities and 68.40 per cent in tertiary activities. A major component of workers, comprising mainly of females and engaged in primary activities, were cultivators. In contrast to this, most of the workers engaged in "other services" in tertiary sector were males. This analysis of the migration streams revealed that the migrants have a strong tendency to move to areas of similar environment. As such the inter-district migration within the Hill region constituted 46.40 per cent of the total. Next in importance is the relatively rich agricultural plains of Western Uttar Pradesh which accounted for 44.16 per cent of the inter-district migration. The Eastern region, the Central region and the Bundelkhand region shared the rest (9.44 per cent). It must be noted here that Western U.P. is relatively more developed in agriculture and industry and has easy access to the Hill region unlike the Central and the Bundelkand regions.

Migration outside the State

This type of migration relates to the migration in the states of India beyond the state of enumeration. According to the 1971 Census, the total number of migrants in this category figured 3,755 or 3.53 per cent of the total migrants. As in the inter-district type of migration, males outnumbered the females. It would be revealed from Table 5.1 that about 22.51 per cent of the total workers were engaged in primary activities, 5.19 per

TABLE 5.1
Occupational Patterns of Migrant Workers - 1971

Categories of migration	Total No. of migrant workers	Occupational categories (Percentage to the total) Primary			Secondary		Tertiary			
		I	II	III	IV	V	VI	VII	VIII	IX
I. Within the district of enumeration.	114,955	87.47	1.23	1.01	0.01	0.84	0.14	1.34	0.41	7.55
II. Outside the district but within the state of enumeration.	20,455	18.70	1.88	6.50	0,05	4.47	3.15	5.35	3.04	56.86
III. Outside the state of enumberation but within the country.	3,755	10.25	0.28	11.98	-	5.19	0.53	11.37	2.74	57.66
IV. Abroad	2,365	8.03	2.33	29.18	-	1.48	14.58	8.03	5.29	31.08
All categories.	141,530	74.15	1.32	2.58	0.01	1.49	0.83	2,30	0.92	16.40

I. Cultivators.
II. Agricultural labourers.
III. Mining, forestry etc.
IV. Household industry.
V. Manufacturing.
VI. Construction
VII. Trade and commerce.
VIII. Transport and communications.
IX. Other services.

cent in the secondary activities and the majority 72.30 per cent in the tertiary activities. This observation follows the same pattern as in inter district movement i.e. the migrants are mainly absorbed in miscellaneous occupations (more than 80 per cent). In the primary activities, 10.25 per cent of the total workers were engaged as cultivators and slightly a higher percentage in the activities relating to livestock, forestry, orchards etc. Workers engaged in both these activities were confined mainly to the states of Himachal Pradesh and Jammu and Kashmir in the Northern region.

An anlysis of the directions of migration showed that the migration to the adjoining areas was relatively much more than to the areas farther away. The Northern region comprising the states of Himachal Pradesh, Jammu and Kashmir, Haryana and Punjab and the Union territory of Chandigarh, recorded the highest percentages of 30.75 and 33.55 to the total migrant population and migrant workers respectively. The metropolitan city of Delhi, seems to be the most attractive area for the migrants (27.02 per cent of the total). Next to the Delhi region was the Eastern region comprising of the states of Bihar, Orissa, West Bengal, Assam and other eastern states of India (18.76 per cent). The other regions, namely the Central region comprising the states of Madhya Pradesh and Rajasthan; the Western region comprising the states of Maharashtra and Gujarat and the Southern region comprising the states of Andhra Pradesh, Tamilnadu, Karnataka and Kerala absorbed, relatively low proportion of migrants. The percentages to the total migrants in these regions were 13.35, 6.70 and 3.42 respectively.

Migration outside the country

The total number of migrants residing abroad as per the 1971 Census figured 2,705 persons or approximately 1.23 per cent of the total migrants, among different categories of migration from the study area. About 90 per cent of them were male migrants and the remaining female migrants. Of these, the migrant workers numbered 2,365, constituting 87.43 per cent of the total migrant population. Over 98 per cent of them were the male workers. This is to be expected under the prevailing conditions for emigration. Most of the migrant population resided in Nepal (86.88 per cent), Pakistan (11.65 per cent) and Burma (1.11 per cent) and very few resided in other countries of the world. It would be observed from Table 5.1 that 39.53 per cent of the total workers were engaged in primary activities, 1.48 per cent in the secondary activities and the remaining 58.98 per cent in the tertiary activities. This again reveals the unskilled nature of the migrant population, distance from place of living and the lower level of development of the country, which receives migrants mainly for agriculture and household activities. Among the primary activities, livestock, forestry, orchards etc. engaged over 29.18 per cent of the total workers and very few were engaged in others. Likewise, in the secondary sector, only 1.48 per cent of the total workers were engaged. In the services sector, construction activities, trade and commerce, transport and storage etc. and "other services" engaged 14.59 per cent, 8.03 per cent, 5.29 per cent and 31.08 per cent of the total workers respectively.

The above analysis of the secondary data on migration has brought out vividly the magnitude of outmigration, male selectivity, areas of absorption and type of occupation, keeping with socio-economic backwardness of the area, from which they originate. It would be interesting to study the impact of outmigration on the region, as many families depend on money remittances from the male migrants, who mostly keep their female members, the aged and the children at home. For this purpose, field enquiry was conducted in 218 households, selected by systematic stratified sampling in which the strata cover the spatial units and households of different socio-economic backgrounds.

A study of the physical characteristics of the land, cropping pattern, the productivity and other resources was conducted to provide a spatial framework for selecting sample villages and in turn, from within them the households. In all, 42 sample villages were selected for understanding the socio-economic conditions of the villages of outmigrant population. Of these, 42 villages where the field enquiry was conducted, 33 villages comprising 2,804 households and a population of over 17,000 had migrants, on whom the household and in turn the village economy, largely depended. It was found that 8.59 per cent of the households, comprising 5.87 per cent of the population, in these villages had permanently migrated to various places, particularly in the adjoining small towns of the district, during the last three decades (Table 5.2). In addition, as would be observed from Table 5.3, 112 households or 51.38 per cent of the total households surveyed, reported outmigration of temporary nature. On an average, there were 4 workers per household and 45 per cent of them were migrant workers. The percentage variations of migrant workers to the total workers, among different villages, ranged from 20 per cent to as high as 100 per cent, though in different size range of holdings, the variations ranged from 40.35 per cent to 50.50 per cent.

The outmigration of the people to different destinations can be viewed from an examination of Table 5.2. It would be observed that 69 households (28.51 per cent) had migrated permanently within the district, 152 (62.81 per cent) outside the district but within the state of U.P. and the remaining 21 (8.68 per cent) outside the state.

The pattern of outmigration, in the sample study reveals that it is not area or location specific but is diffused spatially. It is observed that the magnitude of outmigration is weak in those settlements which are devoid of accessibility conditions and are cut off from the main streams of modernisation. Despite stark poverty and economic distress, people are clinging to their traditional subsistence agriculture. This seems to dispel the popular belief that poverty leads to outmigration. The magnitude of the migration is greater in settlements and areas which had the initial advantage of educational facilities, access to traditional routes of transportation and communication and above all the initiative of the educated rural elites, who motivate these migrants to shift to the urban centres. Thus, the **city's pull factor has been more dominant than the push factor of the region.**

There appears to be a relationship between the size of the settlements and strength of migration stream because of the information flow and relatively more interaction among people. Settlements, small and large alike share the migration characteristics, the intensity of migration appears more closely associated with accessibility and traditions of migration.

The pattern of outmigration, as would be revealed from Table 5.4 shows a diversified pattern in respect of destinations of the migrants. The small towns of Pauri, Kotdwara, Lansdowne, Dogadda, Srinagar, Bah Bazar (Deoprayag) within the district, absorbed only 6.47 per cent of the total migrants due to limited job opportunities in them. About 23.38 per cent of the migrants have moved out to the urban centres of the state though a sizeable number of them migrated to adjoining towns. The migrants who moved out of the state were 138 or 68.66 per cent of the total migrants from the district. Among the various regions of India, Delhi region topped with 20.90 per cent, followed by Central region (13.93 per cent), Northern region (11.94 per cent), Western region (8.96 per cent), Eastern region (9.95 per cent) and Southern region (2.99 per cent) to the total migrants from the district. These trends are comparable with those based upon the analysis of secondary data for the year 1971.

TABLE 5.2

Destinations of migrant households from Pauri Garhwal district

(Sample Survey - 1977-78)

To	No. of households		Total
I. Within the District	-	-	69 (28.51 Per cent)
(a) Urban	-	18	
(i) Pauri	8		
(ii) Kotdwara	10		
(b) Rural	-	51	
(i) Kotdwara Bhaber	41		
(ii) Kalagarh Bhaber	10		
II. Within the state (But outside the District)	-	-	152 (62.81 Per cent)
(a) Adjoining Towns	-	120	
(i) Almora	4		
(ii) Haldwani	11		
(iii) Ramnagar	12		
(iv) Kashipur	11		
(v) Rishikesh	35		
(vi) Dehradun	34		
(vii) Hardwar	13		
(b) Other Towns	-	32	
(i) Moradabad	4		
(ii) Bareilly	7		
(iii) Roorkee	3		
(iv) Saharanpur	1		
(v) Lucknow	8		
(vi) Allahabad	6		
(vii) Meerut	2		
(viii) Kanpur	1		
III. Out of the State	-	-	21 (8.68 Per cent)
(i) Maharashtra	6		
(ii) Delhi	8		
(iii) Madhya Pradesh	2		
(iv) Punjab & Haryana	5		
All Categories	-	-	242

Occupational structure of the outmigrants also shows a

TABLE 5.3

Outmigrant households, population and workers in different size-range of holdings Sample Survey - 1977-78

Size-range of holdings	Total No. of house-holds surveyed	Households reporting outmigra-tion		Population of house-holds surveyed	Migrant Population of house-holds		Total workers in house holds surveyed	Total No. of migrant workers in the house-holds	
		No.	%		No.	%		No.	%
I. Below 0.25 hectare	44	13	29.55	252	84	33.33	43	20	46.51
II. 0.25 - 0.50 hectare	53	28	52.83	357	284	79.55	104	42	40.38
III. 0.50 - 1.00 hectare	63	37	58.73	465	334	71.83	148	65	43.92
IV. 1.00 - 2.00 hectares	41	23	56.10	327	204	62.39	101	51	50.50
V. Over 2.00 hectares	17	11	64.71	189	120	63.49	57	23	40.35
All Categories	218	112	51.38	1,591	1,026	64.42	453	201	44.37

TABLE 5.4
Destinations of Migrant Workers from Pauri Garhwal District
Sample Survey - 1977-78

To	No. of workers		Total
I. **Within the District**	-	-	13 (6.47%)
(i) Pauri	3		
(ii) Kotdwara	5		
(iii) Lansdowne	3		
(iv) Srinagar	1		
(v) Deoprayag	1		
II. **Within the State but outside the District**	-	-	47 (23.38%)
1. Adjoining Towns	-	30	
(i) Dehradun	3		
(ii) Rishikesh	14		
(iii) Saharanpur	2		
(iv) Roorkee	7		
(v) Nainital	1		
(vi) Hardwar	1		
(vii) Ranikhet	1		
(viii) Ramnagar	1		
2. Other Towns	-	17	
(i) Lucknow	6		
(ii) Moradabad	1		
(iii) Shahjehanpur	1		
(iv) Bareilly	5		
(v) Allahabad	2		
(vi) Moradabad	1		
(vii) Amroha	1		
III. **Outside the state**	-	-	138 (68.66%)
(i) Delhi Region	-	42	
(ii) Northern Region	-	24	
(iii) Central Region	-	28	
(iv) Western Region	-	18	
(v) Eastern Region	-	20	
(vi) Southern Region	-	6	
IV. **Abroad**	-	-	3 (1.49%)
(i) U.K.	-	1	
(ii) Iran	-	1	
(iii) Zambia	-	1	
All Categories	-	-	201 (100.00)

diversified character. They are engaged in various professions ranging from menial and clerical service to the services of high intellectual cadre. Traditionally, the region has been a recruiting ground for armed forces, especially since the time of inception of Military Cantonment at Lansdowne in the last century. A sizeable number of outmigrants, 69 out of 201 or 34.33 per cent were engaged in defence forces such as military, police, Indo-Tibetan Border Force, Border Security Force etc. Another 35.82 per cent are engaged in civil services of central and state governments. There were 29.85 per cent of the outmigrants who were engaged in private services.

TABLE 5.5
Educational Levels of outmigrants
Sample Survey - 1977-78

Educational Level	No. of migrants	Percentage to the total
Without any education.	13	6.47
Primary and middle level.	45	22.39
Secondary level. (High School/Higher Secondary/Intermediate):	88	43.78
Graduate level.	39	19.40
Post-graduate level.	16	7.96
All levels	201	100.00

TABLE 5.6
Age Structure of the Migrants
Sample Survey - 1977-78.

Age-group	No. of migrants	Percentage
Below 20 years	14	6.96
21 - 30 years	102	50.75
31 - 40 years	48	23.88
41 - 50 years	27	13.43
51 and above	10	4.98
All categories	201	100.00

TABLE 5.7
Period of Migration
Sample Survey - 1977-78

Period	No. of migrants	Percentage to the total
Less than 5 years	55	27.36
5 - 10 years	62	30.85
10 - 15 years	38	18.95
15 - 20 years	22	10.95
Over 20 years	24	11.94
All categories	201	100.00

The educational levels of the outmigrants (Table 5.5) was high and was in tune with the high literacy levels of the district. There were 13 migrants without any educational level and 45 with primary and middle level of education. The majority of the migrants 88 (43.78 per cent) out of 201 had secondary level of education. Those who had undergraduate and post-graduate level of education figured 55 (27.36 per cent).

It would be revealed from Table 5.6 that out of the total outmigrants, nearly 50 per cent were in the age-group of 21-30 and another 23.88 per cent in the age-group of 31-40. The remaining outmigrants were in other age groups. This is another important factor which retards the development of the region by way of the exodus of energetic people of younger age-group.

As to the period of outmigration, 46 migrants had been away over 15 years, 38 between 10-15 years, 62 between 5-10 years and 55 less than 5 years.

A majority of migrants leave behind their parents, wives and children in their home places, particularly those who are employed in the defence forces getting annual leave for 2 months. In our sample study, 128 (63.68 per cent) out of 201 migrants visited their home places once a year. Since frequent visits to home places involves additional monetary burden, monthly or quarterly visits are relatively infrequent except by those migrants who are employed within the district or in the adjoining towns of the district. The number of migrants making monthly and quarterly visits figured 8 (3.98 per cent) and 18 (8.96 per cent) respectively. Those who visited their home places after the lapse of one year numbered 13 (6.46 per cent) and were generally those who were relatively better placed, serving in far off places and having weaker links with their home places.

The levels of incomes of the outmigrants are relatively low. This is revealed from the fact that over 55 per cent of these fall in the income ranges of less than Rs.5,000 per annum or Rs.400.00 per month. In the higher income ranges, the percentage of migrants diminishes (Table 5.8).

TABLE 5.8
Annual Income of outmigrants Sample Survey - 1977-78

Range of income	No. of migrants	Percentage to the total
Below Rs.1,000.00	6	2.97
Rs.1,001 - 3,000	32	15.92
Rs.3,001 - 5,000	74	36.82
Rs.5,001 - 7,000	33	16.42
Rs.7,001 - 10,000	23	11.44
Rs.10,001 - 15,000	18	8.96
Over Rs.15,001	15	7.45
All Ranges	201	100.00

The lower levels of earning of the migrants leads to lower levels of remittances. All those who migrate do not remit money. In our sample study, 65 per cent of the outmigrants had remitted less than Rs.1,000.00 per annum. The remittance by another 25 per cent of the migrants was in the range of Rs.1,000 to Rs. 2,000 per annum and the remaining 10 per cent of the outmigrants in the higher ranges (Table 5.9).

Although the average annual income of the outmigrants amounted to Rs.7,000 per annum or Rs.585.00 per month, the range varied very widely among different income slabs. Its variation was between Rs.743.00 per annum in the lowest income slab to Rs.27,850.00 per annum in the highest income slab. The average annual remittances of 157 outmigrants worked out Rs.1,069.00 per annum or Rs.90.00 per month. The variation of remittances, however, was between Rs.30.00 per month in the lowest income group to Rs.170.00 per month in the highest income group.

The remittances are being made by the migrants through different modes but a majority of them 113 out of 157 (71.97 per cent) remitted by way of moneyorders. Another 13.38 per cent of the migrants remitted through the medium of friends and relatives. Those who remitted by means of cheques/drafts figured 6 or 3.82 per cent only. The remittances to the extent of 87.52 per cent were made on monthly basis, 12.74 per cent on quarterly basis, 9.55 per cent on six-monthly basis and the remaining 10.19 per cent on annual basis. This reflects upon the meagre inflow of money to the households and perpetuation of poverty and subsistence economy.

TABLE 5.9
Inflow of money (remittances by migrants)*
Sample Survey - 1977-78

Range of remittances per annum.	No. of migrants	Percentage to the total
Below Rs.500.00	46	29.30
Rs. 501 - 1,000	55	35.03
Rs.1,001 - 1,500	20	12.74
Rs.1,501 - 2,000	20	12.74
Rs.2,001 - 2,500	7	4.46
Rs.2,501 and above	9	5.73
All Ranges	157	100.00

*44 outmigrants out of 201 did not remit.

MONEYORDER REMITTANCES

Analysis of the magnitude of outmigration and money flow to the households and its variations led us to examine to what extent the region depends upon remittances from migrants. Though the households receive a small amount regularly, the total inflow of money through migrants is substantially large and has a decisive impact on the regional economy. This study was conducted on the basis of secondary data[1] for different Postal regions under Pauri Garhwal District. Before an analysis of the extent of moneyorder remittances and their regional variations is made, it would be desirable to throw light on the demarcation of geographical Postal regions and the Regions of India under reference.

Postal Regions of Pauri Garhwal District

The demarcation of geographical regions in respect of the inflows of moneyorder remittances under Pauri Garhwal District was based upon the Postal Organisational structure of post offices existing as on 1st April, 1973[2]. The Head Post Offices/ Delivery Sub-Post Offices, from which the moneyorder flow data were available at the Head Post Offices of Pauri and Lansdowne were considered suitable units for the purposes of the demarcation of Postal regions. The other considerations taken into account were: first, those Delivery Sub-Post Offices which had too small spatial linkages to form a separate Postal regions were merged with other Sub-Post Offices nearby having larger spatial linkages;[3] secondly, the Non-Delivery Sub-Post Offices were merged with the nearest Delivery Post Offices;[4] and lastly the changes in the organisational structure during 1972-73 were not taken into account[5] owing to constraints of data analysis.

After taking into account all these considerations, 2 Head Post Offices and 41 Sub-Post Offices emerged as the basic postal units for purpose of demarcating the Postal regions. The spatial linkages of each of these Postal units were marked since each of these is linked spatially with a number of Branch Post Offices and each Branch Post Office in turn is linked with a number of geographically distributed settlements/postal villages.[6] With the help of topographical sheets (1" = 1 mile), the Postal regions were demarcated by pooling all the connecting Branch Post Offices[7] along with their linked settlements/postal villages. The total number of Postal regions thus demarcated numbered 43, 19 under Pauri Head Post Office and 24 under Landowne Head Post Office. The names of these Postal regions are given below: (Figure 18).

I. **Postal Regions under Pauri Head Post Office**:

1. Pauri	6. Kanskhet	11. Mawadhar	16. Patisain
2. Chipalghat	7. Khirsu	12. Naithana	17. Rudraprayag
3. Deolchauri	8. Kot	13. Pabau	18. Srinagar
4. Deoprayag	9. Laxmanjhula	14. Paidul	19. Thalisain
5. Kaljikhal	10. Lwali	15. Parsundakhal	

II. **Postal Regions under Lansdowne Head Post Office**:

1. Landsdowne	7. Dudharkhal	13. Jaharikhal	19. Paukhal
2. Baijro	8. Dwarikhal	14. Kalagarh	20. Pokhra
3. Bhrighukhal	9. Dhumakot	15. Kotdwara	21. Rikhnikhal
4. Bironkhal	10. Dadamandi	16. Kandakhal	22. Syunsinagar
5. Cheulsain	11. Dogadda	17. Naugaonkhal	23. Satpuli
6. Deorajkhal	12. Ekeswar	18. Nainidanda	24. Silogi

These 43 Postal regions varied much both in respect of the size of population and the number of households. The average size of population for each Postal region worked out to 12,861 persons ranging between a population of 33,890 persons in Kotdwara Postal Region to a population 1,440 persons in

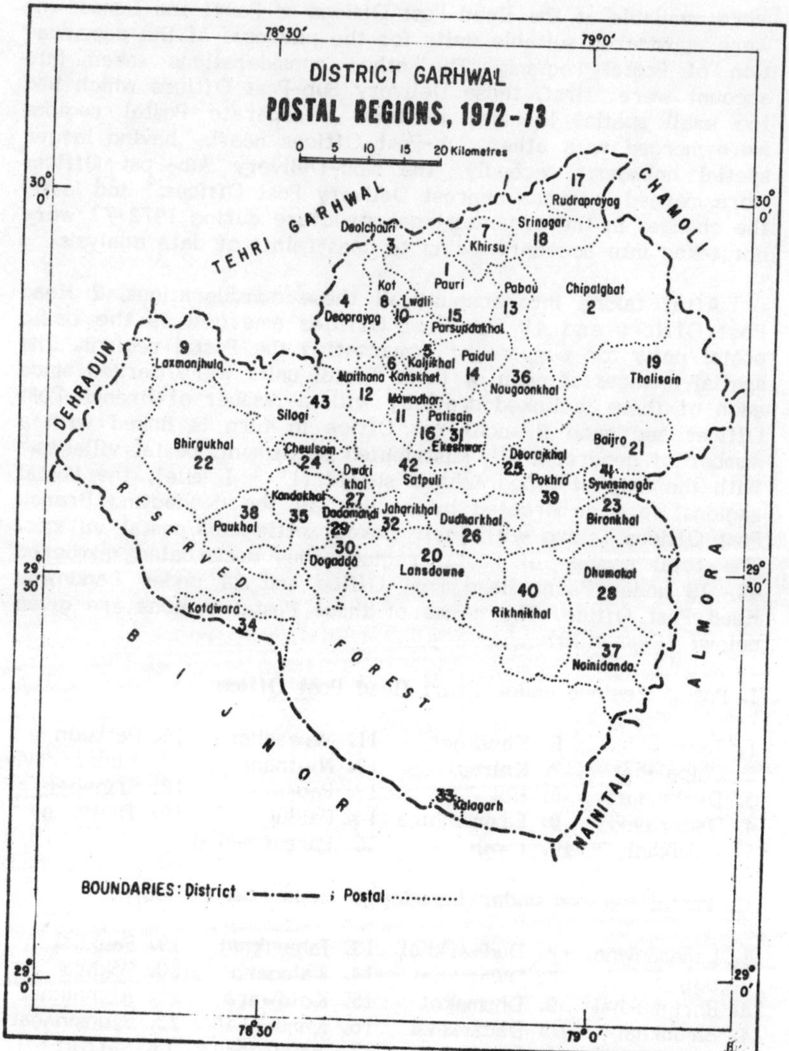

DISTRICT GARHWAL
POSTAL REGIONS, 1972-73
0 5 10 15 20 Kilometres
78°30′
79°0′
30° 0′
29° 30′
29° 0′
TEHRI GARHWAL
CHAMOLI
DEHRADUN
RESERVED FOREST
BIJNOR
NAINITAL
ALMORA
17 Rudraprayag
18 Srinagar
7 Khirsu
3 Deolchauri
1 Pauri
Pabau 13
Chipalghat 2
Kot 8
Lwali 10
4 Deoprayag
15 Parsundakhal
5 Kaljikhal
6 Kanskhet
Paidul 14
36 Nougaonkhal
19 Thalisain
9 Laxmanjhula
Naithana 12
43 Silogi
Mawadhar 11
Patisain 16 31
Ekeshwar
Baijro 21
Bhirgukhal 22
Cheulsain 24
Dwarikhal 27
42 Satpuli
Deorajkhal 25
Pokhra 39
41 Syunsinagar
23 Bironkhal
Kandakhal 35
38 Paukhal
Dadamandi 29
Jaharikhal 32
Dudharkhal 26
30 Dogadda
20 Lansdowne
Dhumakot 28
40 Rikhnikhal
Kotdwara 34
37 Nainidanda
33 Kalagarh
BOUNDARIES: District ; Postal

Fig. 18

Kanskhet Postal Region. The corresponding average number of households per Postal region came to 2,866, varying between 7,177 households in Lansdowne Postal Region to 424 households in Kanskhet Postal Region.

Postal Regions of India

Moneyorder remittances, in the study region, flow from every part of the country. It was, therefore, found necessary to delineate the entire country into different regions. Our demarcation of the country into different regions was based upon 13 Audit Regions existing at present under the Posts and Telegraphs Directorate. These Audit Regions are Calcutta, Delhi, Kapurthala, Madras, Hyderabad, Nagpur, Jaipur, Cuttack, Trivandrum, Lucknow, Bangalore, Bhopal and Patna and cover the entire country. Moreover, moneyorder flow data was available by Audit Region only at the Head Post Offices. Considering both the data constraints and data analysis, it was found appropriate to delineate the entire country into 7 regions by merging some of the Audit Regions. The regions thus emerged, their Audit Head quarter(s) and the State(s) covered by each of them are as follows.

Postal Regions of India

Sl. No.	Name of the Region	Name of the Audit H.Q.(s)	State(s) covered
1.	Uttar Pradesh	Lucknow	Uttar Pradesh.
2.	Delhi	Delhi	Delhi.
3.	Northern	Kapurthala	Punjab, Haryana, Himachal Pradesh, Jammu & Kashmir and the Union Territory of Chandigarh.
4.	Eastern	Calcutta Cuttack Patna	West Bengal, Orissa, Bihar, Assam, Arunachal Pradesh, Nagaland, Meghalaya, Mizoram, Manipur, Tripura and the Union Territory of Andaman and Nicobar Islands.
5.	Central	Bhopal Jaipur	Madhya Pradesh and Rajasthan.
6.	Western	Nagpur Ahmedabad	Maharashtra, Gujarat and the Union Territory of Goa.
7.	Southern	Hyderabad Madras Bangalore Trivandrum	Andhra Pradesh, Tamilnadu, Karnataka, Kerala and the Union Territory of Pondicherry.

EXTENT OF MONEYORDER REMITTANCES

The district's economy depends to a large extent on outside incomes chiefly by way of moneyorder remittances from its migrant population working outside the region. This dependence has, over the years, increased steadily. In 1933, Ibbotson, on a conservative scale had estimated an annual flow of Rs.4,000,000 from all sources from outside.[8] By 1945, the inflow of remittances increased further[9] and the phenomenon gained momentum after Independence in 1947.[10] In 1965-66, the total value of moneyorder remittances had increased to Rs.33,047,000 and further to Rs.45,908,000 in 1969-70 with an annual average growth of over 8.59 per cent.[11] The inflow of moneyorder remittances into Pauri Garhwal District continued to be phenomenally high, even after the creation of a separate Postal Division for Chamoli District and consequent bifurcation of flows of remittances. In 1972-73 the inflow of moneyorder remittances in Pauri Garhwal District alone amounted to Rs.41,172,000 which increased to Rs.70,445,000 by 1980-81 indicating thereby an overall growth of 71 per cent or approximately 9 per cent per annum.

In 1972-73, the total inflow of moneyorder remittances into the district was Rs.41,172,000 recording a growth of 9.31 per cent over the preceding year.[12] The monthly average comes to Rs.3,431,000 and distributed through over 37,000 moneyorders. Roughly, these figures indicate that about 37,000 families in the district receiving these external moneyorder remittances depend on the number of families/individuals, who have migrated keeping some of their dependent members of their family at home. Nearly one-third of the total disbursements are made in the first fortnight and the remaining two-thirds in the second fortnight of the month. The relatively higher income flow, in the second fortnight might be on account of high percentages of workers, engaged in the tertiary sector, outside the district. Such workers are likely to belong to fixed income groups, getting their monthly wages and salaries in the first week of the month. On the other hand, unskilled migrants who work as domestic servants generally do not get their wages in the first week of the month. Moreover, inaccessibility sometimes causes undue delay in the disbursements of moneyorders.

Out of the total monthly inflow of moneyorder remittances of Rs.3,431,000 in the district during 1972-73, an amount of Rs.1,517,000 or 44.17 per cent of the total were disbursed by way of 16,993 moneyorders among the 19 Postal Regions under Pauri Head Post Office and comprising together a population of 222,305 persons and households numbering 49,111 (1971 Census).

The remaining amount of Rs.1,914,000 or 55.83 per cent of the total were disbursed by way of 20,705 moneyorders among the 24 Postal regions under Lansdowne Head Post Office and comprising together a population of 330,855 persons and households numbering 74,129. The range of variations of moneyorder remittances among these 43 Postal regions was very wide and lay between Rs.12,591 (0.37 per cent) in Kanskhet Postal Region to Rs.225,784 (6.58 per cent) in Pauri Postal Region. Table 5.10 below provides the details of the value and number of moneyorder remittances per month in different size-range of remittances. From Table 5.10, it would be observed that the inflow of moneyorder remittances in each of the 4 Postal regions of Pauri, Chipalghat, Kotdwara and Landsdowne exceeded over Rs.150,000 per month during 1972-73. Their disbursements together amounted to Rs.766,000 (22.33 per cent) by way of 8,717 moneyorders (23.12 per cent). Postal regions whose inflows of moneyorder remittances ranged between Rs.100,000 and Rs.150,000 per month figured 9 only. Their aggregate inflow of moneyorder remittances amounted to Rs.1,160,000 (33.88 per cent) and were disbursed by 4,185 moneyorders (11.11 per cent) per month. However, the largest number of Postal regions numbering 15 lay in the size range between Rs.50,000 and Rs.100,000. They together accounted for a total of Rs.1,063,000 (31.00 per cent) and disbursed through 12,410 moneyorders (32.92 per cent) per month. The remaining 15 Postal regions lay in other size ranges - 11 in the size range of Rs.20,000 to Rs.50,000 and 4 in the size range of less than Rs.20,000. These together accounted for a disbursement of Rs.442,000 (12.79 per cent) through 12,386 moneyorders (32.85 per cent) among various Postal regions of the district.

REGIONAL VARIATIONS IN MONEYORDER REMITTANCES

The moneyorder remittances flow into the district from all the regions of India, their intensity varying from region to region. The total monthly inflow of moneyorder remittances of Rs.3,431,000 from all the 7 regions of India is disbursed among 43 Postal regions of the district (Table 5.11). Table 5.12 and Figure 19 give a detailed account of the flows of moneyorder remittances into each of the 43 Postal regions from each of the 7 regions of India. Of the total inflow of Rs.41,172,000 during 1972-73, Uttar Pradesh region comprising the whole of the state provided the highest inflow of moneyorder remittances of Rs.13,444,000 or 32.65 per cent of the total remittances. Among these 43 Postal regions, the percentage variations of the inflow of moneyorder remittances from U.P. region were also the largest and ranged from 22.40 per cent in Baijro Postal region to 57.15 per cent in Kalagarh Postal region. The Postal regions

TABLE 5.10
Monthly value and number of remittances - 1972-73[13]

Range of remittances	No. of Postal regions	Value Rs.	Value Per cent	Moneyorders No.	Moneyorders Per cent	Average amount per money-order
Above Rs. 150,000	4	766,000	22.33	8,717	23.12	88.56
Rs.100,000-150,000	9	1,160,000	33.88	4,185	11.11	253.05
Rs. 50,000-100,000	15	1,063,000	31.00	12,410	32.92	85.66
Rs. 20,000- 50,000	11	377,000	10.94	11,765	31.21	32.05
Below Rs. 20,000	4	65,000	1.85	621	1.64	104.67
All ranges	43	3,431,000	100.00	37,698	100.00	91.01

of Kalagarh, Kotdwara and Srinagar had relatively higher percentages of 57.15, 48.25 and 43.84 respectively. But in a majority of Postal regions, the variations ranged between 25 per cent and 35 per cent. Both the magnitude and regional variations of moneyorder remittances strongly suggest the relative importance of migrant population in the areas within the State.

The Western region comprising the states of Maharashtra and Gujarat, ranked second in moneyorder remittances into the district (Rs.11,857,000 or approximately 28.81 per cent of the aggregate inflow). The monthly flow works out to Rs.988,000. Among 43 Postal regions, the inflows of moneyorder remittances from Western region ranged from 15.35 per cent in Kalagarh Postal region to 45.42 per cent in Lansdowne Postal region. Within these limits, 14 Postal regions lay in the range between 30 to 35 per cent; 24 Postal regions between 20 and 30 per cent and the remaining 3 below 20 per cent. The high intensity of moneyorder remittances and their wide variations may be attributed to two main reasons. First, the industrial centres of Maharashtra and Gujarat, particularly that of the metropolitan city of Bombay exercises strong pulls to the working population from the study area. Secondly, military personnel, as a matter of special concession while on field duties, are not required to pay the moneyorder commission. While this concession is availed of by them throughout the country, our field enquiries revealed that this is a particularly strong feature of this region.

As compared with other regions of India, Delhi region covers a much smaller geographical area of the Union Territory of Delhi. Yet the moneyorder remittances from this region amounted to Rs.5,384,000 or 13.07 per cent of the total inflow of moneyorder remittances into the district during 1972-73. The monthly average worked out to Rs.449,000 according to which the region ranked third among all the regions of India. The variations of the flow of moneyorder remittances from Delhi into the different Postal regions of the district ranged from 5.44 per cent in Jaharikhal Postal region to 26.63 per cent in Lwali Postal region. Between these two limits, 8 Postal regions lay above 20 per cent; 23 Postal regions between 10 per cent and 20 per cent and the remaining 12 Postal regions below 10 per cent. The high inflow of money from the metropolitan city of Delhi reflects a high level of outmigration of working population, from the study area, on the basis of the small amount involved in money remittance. The nearness of the region from the study area, the increasing interactions among the people, large information flow and urban influences etc. exert strong pulls to many a migrant from this city.

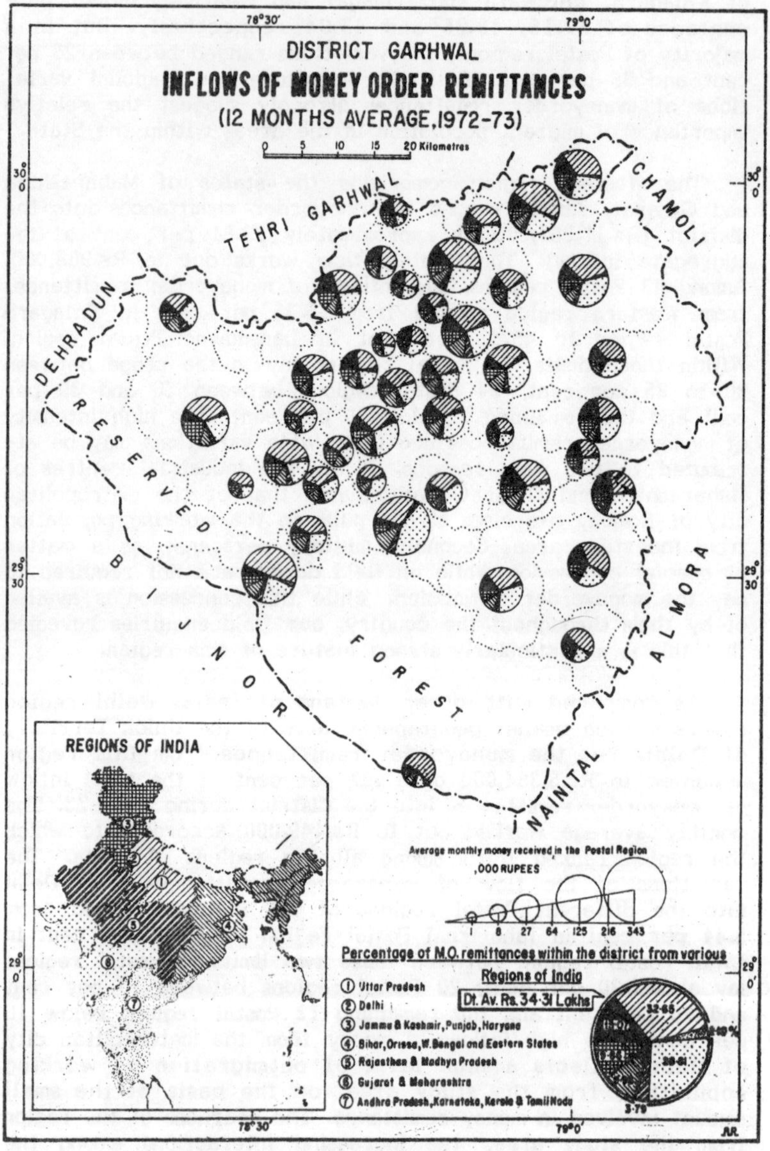
DISTRICT GARHWAL
INFLOWS OF MONEY ORDER REMITTANCES
(12 MONTHS AVERAGE, 1972-73)
0 5 10 15 20 Kilometres
78°30'
79°0'
30° 0'
29° 30'
29° 0'
TEHRI GARHWAL
CHAMOLI
DEHRADUN
RESERVED FOREST
BIJNOR
ALMORA
NAINITAL
REGIONS OF INDIA
Average monthly money received in the Postal Region
,000 RUPEES
1 8 27 64 125 216 343
Percentage of M.O. remittances within the district from various Regions of India
Dt. Av. Rs. 34·31 Lakhs
32·65
3·79
① Uttar Pradesh
② Delhi
③ Jammu & Kashmir, Punjab, Haryana
④ Bihar, Orissa, W. Bengal and Eastern States
⑤ Rajasthan & Madhya Pradesh
⑥ Gujarat & Maharashtra
⑦ Andhra Pradesh, Karnataka, Kerala & Tamil Nadu
AR.

Fig. 19

The inflow of money from the Eastern region was Rs.4,084,000 during 1972-73. Although it covered the States of Bihar, Orissa, West Bengal, Assam and other eastern States/ Union Territories of India, its monthly flow of Rs.340,000 or 9.92 per cent of the total remittances was relatively low. The regional variations of moneyorder remittances from this region among various Postal regions were also low and ranged between 5.16 per cent in Dhumakot Postal region and 16.00 per cent in Mawadhar Postal region. Mawadhar (16.00 per cent) and Dogadda (15.80 per cent) were the only two Postal regions where the inflow of moneyorder remittances exceeded 15 per cent to their respective total inflow of moneyorder remittances from the country. Besides, 21 Postal regions lay in the range between 10 per cent and 15 per cent and the remaining 20 Postal regions in the range of less than 10 per cent of their respective total moneyorder remittances.

The Northern region comprises the States of Haryana, Punjab, Himachal Pradesh, Jammu and Kashmir and the Union Territory of Chandigarh. Its flow of moneyorder remittances in the study area was Rs.3,979,000 or 9.66 per cent of the total inflow of remittances during 1972-73. The percentage variations in respect of moneyorder remittances from the region to the total remittances among 43 Postal regions ranged between 4.16 per cent in Lansdowne Postal region to 21.67 per cent in Bhrigukhal Postal region. Between these limits, 4 Postal regions lay in the range of over 15 per cent, 16 Postal regions between 10 per cent and 15 per cent and 22 Postal regions between 5 per cent and 10 per cent. Lansdowne Postal region was the only exception which had less than 5 per cent of the total remittances from the Northern region.

The moneyorder remittances from the Central region comprising the States of Rajasthan and Madhya Pradesh totalled Rs.1,560,000 or 3.79 per cent of the total remittances during 1972-73 in the district. This was relatively low when compared with the percentages of other regions of India. The percentage variations, too, were small and varied between 1.74 per cent in Lwali Postal region and 8.23 per cent in Laxmanjhula Postal region. Similarly, for Southern region, comprising the States of Andhra Pradesh, Tamilnadu, Karnataka and Kerala, the flow of moneyorder remittances was only Rs.864,000 or 2.10 per cent of the total inflow of remittances during 1972-73. The percentage variations also ranged between 0.82 per cent in Dwarikhal Postal region and 3.14 per cent in Kanskhet Postal region. The low proportions of moneyorder remittances from these regions may be attributed to the fact that migrant population, especially the unskilled one, prefers job opportunities, usually nearer to his home places rather than far away from their relatives.

INTRA-DISTRICT VARIATIONS IN MONEY-FLOW

A study of the total flow of moneyorder remittances from various regions of India into the various Postal regions of the study area has been made in the preceding pages. It has been stated that the monthly flow of moneyorder remittances of Rs.3,431,000 is disbursed among 43 Postal regions comprising together of 123,240 households and a population of 553,000. The average monthly value of moneyorder remittances paid per household worked out to Rs.27.84 for the district. The spatial variations in the extent of inflow of money is brought out in the accompanying map (Figure 20).

Areas of High Intensity in money flow:

This category covered those areas where monthly average inflow of money exceeded Rs.40.00 per household. It comprises two contiguous areas - in the centre and north-eastern part of the district. The first one consisting of 7 Postal regions of Jaharikhal, Dadamandi, Dwarikhal, Satpuli, Ekeswar, Mawadhar and Paidul is connected by the main transport line from Kotdwara. The second block, consisting of the Postal regions of Srinagar and Rudraprayag is not only linked by the main highway from Rishikesh to Badrinath but also by the main road connecting Kotdwara with Pauri and Srinagar. These Postal regions taken together, contained in all 18,673 households with a total population of 88,293 persons (1971 Census). The total monthly inflow of moneyorder remittances in this category of Postal regions during 1972-73, amounted to Rs.797,000 or 23.24 per cent of the total moneyorder remittances into the district and were disbursed through 8,037 moneyorders. The monthly average value of the inflow of moneyorder remittances per household for this category worked out to Rs.42.72 as against the district average of Rs.27.84.

Areas of High Medium Intensity in money flow:

Postal regions whose monthly average value of moneyorder remittances ranged between Rs.35.00 and Rs.40.00 per household were included in this category. It covered in all 8 Postal regions, grouped into 3 separate compact blocks. The first block lying on the western part of the district covered three contiguous Postal regions of Cheulsain, Silogi and Deoprayag. The second block lying on the northern part of the district covered the four contiguous Postal regions of Kaljikhal, Parsundakhal, Pauri and Pabau. Pokhra Postal region, lying on the eastern part

TABLE 5.11

Monthly inflow of Moneyorder Remittances in Pauri Garhwal District from various Regions of India April 1972 – March 1973

(Value in thousand rupees)

Month (1972-73)	Total Value of M.O. remittances	Regions of India						
		U.P.	Delhi	Northern	Eastern	Central	Western	Southern
April, 1972	3,248	1,092	417	307	290	125	954	63
May	3,300	1,176	353	335	348	138	886	64
June	3,209	1,040	409	309	327	128	925	71
July	3,753	1,209	538	384	364	154	1,045	59
August	3,727	1,199	599	405	367	134	966	57
September	3,690	1,147	546	381	357	130	1,062	67
October	2,939	896	358	332	306	98	893	56
November	2,914	981	361	243	284	99	891	55
December	3,470	1,122	448	296	355	129	1,042	78
January, 1973	3,651	1,186	497	329	340	150	1,061	88
February	3,333	1,123	371	291	304	138	1,039	67
March	3,938	1,273	487	367	442	137	1,093	139
Total for 1972-73	41,172	13,444	5,384	3,979	4,084	1,560	11,857	864
Monthly Averages	3,431	1,120	449	332	340	130	988	72
Percentage to the total	100.00	32.65	13.07	9.66	9.92	3.79	28.81	2.10

TABLE 5.12

Monthly inflow of moneyorder remittances into various Postal regions of Pauri Garhwal District from various regions of India - 1972-73

S.No.	Name of the Postal region	Total Value of M.O. remittances (Rs.)	From regions of India (Percentage to total)						
			U.P.	Delhi	Northern	Eastern	Central	Western	Southern
(1)	(2)	(3)	(4)	(5)	(6)	(7)	(8)	(9)	(10)
	Postal regions under Pauri Head Post Office								
1.	Pauri	225,784	36.34	13.60	7.08	7.26	2.65	31.42	1.65
2.	Chipalghat	154,998	31.59	11.99	10.59	8.00	2.52	23.83	1.48
3.	Deolchauri	19,439	31.27	24.00	15.87	6.81	4.31	16.37	1.36
4.	Deoprayag	109,905	27.27	18.17	13.52	8.01	5.27	25.49	1.77
5.	Kaljikhal	23,282	24.93	19.45	7.91	14.06	5.37	26.67	1.61
6.	Kanskhet	12,591	35.30	21.98	11.13	8.05	3.07	16.65	3.14
7.	Khirsu	58,954	33.32	12.60	8.32	11.33	2.21	30.01	2.01
8.	Kot	49,854	27.35	24.74	10.35	10.62	3.14	21.52	2.28
9.	Laxmanjhula	52,541	22.60	12.05	13.20	12.81	8.23	28.75	2.26
10.	Lwali	22,856	26.32	26.63	10.94	8.14	1.74	24.72	1.51
11.	Mawadhar	65,318	31.86	11.21	7.98	16.00	6.60	24.32	2.03
12.	Naithana	69,871	27.45	22.05	12.27	10.81	4.57	20.75	2.10
13.	Pabau	67,286	25.19	14.43	8.64	9.32	7.59	32.64	2.23
14.	Paidul	137,757	29.48	14.06	9.80	14.42	4.91	24.75	2.58
15.	Parsundakhal	33,719	26.12	16.61	10.43	12.48	6.67	25.32	2.37
16.	Patisain	73,636	25.65	15.57	7.92	14.22	5.20	29.40	2.04
17.	Rudraprayag	127,653	36.07	12.54	11.75	5.78	2.22	30.30	1.34
18.	Srinagar	144,000	43.84	12.70	8.08	7.05	2.66	24.25	1.41
19.	Thalisain	60,016	34.59	14.56	10.51	5.58	2.05	31.50	1.21

Table 5.12 (contd.)

(1)	(2)	(3)	(4)	(5)	(6)	(7)	(8)	(9)	(10)
Postal regions under Lansdowne Head Post Office									
20.	Lansdowne	221,260	28.65	6.23	4.16	10.19	3.32	45.42	2.33
21.	Baijro	82,335	22.40	22.06	14.41	6.10	5.04	27.91	2.08
22.	Bhirgukhal	121,441	33.88	9.36	21.67	8.15	3.43	21.63	1.88
23.	Bironkhal	127,330	28.36	21.72	8.22	5.67	4.92	29.06	2.51
24.	Cheulsain	34,653	35.84	8.13	10.60	8.70	5.30	29.28	2.15
25.	Deorajkhal	18,726	27.41	19.28	10.00	10.06	3.42	28.44	1.40
26.	Dudharkhal	65,213	28.86	9.69	5.93	12.14	3.70	32.09	2.59
27.	Dwarikhal	24,525	32.56	6.68	8.21	14.08	8.07	29.58	0.82
28.	Dhumakot	82,552	36.85	20.02	9.19	5.11	3.15	23.96	1.71
29.	Dadamandi	50,155	36.27	6.09	7.15	13.75	2.22	31.57	2.95
30.	Dogadda	48,550	39.04	8.03	7.26	15.80	3.67	23.97	2.23
31.	Ekeswar	83,458	30.63	13.16	5.71	13.30	3.36	31.47	2.37
32.	Jaharikhal	29,506	37.71	5.44	6.06	11.79	3.21	33.30	2.50
33.	Kalagarh	33,114	57.15	6.25	6.14	10.18	3.36	15.35	1.57
34.	Kotdwara	163,576	48.25	6.29	7.06	9.28	3.11	23.87	2.14
35.	Kandakhal	97,432	36.65	7.11	15.45	10.75	4.31	23.20	2.54
36.	Naugaonkhal	108,952	27.46	10.73	10.61	12.08	4.12	32.85	2.16
37.	Nainidanda	39,839	43.50	13.93	8.22	6.52	2.76	22.33	2.74
38.	Paukhal	13,828	42.85	7.92	9.04	11.35	3.60	23.02	2.22
39.	Pokhra	149,141	30.58	14.49	8.51	10.10	2.72	31.55	2.05
40.	Rikhnikhal	88,778	29.35	13.21	10.77	8.98	3.60	32.08	2.01
41.	Syunsinagar	38,161	26.06	19.09	15.02	6.48	3.19	28.96	1.20
42.	Satpuli	135,330	28.55	11.69	8.75	13.13	4.67	30.66	2.55
43.	Silogi	65,689	30.34	13.22	12.09	7.48	3.48	31.24	1.65
Monthly Average inflow into Pauri Garhwal		3,431,009	32.65	13.07	9.66	9.92	3.79	28.81	2.10

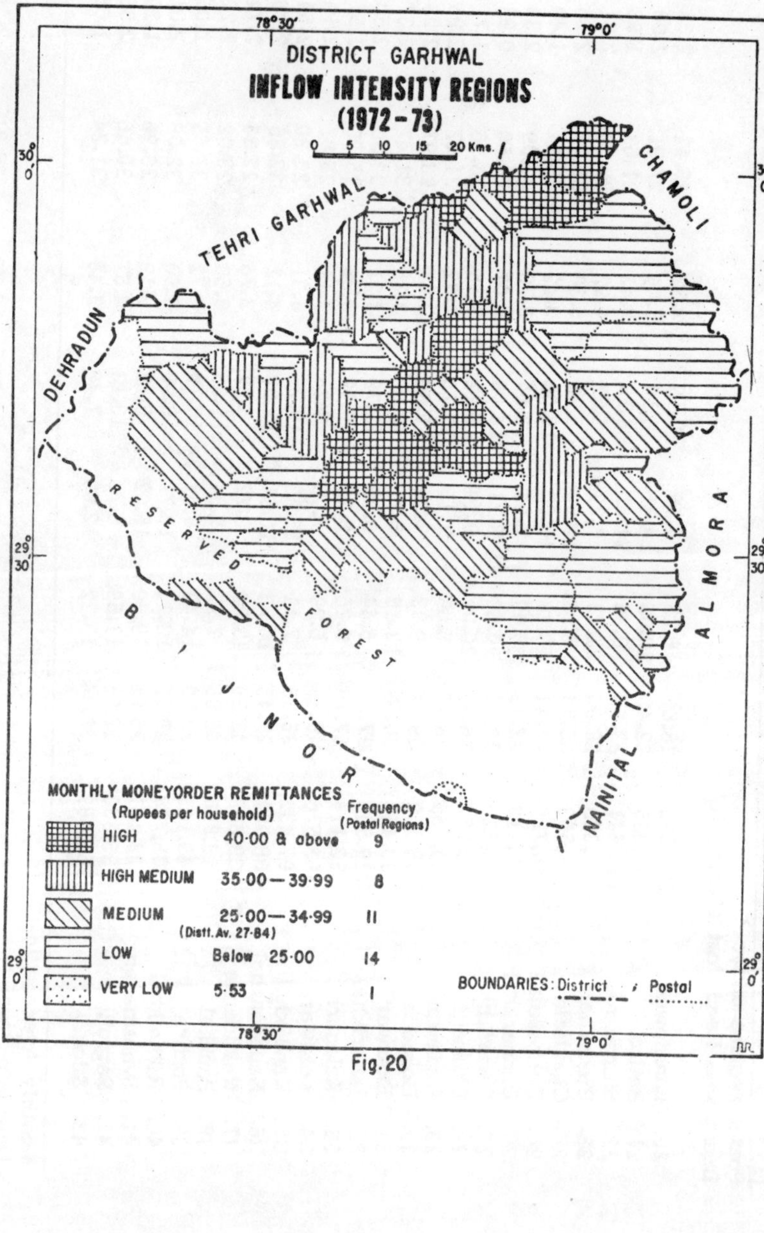
78°30'
79°0'
DISTRICT GARHWAL
INFLOW INTENSITY REGIONS
(1972-73)
0 5 10 15 20 Kms.
30° 0'
29° 30'
29° 0'
TEHRI GARHWAL
CHAMOLI
DEHRADUN
RESERVED FOREST
BIJNOR
ALMORA
NAINITAL
MONTHLY MONEYORDER REMITTANCES
(Rupees per household)
Frequency (Postal Regions)
HIGH 40·00 & above 9
HIGH MEDIUM 35·00—39·99 8
MEDIUM 25·00—34·99 11
(Distt. Av. 27·84)
LOW Below 25·00 14
VERY LOW 5·53 1
BOUNDARIES: District / Postal

Fig. 20

of the district formed the third block. These Postal regions together contained in all 19,734 households with a population of 87,110 persons. The total monthly inflow of moneyorder remittances in this category of Postal regions amounted to Rs.710,000 or 20.67 per cent of the total moneyorder remittances in the district and were disbursed through 7,413 moneyorders. The monthly value of moneyorder remittances for this category worked out to Rs.35.97 per household. The variations among the 8 Postal regions ranged between Rs.35.20 per household in Silogi Postal region and Rs.36.68 per household in Cheulsain Postal region.

Areas of Medium Intensity in money flow:

This category includes those Postal regions whose monthly average value of moneyorder remittances ranged between Rs.25.00 and Rs.35.00 per household. It included 11 Postal regions: Bhrigukhal Postal region in the west; Kotdwara, Dogadda and Lansdowne Postal regions in the south; Nainidanda Postal region in the south-east; Bironkhal and Baijro Postal regions in the east; Kanskhet, Patisain and Naugaonkhal Postal regions in the centre and Khirsu Postal region in the north of the district. Kotdwara Postal region is the most significant Postal region, lying on the contact zone between the hills and the plains and covers the urban area of Kotdwara town. Better agricultural conditions in this area attract the migrant population from the hills to settle down. At the same time, outmigration so characteristic of other regions is not pronounced. The Postal regions included in this category contained in all 37,708 households having a total population of 174,715 persons (1971 Census). The total monthly inflow of moneyorder remittances in this category amounted to Rs.1,058,000 or 30.81 per cent of the total moneyorder remittances in the district. These were disbursed by means of 11,559 moneyorders. The monthly value of moneyorder remittances for this category worked out to Rs.28.37 per household as against Rs.27.84 per household for the district. The variations among the 11 Postal regions ranged between Rs.25.16 per household in Bironkhal Postal region to Rs.32.57 per household in Patisain Postal region. Both the district average value of Rs.27.84 per household and the median value of Rs.29.01 per household fall in this category.

Areas of Low Intensity in money flow:

Postal regions whose monthly average value of moneyorder remittances were less than Rs.25.00 per household were covered by this category. It included 14 Postal regions spread out throughout the district. They, however, formed 4 separate compact blocks. The first block covered five contiguous Postal regions of Dehalchauri, Kot, Lwali, Naithana and Laxmanjhula; All of them lie in the north-western part of the district. The second block, on the north-east is rather a big tract of two contiguous but relatively inaccessible Postal regions of Thalisain and Chipalghat. The third block comprised the contiguous Postal regions of Dhumakot, Rikhnikhal and Dudharkhal Postal regions and lie in the south-eastern part of the district. The last block consists of the Postal regions of Paukhal and Kandakhal on the west of the district. Deorajkhal and Syunsinagar are the only Postal regions, which do not form contiguous parts of any of the blocks under this category. Ths Postal regions included in this category contained in all 41,444 households with a population of 184,944 persons. The total monthly inflow of moneyorder remittances in this category amounted to Rs.834,000 or 24.33 per cent of the total remittances and were disbursed through 10,145 moneyorders. The monthly value of moneyorder remittances for this category came to Rs.26.53 per household as against the district average of Rs.27.84 per household. These areas are in most cases hilly interiors where outmigration is not so pronounced. This corroborates our earlier observation that inaccessible areas even under extreme conditions of poverty have not induced outmigration. At the other end of the scale there is evidence that areas like the Bhaber plains in the south-west have a relatively stable population and they have attracted people from the plains as well as the Hill region.

Areas of Very Low Intensity in money flow:

Kalagarh Postal region, in the extreme south of the district, is the exceptional Postal region having a very low intensity of moneyorder remittances. The monthly value of moneyorder remittances came to Rs.5.53 per household which is much less than the district average of Rs.27.84 per household. In 1971, it had in all 5,980 households with a population of 16,088 persons. The main reason for the very low intensity of moneyorder remittances in this Postal region was the influx of large number of workers at the dam site of Ramganga Project. Most of the workers remitted money through moneyorders to their relatives outside the district rather than received from outside. As such the outflows rather than the inflows of moneyorder remittances became the phenomenon in this Postal region.

The above analysis of the extent of the inflow of moneyorder remittances and their variations among 43 Postal regions of the district highlights some important observations. First, the monthly inflow of moneyorder remittances to the tune of Rs.3,431,000 and its progressively increasing magnitude reflects the high dependence of the district on outside incomes. Secondly, most areas showing high intensity of the flow of moneyorder remittances are linked by the main transport lines from Kotdwara and Rishikesh reflecting better accessibility conditions, linkage effects and greater interactions among the people. All of the urban centres, with the exception of Kotdwara (Figure 20) lie in this tract. They, being the centres of activities and under the impact of outside contacts, are instrumental in spreading out the urban influences and information flow to the surrounding regions. In contrast to these, areas which are relatively more isolated and deprived of the advantages of accessibility, interactions, functional linkages, urban influences and information flow have low levels of inflow of money. This indicates the dominance of pull factor rather than push factor in respect of outmigration of the people. Thirdly, among the various regions of India, the regions which lie in close proximity to the study area or those who exercise strong pulls to the migrant population like Delhi, constitute a high proportion of the total inflows of moneyorder remittances into the district except metropolitan cities like Calcutta and Bombay. Lastly, the inflows of moneyorder remittances are widely dispersed spatially within the district though intra district variations do reveal, interestingly, the impact of physical and socio-economic conditions.

IMPACT OF OUTMIGRATION AND MONEYORDER REMITTANCES

The foregoing analysis demonstrates vividly that the phenomena of outmigration and moneyorder remittances have decisive impact on the region's economy. It is reflected, in terms of growing dependency of the economy on outside incomes, the slow growth of the economy and others.

Outmigration and the Growing Dependency

The phenomenon of outmigration of working population has led to the dependency of the region on outside incomes, chiefly by way of moneyorder remittances. It is widely distributed. Its magnitude varied from region to region, depending upon the size of population, the number of households and other demographic and socio-economic attributes of population. The dependency as a result of outmigration has over the years increased steadily. In 1972-73, the inflow of moneyorder remittances, as pointed out earlier, was to the extent of Rs.41,172,000 or Rs.3,431,000 per month and distributed through over 37,000 moneyorders throughout the district comprising of 123,240 households and a population of over 553,000 persons (1971 Census). Since then the moneyorder remittances are increasing with an annual average growth of 9 per cent (Rs.70,445,000 in 1980-81). The per captia and per household value of moneyorder remittances in the district worked out to Rs.6.20 and Rs.27.84 respectively. The corresponding value of moneyorder remittances per moneyorder was Rs.91.01. From our sample survey, the average net annual income per household worked out to be Rs.6,550.00 of which income from agriculture and its allied activities constituted 67.64 per cent and the rest by other sources. Among the sources, other than agriculture and its allied activities, the income through moneyorder remittances was the highest and constituted 13.16 per cent of the total net annual income from all sources (40.70 per cent of the net annual income from sources other than agriculture and its allied activities). These high values of moneyorder remittances, both in absolute and relative terms, demonstrate the low levels of standard of living and productivity due to high level of outmigration.

Outmigration and Levels of Productivity and Income

The initial nature and character of spatio-economic and socio-cultural dimensions of the district under study, kept the development of its actual and potential resources at a very low level. The low level of underdevelopment, in turn, led to low levels of productivity, output, income and employment. These low levels have been decelerated by the outmigration of active and working population. Agriculture is the mainstay of the people and therefore, most of the incomes originate from agriculture. In 1955-56, of the total income of Rs. 13.24 cores in the district (then comprising of both the Chamoli and Pauri Garhwal Districts) 76.36 per cent originated from agriculture, 4.13 per cent from manufacturing and the rest 19.41 per cent from services sector.[14] This itself is a sign of underdevelopment, wherein an area less suited to large scale agriculture, derives its income mainly through it. This district was not only the top ranking among all the districts of U.P. but was also among the first 10 districts in India, having such a high percentage of income originating from agriculture. The per capita income in the district was as low as Rs.294.00 and per agricultural household annual income was Rs.1,074.00 in 1961-62. Our sample study of 218 households in 42 villages during 1977-78 also throws light on the levels of productivity and income and also the extent of utilisation of agricultural inputs in the region.[15] It is revealed that the yield per hectare of almost all the crops are low except in irrigated lands, which account for 20.84 per cent of the net area sown. The average yields of paddy in irrigated and unirrigated areas accounted for 15.66 and 10.09 quintals per hectare. The corresponding figures for wheat are 11.42 and

9.14 respectively. As compared to these the yields for paddy and wheat for U.P. are 11.59 and 15.50 quintals (1978-79) per hectare respectively. These low levels are reflected in low levels of incomes. It is observed that average net annual income per household from agriculture and allied activities came to Rs.4,431.00 at 1977-78 price level which is 67.84 per cent of the total net income from all sources. Among different size range of land-holdings the variations are between Rs.1,683.00 and Rs.10,647.00. These variations were still larger among the different villages and ranged between Rs.1,916.00 and Rs.18,745.00. Similarly, per capita income ranges from Rs.510.00 and Rs.3,398.00 in different villages and average comes to Rs.909.00. The variations among different categories of land-holdings were less marked. These figures are comparable with those of the state. The per capita income of U.P. was estimated to be Rs.949.00 at current prices (1977-78)[16] as against Rs.1,210.00 for India as a whole. It ranked 12th among all the states of India.

A pertinent question naturally arises as to why the growth of the region's economy remained more or less stagnant and its productive capacity does not increase despite large flows of income from outside? The answer is obvious. Initial nature and character of spatio-economic and socio-cultural dimensions of the district kept the development of its vast resources at a low level. Low level of underdevelopment in turn led to low levels of productivity, output, income and employment. These in turn, kept the levels of savings, investments and capital formation at low levels. These gave rise to the phenomena of outmigration and of flow of incomes from outside, chiefly by way of moneyorder remittances. The income generated inside the region together with the income from outside are channelised mainly for the purchase of consumer goods and do not influence the levels of savings and investments. The demand for consumers' goods is high due to changes in consumers' behaviour pattern by demonstration or emulation effects of migrants who have acquired urban ways of life and consumption of goods produced in towns. Great attachment to land and other tangible assets for prestige and social reasons vigorously act as instruments of dissaving. Simultaneously, the margin of savings of the working force outside the district, is reduced which in turn has an important bearing on their standards of living. Low levels of savings, thus, lead to low levels of investments. Investments, in addition to low capacity to save, depend to a large extent on the willingness to invest, the conditions for production and the role of government. All of them affect the structure of the economy and the direction and intensity of economic activity. Unfortunately, they are awfully lacking. Thus, the low levels of savings and investments have made capital accumulation extremely difficult to rise endogenously and set the process of development of the economy in motion.

Outmigration and Consumption Pattern

The impact of the phenomenon of outmigration has primarily been on the consumption levels through the inflows of remittances, chiefly by way of moneyorders. An overwhelming majority of outmigrants leave behind their parents, wives and children at their respective homes; their subsistence and maintenance inevitably necessitate frequent remittances of incomes from outside as the existing low levels of productivity in agriculture do not generate sufficient food and incomes to support the population. As such, these remittances are channelised chiefly for the purchase of consumers' goods rather than for the producers' goods. This is evident from the analysis of consumption pattern based upon our sample study. The total expenditure per household on different items of consumption at 1977-78 price levels, worked out to Rs.6,217.00 per annum or approximately Rs.518.00 per month. Of this, the expenditure on food items constituted 69.20 per cent, the expenditure on non-food items 20.79 per cent and the remaining 10.01 per cent on items of miscellaneous character such as marriage and other religious functions etc. A sizeable portion of the total expenditure on food items is incurred on cereals and pulses (48.40 per cent) of which rice and wheat are the dominant ones. The expenditure on items such as ghee, dalda, oil, milk and other milk products accounted for another 35.46 per cent of the total expenditure. Besides, sugar and gur̥ (6.23 per cent), tea (4.21 per cent), tobacco and cigarettes (2.24 per cent) were the other food items of importance. Clothing is the most important among non-food items. It covered 37.52 per cent of the total expenditure on non-food items. This was followed by expenditure on education (19.96 per cent), items of toilets (9.57 per cent), footwear (8.16 per cent), fuel and lighting (7.27 per cent), conveyance (6.62 per cent) and medicine (5.90 per cent). The pattern of consumption also revealed that the percentage variations of expenditure per household both on food and non-food items were marked more widely among different villages than among different size-range of land holdings. The percentage of expenditure on food items per household in small sized land holdings was relatively higher than in the large-sized land-holdings. In contrast to this, the percentage of expenditure on non-food items per household increased with the increase in the size range of land holdings.

The above analysis of consumption pattern indicates that

bulk of the incomes of the people either generated through agriculture and its allied activities or received through outside remittances are absorbed in meeting the consumption expenditure, leaving thereby little room for savings to accummulate. Simultaneously, the margin of savings of the working force, outside the region is also reduced due to disruption in family organisation and resultant maintenance of two and sometimes three establishments. The productive capacity of the region does not increase as the levels of savings and investments are not influenced and process of capital formation does not take place. As such, the demand for both agricultural and non-agricultural goods is met through the small traders and retailers, who in turn depend heavily on the big businessmen and wholesalers controlling their commercial transactions from the terminals of Ramnagar, Kotdwara and Rishikesh. Thus, the large inflow of remittances drains out of the region immediately in the form of consumption expenditure.

Outmigration and Expropriation of Profits

The outmigration of working population has, however, been beneficial to the trading and merchant community. The phenomenon of outmigration has led to the inflow of moneyorder remittances. The inflow of moneyorder remittances increases the purchasing power of the people, reflected in the increasing demand for agricultural and non-agricultural goods and services from the small retailers and traders. This, in turn, increases the demand for goods and services from the big businessmen and wholesalers. Taking advantage of the situation, they expropriate large profits. Most of them who are outsiders, have the stronghold on the economy as the indigenous businessmen have neither the skill-hereditary or otherwise, nor the economic competence to compete with them. Their economic competence and resourcefulness have enabled them to have access to the right persons at right places in right time. They are controlling the region's economy from the terminals of Ramnagar, Kotdwara and Rishikesh by carrying out their monetary and barter transactions in food, cloth, cement, forestry, transport and others. The considerable expropriation of profits by this community has led them to the geographical expansion of their economic universe. The expansion, however, was limited in the past, by the constraints of inaccessibility conditions. But with the construction of roads, their stronghold has increased by setting up trading posts, monopolising the transport services and developing closer contacts with the isolated settlements. Their agents carry out barter transactions of agricultural goods like pulses, turmeric, ginger, chillies, onions, potatoes etc. by the manufactured goods such as utensils, cloth, artificial ornaments, footwears and similar others. There is a parallel evidence in several underdeveloped regions of the country which are reeling under the metropolitan dominance e.g. Konkan region of Maharashtra **vis-a-vis** Bombay and Bankura-Purulia tract of West Bengal in relation to Calcutta. An important finding which is corroborated in this study is that the investment on transport without matching economic inputs accentuates the problem of regional stagnation and rural-urban dichotomy.[17] Such transactions with the ignorant rural folk, quite unaware of the prevailing market prices and fluctuations therein; fetch them abnormal profits, sometimes over 500 per cent. The expropriation of more and more profits, results into more and more exploitation of the simple and unsophisticated rural folk. Enjoying a situation of total or partial exclusivity to purchase or sell, this group manipulates prices in such a manner as to achieve the highest profits. The accummulation of resources in the hands of the merchants makes it possible for them to finance lands, purchase of real estates and so on. Growth in their system hinges basically on the opening up of new markets, deep in the interior of region and once opened up, their maintenance implying the generation for a permanent flow of profits towards those controlling trade and business. Thus, by such a process of exploitation and expropriation of profits, most of the incomes of the people drains out of the region in the form of consumption expenditure and passes on virtually in the hands of these expropriators.

The foregoing study of outmigration of working population and of magnitude and spatial disbursements of the inflows of moneyorder remittances and their impact on the region's economy reveals that the economy is constrained by the operation of a number of negative factors keeping thereby the economy at a low level of equilibrium. The phenomenon of outmigration has deprived the economy of its best managerial skills and entrepreneurial ability. There is a rapid deterioration of population structure, disruption of agrarian organisation and progressive underuse and decline of private and social assets. Industrial potentialities, in the absence of local entrepreneurship are being exploited by the outsiders. The level of outmigration, as revealed from our study, is progressively increasing and has a decisive impact on the growth of the economy. The growth has further been dampened by the exploitation of the region by the outsiders by monopolising trade and business, expropriating abnormal profits and manipulating the prices. As such, these end-products of the phenomenon of outmigration have been detrimental to the growth of the economy and would continue to be so in future, for lack of the formulation of a spatial development strategy, close to the regional structure, processes of development over time and its diffusion in space.

The study also reveals that the region's economy is caught up in a spiral pattern, ever increasing in height and radius as it were. The sequence of factors leading to such a phenomenon is as follows. The initial nature and character of spatio-economic and socio-cultural dimensions of the district under study, have so far constrained the development of its actual and potential resources to a very low level. The low level of underdevelopment, in turn, led to low levels of productivity, output, income and employment. Existing inaccessibility conditions have maintained the geographical immobility and isolation intact and have not permitted much interaction of the people with the outside world. Push factors could only motivate outmigrants to a very limited extent. Consequently, the district has in the past remained economically backward, rurally stagnated, socially isolated and cut off from the main streams of modernisation. In the subsequent stage and in recent times, however, the advent of development and planning have facilitated better accessibility conditions, wider linkages and greater interactions of greater amplitude, so stepping up the process of outmigration of the people. As an overwhelming majority of outmigrants left their parents, wives and children at their respective homes, their subsistance and maintenance inevitably necessitate frequent remittances of income from outside. This has led to the phenomenon of inflows of remittances, mainly by way of moneyorders. These remittances canalised chiefly towards the purchase of consumers' goods rather than producers' goods. In course of time, the structure of demand underwent a change, accentuated further by demonstration or emulation effects in the consumers' behaviour patterns on the one hand and on the other the structure of supply remained more or less static because of the low levels of savings, investments, capital formation, output, income and employment. Increasing demand for consumers' goods without a corresponding increase in producers' goods led to a further increase in demand for moneyorder remittances from still further outmigration of working population, aggravated further by increasing pressure of population and accessibility conditions due to development of transportation. Thus the vicious circle of outmigration → inflow of moneyorder remittances → increasing demand for consumers' goods without corresponding increase in producers goods, → outmigration spirals at every subsequent stage. The increasing spirals as revealed by our analysis is accounted for more by the pull factors than by the push factors. This is especially so in areas within the district which had the initial advantages of urbanisation, infrastructure development, accessibility conditions, interactions and outside contacts of the people and above all the leadership of rural elites equipped with knowledge and information providing motivation for outmigration to the working population. Thus the phenomenon of outmigration under initially unfavourable conditions of land-man relationship has qualitatively changed and reinforced itself into the new one in which the rural-urban relationship under the impact of the development strategy adopted at the national and state level is rendering the Hill region as a periphery to the core of development which is largely in the plains and elsewhere outside the region.

NOTES AND REFERENCES

1. The postal data were compiled for the year 1972-73 from the Head Post Offices of Pauri and Lansdowne and Sub-Post Office of Kalagarh under Pauri Postal Division. These data pertained to 2 Head Post Offices of Pauri and Lansdowne, 53 Sub-Post Offices and 274 Branch Post Offices. The data so compiled had to be averaged 12 monthly for the year 1972-73 in order to yield reliable monthly averages.
2. Under the Postal Organisational structure, Pauri Garhwal District has a single Postal Division called Pauri Garhwal Postal Division. It comprises different types of post offices performing diversified functions and connecting every nook and corner of the district by its network of postal services. As on 1st April, 1973, the Division had 2 Higher Selection Grade Post Offices of Pauri and Lansdowne; 10 Lower Selection Grade Post Offices of Rudraprayag, Srinagar, Bhrigukhal, Bironkhal, Dogadda, Kalagarh, Kotdwara, Naugaonkhal, Pokhra and Satpuli; 1 Class I Sub-Office of Deoprayag; 14 Class II Sub-Offices of Chipalghat, Khirsu, Laxmanjhula, Naithana, Pabau, Patisain, Swarg Ashram, Baijro, Dhumakot, Ekeswar, Jaharikhal, Kandakhal, Rikhnikhal and Silogi; 14 Class III Sub-Offices of Chakisain, Kaljikhal, Kot, Mawadhar, Paidul, Parsundakhal, Thalisain, Toli, Dadamandi, Dwarikhal, Dudharkhal, Nainidanda, Syunsinagar and Sri Sankaracharyanagar; 9 Experimental Delivery Sub-Offices of Dehalchauri, Kandoliya, Kanskhet, Lwali, Cheulsain, Deorajkhal, Paukhal, Rithakhal and Vedikhal and 5 Non-Delivery Town Sub-Offices of Kamleshwar (Srinagar), Upper Bazar (Pauri), Kotdwara Railway Station, Lansdowne Cantonment and Ramganga Project (Kalagarh). Besides, 274 Branch Post Offices were functioning throughout the district.
3. There were 4 such Sub-Post Offices. Thus, Kandoliya was merged with Pauri Postal region; Swarg Ashram and Sri

Sankaracharyanagar with Laxmanjhula Postal region and Vedikhal with Syunsinagar Postal region.

4. The 5 Non-Delivery Sub-Post Offices of Kamleshwar (Srinagar), Upper Bazar (Pauri), Kotdwara Railway Station; Lansdowne Cantonment and Ramganga Project (Kalagarh) were merged with the Delivery Post Offices of Srinagar, Pauri (H.P.O.), Kotdwara, Lansdowne (H.P.O.) and Kalagarh respectively.
5. A few changes took place during the year 1972-73. On 1st November, 1972, Jakholi Sub-Office was transferred to Chamoli Postal Division. Toli, a Branch Post Office of Paidul was upgraded to a Class III Sub-Office with effect from 1st January, 1973. Subsequently, with effect from 1st March, 1973, Chakisain, a Branch Post Office of Chipalghat Sub-Office and Rithakhal, a Branch Post Office of Satpuli Sub-Office too were upgraded to Class II Sub-Office and Experimental Delivery Sub-Office respectively.
6. A Postal village is different from a Revenue or a Census village. It is a compulsory **dak** (post) delivery place/point such as a village, a school, a dispensary, a hospital or a shop etc. There were over 4,000 Postal villages inclusive of 3,236 inhabited settlements in 1972-73 in the entire district.
7. The spatial linkages of these Branch Post Offices covered by the Pauri Garhwal Postal Division but lying outside the geographical boundaries of the district were dispensed with. There were 7 such Branch Post Offices: Narkota and Sera Bhardar under Srinagar Sub-Post Office and Jawari, Kurjan, Saterkhal, Haretakhal and Chopra under Rudraprayag Sub-Post Office.
8. Ibbotson, A.W. : **Final Report of the 11th Revenue Settlement of Garhwal District,** Government Press, Allahabad, 1933; quoted in "Garhwal Mein Kaun Kahan" (in Hindi) by Barthwal, M.S. : Naya Hindustan Press, 1950, p.125.
9. Dhoundiyal, S.P. : **The Economic Life of Garhwal** : An unpublished Ph.D. Thesis; Agra University, Agra, 1945, p.310.
10. It appears that no systematic study on the flow of moneyorder remittances in the district has been conducted during the post independence period. The first preliminary analysis of the income flow into the district through moneyorder remittances was attempted in 1972 as an illustration of low levels of income and standard of living in the region and its high dependency on the earnings of the outmigrants. For details refer: Dobhal, G.L.: **Pauri Garhwal – A Regional Study,** M.Phil. Dissertation, Centre

for the Study of Regional Development, School of Social Sciences, Jawaharlal Nehru University, New Delhi, 1972, pp.100-110.

11. **Ibid,** p.102. The data relate to the present districts of Chamoli and Pauri Garhwal as there was only one Postal Division covering them. The separate Postal Division for Chamoli was created in September, 1970.
12. The flow of moneyorder remittances is supplemented by other modes of remittances through friends and relatives, insured posts, banks, pensions etc. The total pension flow in the district during 1972-73 was to the tune of Rs.7,292,000, over 75 per cent of which by way of military pensions. This was outside the scope of the present study.
13. In contrast to the inflow, the outflow of moneyorder remittances has been insignificant. In 1972-73, the average monthly outflow of moneyorder remittances, amounted to Rs.1,172,000 by way of 15,000 moneyorders. Among the 43 Postal regions, the monthly average of outflow of moneyorder remittances per household ranged widely and lay between Rs.0.47 and Rs.57.36 against the district average of Rs.9.47. However, over 80 per cent of the value of outflow of moneyorder remittances through 76 per cent of moneyorders was accounted for by the 8 Postal regions of Pauri, Srinagar, Deoprayag, Laxmanjhula, Rudraprayag, Lansdowne, Kalagarh and Kotdwara. They include the urban centres which have outside contacts and are instrumental in spreading out urban influences. Lansdowne town alone covered over 40 per cent of the total outflow of the district. In contrast to these, the Postal regions relatively inaccessible and having less interaction with outside world have low levels of outflow of moneyorder remittances. On account of the constraints of data analysis, the study of the outflow of moneyorder remittances had to be kept outside the purview of our study.
14. National Council of Applied Economic Research: **Inter-District and Inter-State Income Differentials;** Occasional paper No. 6, 1955-56.
15. For details refer Chapter IV.
16. Government of Uttar Pradesh, Economic & Statistical Division : **Statistical Diary,** 1980, p.47.
17. Deshpande, C.D. **et.al. : Impact of Metropolitan City on the Surrounding Region;** Concept Publishing House, New Delhi, 1980.

SIX

Spatial Processes and Variations in the Levels of Development.

In the foregoing chapters, various facets of the district economy in their spatial framework, have been analysed in detail. Based on this background, the present chapter is an attempt to highlight, the spatial processes and variations, in the levels of development. In this context, the relationship between demographic and socio-economic variables is evaluated, leading on to the areal differentiation in the levels of development between different sets of variables within the district taking into account 169 patwari circles as the units of study.

In order to examine the mutual interdependence among different characteristics of the region, a correlation matrix of 29 selected demographic and socio-economic variables was designed and evaluated applying Karl Pearson's correlation coefficient technique using patwari circle-wise data (Table 6.1). The results are summarised as under.

A weak positive correlation exists between (1) population size of settlements and primary sector work force, (2) growth of population and literacy, (3) density of population and literacy, (4) density of population and health facilities, (5) non-primary sector work-force and growth of dependency, (6) primary sector work-force and area under **jhangora,** (7) overall work participation and area under **mandua,** (8) female work participation and area under **mandua,** (9) net area sown and land revenue, (10) intensity of cultivation and land revenue, (11) health facilities and land revenue, (12) postal facilities and secondary school facilities.

Weak negative or inverse association is found between : (1) size of settlements and electrification, (2) small-sized settlements and land revenue, (3) growth of population and culturable waste, (4) scheduled caste population and area under forests, (5) primary sector work-force and growth of dependency, (6) non-primary sector work-force and area under **jhangora,** (7) female work participation and area under irrigation and (8) culturable waste and area under irrigation. This is because in most cases they do not mutually co-exist.

While the above enumerated positive and negative associations are apparent and understandable by and large, the positive weak association between population size of settlements and primary sector work-force is indicative of the dominance of small-sized settlements in various patwari circles of the district. (2) The weak positive association between nonprimary sector work-force and dependency spells out the outmigration of working population leaving behind the dependent population, mainly the young children and the aged, at their respective home places. (3) The impact of imbalanced sex ratio, in which females outnumber the males is also reflected in weak positive associations between (a) primary sector work-force and area under **jhangora**; (b) overall work participation and area under **mandua**; and (c) female work participation and area under **mandua**. This is because of the fact that the female workers perform solely most of the agricultural operations involved in the cultivation of both the **jhangora** and mandua. (4) The positive weak associations of land revenue per acre net cultivated area with other variables may be analysed as follows. The land revenue, including land development tax from a villages, depends not only upon the size of settlement and the area under cultivation, but also on the quality of land and the extent of area under irrigation. The relatively large-sized villages, possessing irrigation facilities and large area under cultivation, have been paying large shares of land revenue than their counterparts, the small-sized villages. The access to irrigation facilities and to good quality of land not only helps concentrate on growing of superior crops of paddy and wheat rather than on inferior crops of **jhangora** and **mandua**, but also keeps intensity of cultivation high. Such villages, in course of time, have emerged as nodal villages for locating postal, health and education facilities in them.

The negative correlation between the population size of settlements and electrification is indicative of the existing policy of the government to give priority to the large-sized villages on account of relatively higher per unit cost on transmission and distribution works to the small-sized villages. (2) The negative association between scheduled caste population and the area under forests throws light on two counts. First, forest resources continue to be the means of livelihood which have been depleted due to excessive exploitation. Secondly, the quest for the barest minimum land for cultivation has forced them to resort to more and more terracing by clearing the forested area. (3) The negative association between female work participation and area under irrigation highlights the nature of such agricultural operations as are exclusively performed by the male work-force in the irrigated areas.

Positive correlation exists mildly but significantly (values ranging between 0.25 and 0.50) between (1) population growth rate and density of population - a tendency for clustering and intra-district migration as revealed in the study of migration data, (2) population growth rate and non-primary sector work-force, (3) population growth rate and secondary school facilities, (4) density of population and non-primary sector work force, (5) density of population and electrification, (6) density of population and net irrigated area, (7) density of population and area under paddy, (8) density of population and area under wheat, (9) density of population and secondary school facilities, (10) scheduled caste population and area under barley, (11) electrification and net irrigated area, (12) electrification and area under paddy, (13) electrification and area under wheat, (14) electrification and secondary school facilities, (15) net irrigated area and area under paddy, (16) net irrigated area and area under wheat, (17) net irrigated area and secondary school facilities, (18) net irrigated area and health facilities, (19) land revenue and area under paddy, (20) land revenue and area under wheat, (21) land revenue and secondary school facilities, (22) area under **jhangora** and area under barley, (23) primary school facilities and postal facilities and (24) secondary school facilities and health facilities.

Negative correlation exists mildly but significantly between: (1) percentage of small-sized settlements and growth rate of population, (2) percentage of small-sized settlements and primary school facilities, (3) percentage of small-sized settlements and secondary school facilities, (4) percentage of small-sized settlements and postal facilities, (5) percentage of population of small-sized settlements and growth rate of population, (6) percentage of population of small-sized settlements and primary school facilities, (7) percentage of population of small-sized settlements and secondary school facilities, (8) density of population and primary sector work-force, (9) density of population and area under forests, (10) density of population and culturable waste, (11) density of population and area under barley, (12) overall literacy and primary sector work-force, (13) overall literacy and overall work participation, (14) overall literacy and female work participation, (15) sex ratio and net irrigated area, (16) non- primary sector work-force and overall work participation, (17) non-primary sector work-force and female work participation, (18) overall work particpation and growth of dependency, (19) female work participation and growth of dependency, (20) culturable waste and net area sown, (21) intensity of cultivation and area under **mandua**, (22) land revenue and area under **mandua**, (23) land revenue and area under **jhangora** and (24) area under wheat and area under **mandua**. The above pattern of association is a reflection of the need for certain level of population to utilise the available inputs and the tendency for clustering of facilities and amenities. It should however be noted that the concept of economies, resulting from clustering of facilities and amenities or concentration of inputs, in better off areas, tends to accentuate the problem of spatial inequalities in development in area, where large proportion of population lives in scattered hamlets.

The significant positive correlation between population growth rate and density of population and their positive associations with other variables, mentioned above, may be analysed as follows. The growth of population has progressively been putting constant pressure on its limited supply of cultivated land comprising a small proportion of area under irrigation. In villages where the quality of land was inferior and scope of irrigational facilities poor, the existing cultivated area was extended by bringing in more culturable waste under cultivation to meet the growing needs of increasing population. But where the culturable waste had reached its lower limit and possibility of extension of area under cultivation became remote, the only option left with the masses was to migrate to some other areas in proximity or otherwise within the district or even beyond. Nevertheless, such cases at least in initial stages were rare. Alternatively, in villages where quality of land was relatively better, the growing population not only extended the existing limited cultivated area by bringing in more culturable waste under cultivation but also made concerted efforts to extend more area under irrigation. Both the better quality of land and increasing irrigational facilities help motivated people to concentrate on growing of superior crops of paddy, wheat etc. These factors led to the concentration of population in such villages rather than getting diffused in some other villages. In due course, the increasing density of population led to a corresponding increase in demand for basic services and facilities. To cope up with the demand, the requisite facilities such as postal, educational and health and more recently electrification, were provided in such villages. Thus, the increase in educational facilities led to an increase in levels of literacy which in turn have been instrumental in enhancing the size of working population of non-primary sector.

The significant positive association between area under

jhangora and area under barley throws light on the relatively inferior quality of lands under cultivation. Both these crops of jhangora and barley are grown in such lands during kharif and rabi seasons respectively. Similarly, the positive correlation between scheduled caste population and the area under barley also highlights the relatively inferior area under cultivation possessed by the scheduled caste population.

Negative correlation exists mildly but significantly enough between the growth rates of population of patwari circles and the percentage of settlements/population of small-sized villages to the total number of settlements/population of the patwari circles. These and other negative correlations indicate the vital roles played by the relatively large-sized villages not only in pushing up the growth rates of population but also in attracting educational, postal and other facilities in their respective patwari circles.

The negative associations between density of population and area under forests, between density of population and area under culturable waste and between density of population and area under barley bring into light the increasing pressure of population on limited cultivated lands in various patwari circles of the district. Such a phenomenon has led to the depletion of forested lands as well as of the culturable wastes. Lands hitherto cultivated for growing inferior crops were also put to better uses. Consequently, the scarcity of cultivated lands became acute and the existing working population in primary sector has started shifting to the non-primary sector for getting gainful employment.

The negative association between overall literacy and female work participation, overall literacy and overall work participation, and overall literacy and primary sector workforce reflect the impact of literacy levels on the existing working population. Increase in literacy levels have usually been accompanied by shifts of working population from primary sector to non-primary sector. This is on account of the fact that working population possesses strong preference for white-collar type jobs in non-primary sector to those of the menial and other odd jobs in the primary sector. Since the female workers constitute a sizeable proportion of total working population, as also of primary sector, owing to highly imbalanced sex ratio, in which the females outnumber the males, the negative associations hold good in the study area.

The negative associations between (1) female work participation and non-primary sector work-force, (2) female work participation and growth of dependency, (3) overall work participation and non-primary sector work force and (4) overall work participation and growth of dependency show an impact of imbalanced sex-ratio wherein female workers constitute a large proportion of total work-force.

Significantly high degree of positive correlation exists between (1) growth rate of population and net irrigated area, (2) density of population and net area sown, (3) density of population and net irrigated area, (4) primary sector work-force and overall work participation, (5) overall work participation and female work participation, (6) electrification and land revenue (7) net irrigated area and land revenue, (8) intensity of cultivation and area under paddy, (9) area under paddy and area under wheat and (10) primary school facilities and secondary school facilities. Some of these are obvious and yet some focus on the reality of the situation.

Significantly high degree of negative correlation exists between (1) primary sector work-force and non-primary sector work-force, (2) non-primary sector work-force and female work participation, (3) area under forests and net area sown, (4) area under irrigation and area under **mandua**, (5) area under paddy and area under **mandua**, (6) area under paddy and area under **jhangora**, (7) area under paddy and area under barley, (8) area under wheat and area under **jhangora** and (9) area under wheat and area under barley.

The very high positive correlations between primary sector work-force and overall work participation and between overall work participation and female work participation reflects the impact of highly imbalanced sex-ratio with females outnumbering the males. In primary activites, an overwhelming proportion of working population is comprised of the females.

The highly negative correlations between area under paddy and area under **jhangora** and between area under wheat and area under barley throw light on the existing nature and quality of lands cultivated for growing of these crops. These lands are mutually exclusive. The best quality of lands including those under irrigation are usually occupied by paddy during kharif season and by wheat during rabi season. This is in contrast to the relatively inferior lands used for cultivation of **jhangora** and **mandua** during the kharif season. Both paddy and **mandua** are grown during the kharif season. While most of the irrigated and other superior quality of lands in **paddy-sar** are occupied by paddy, a sizeable proportion of lands in **mandua-sar** is devoted to growing **mandua**. Hence, the inverse associations

Table 6.1 : Correlation Matrix of Selected Demographic and Socio-Economic Variables in Pauri Garhwal District (1971)

	x_1	x_2	x_3	x_4	x_5	x_6	x_7	x_8	x_9	x_{10}	x_{11}	x_{12}	x_{13}	x_{14}	x_{15}	x_{16}	x_{17}	x_{18}	x_{19}	x_{20}	x_{21}	x_{22}	x_{23}	x_{24}	x_{25}	x_{26}	x_{27}	x_{28}	x_{29}
x_1	1.00																												
x_2	.87	1.00																											
x_3	-.31	-.36	1.00																										
x_4	-.19	-.19	.45	1.00																									
x_5	.01	.01	-.11	-.04	1.00																								
x_6	.12	.12	.24	.25	-.02	1.00																							
x_7	.15	.15	-.35	-.19	.19	.14	1.00																						
x_8	.15	.21	-.37	-.34	.02	-.35	-.31	1.00																					
x_9	-.15	-.21	.37	.34	-.03	.35	-.16	-.99	1.00																				
x_{10}	.09	.06	-.13	-.16	.02	-.41	-.02	.46	-.46	1.00																			
x_{11}	.16	.12	-.19	-.21	.05	-.28	.03	.52	-.52	.94	1.00																		
x_{12}	.17	.18	-.21	-.09	-.01	-.14	.16	-.25	.25	-.36	-.38	1.00																	
x_{13}	.09	-.01	.15	.14	-.01	-.01	-.22	-.31	.31	.06	.03	.20	1.00																
x_{14}	-.22	-.11	.33	.46	.09	.30	-.28	-.47	.47	-.37	-.40	.05	.17	1.00															
x_{15}	-.04	.02	-.13	-.39	-.20	-.07	-.14	.10	-.10	-.01	-.01	.04	-.10	-.08	1.00														
x_{16}	.16	.18	-.21	-.27	.03	.01	.12	.08	-.08	-.06	.08	.05	-.05	-.18	.03	1.00													
x_{17}	-.03	-.05	.13	.54	-.11	.18	.01	-.11	.11	-.10	-.10	-.10	-.02	.17	-.51	-.46	1.00												
x_{18}	-.19	-.12	.52	.41	-.13	.32	-.36	-.21	.21	-.15	-.23	-.25	.13	.38	.01	-.23	.14	1.00											
x_{19}	-.03	-.01	-.03	.01	.04	.02	.01	-.06	.06	-.09	-.08	-.01	-.05	-.01	.19	.08	-.05	.08	1.00										
x_{20}	-.21	-.11	.47	.56	-.01	.36	-.26	-.25	.25	-.23	-.29	-.21	.05	.54	-.13	-.13	.24	.75	.22	1.00									
x_{21}	-.08	-.01	.14	.27	-.08	.23	-.11	-.23	.23	-.18	-.19	-.07	-.10	.27	.05	.01	.16	.29	.51	.39	1.00								
x_{22}	-.05	-.05	.18	.26	-.13	.25	-.16	-.29	.29	-.16	-.18	-.09	.01	.27	.10	.02	.08	.29	.38	.37	.69	1.00							
x_{23}	-.02	-.07	-.25	-.18	.17	-.19	.25	.13	-.13	.20	.24	.13	.03	-.19	-.16	.04	-.01	-.50	-.45	-.44	-.51	-.45	1.00						
x_{24}	.17	.15	-.14	-.26	-.09	-.25	-.05	.24	-.24	.08	.07	.06	-.01	-.27	.08	.02	-.20	-.16	-.21	-.31	-.56	-.54	.13	1.00					
x_{25}	-.01	.01	-.03	-.16	.29	-.15	.12	.17	-.17	.13	.15	-.01	.10	-.16	-.12	-.07	-.14	-.07	-.04	-.16	-.54	-.71	.11	.32	1.00				
x_{26}	-.46	-.39	.06	-.01	.14	-.28	-.08	-.06	.06	.07	-.01	-.04	.15	.11	-.05	.01	-.15	.02	.01	-.03	-.03	-.04	.07	-.06	.15	1.00			
x_{27}	-.31	-.31	.35	.34	-.15	.17	-.31	-.22	.22	-.09	-.11	-.24	-.01	.29	-.02	-.16	.14	.33	.03	.32	.18	.18	-.09	-.15	-.15	.51	1.00		
x_{28}	-.33	-.23	.18	.19	.11	.08	-.07	.11	.11	-.01	-.02	-.15	-.02	20	-.08	-.09	.05	.14	.07	.22	.07	.13	-.05	-.10	-.06	.30	.20	1.00	
x_{29}*	-.18	-.17	.29	.25	.03	.10	-.11	.04	.04	.01	.03	-.17	.08	.06	-.01	-.10	.10	.32	-.04	.28	.03	.02	.08	-.05	.02	.08	.30	.14	1.00

Table 6.1 (continued)

I. Demographic Structure

X_1	-	Percentage of settlements in the size-group of less than 100 persons to the total settlements of the patwari circles (1971).
X_2	-	Percentage of population in the size-group of less than 100 persons to the total population of the patwari circles (1971).
X_3	-	Growth rate of population (1961-71).
X_4	-	Density per square kilometre (1971).
X_5	-	Percentage of Scheduled Caste population to the total population of patwari circles (1971).
X_6	-	Percentage of total literates to the total population of the patwari circles (1971).
X_7	-	Females per 1,000 males (1971).

II. Occupational Structure

X_8	-	Percentage of workers in primary sector to the total workers in the patwari circles (1971).
X_9	-	Percentage of workers in the non-primary sector to the total workers in the patwari circles (1971).
X_{10}	-	Percentage of total workers to the total population in the patwari circles (1971).
X_{11}	-	Percentage of total female workers to the total female population in the patwari circles (1971).
X_{12}	-	Growth rate of dependency (1961-71).

III. Infrastructure

X_{13}	-	Percentage of villages served by pucca roads to the total number of villages in the patwari circles (1975).
X_{14}	-	Percentage of villages electrified to the total number of villages in the patwari circles (1977-78).

Table 6.1 (continued)

IV. Agricultural Resource

X_{15} - Percentage of ara under forests to the total geographical area of the patwari circles (1971).

X_{16} - Percentage of culturable waste to the total geographical area of the patwari circles (1971).

X_{17} - Percentage of net area sown to the total geographical area of the patwari circles (1971).

X_{18} - Percentage of net irrigated area to the net area sown of the patwari circles (1971).

X_{19} - Intensity of cultivation (1971).

X_{20} - Land revenue per acre net cultivated area (1971).

X_{21} - Percentage of area sown under paddy to the gross cropped area of the patwari circles (1971).

X_{22} - Percentage of area sown under wheat to the gross cropped area of the patwari circles (1971).

X_{23} - Percentage of area sown under **mandua** to the gross cropped area of the patwari circles (1971).

X_{24} - Percentage of area sown under barley to the gross cropped area of the patwari circles (1971).

V. Services and Facilities

X_{26} - Percentage of settlements with primary schools to the total settlements in the patwari circles (1971).

X_{27} - Percentage of settlements with secondary schools to the total settlements in the patwari circles (1971).

X_{28} - Percentage of settlements having postal facilities to the total settlements in the patwari circles (1972-73).

X_{29} - Percentage of settlements having health facilities to the total settlements in the patwari circles (1977-78).

between irrigated area and area under **mandua** and between area under **mandua** and area under paddy hold good.

LEVELS OF DEVELOPMENT

For finding out the levels of development, all the 29 variables (Table 6.1) considered for correlation matrix were grouped into 5 sets of variables : (1) demographic structure (7 variables), (2) occupational structure (5 variables), (3) infrastructure (2 variables), (4) agricultural resource (11 variables) and services and facilities (4 variables). By the application of the technique of principal component analysis, the composite scores separately for each set of variables in respect of each of the 169 patwari circle were found out. Finally, composite scores considering all the 29 variables together, in respect of all the 5 sets mentioned above, were also obtained.

The analysis of composite scores in respect of 29 variables for 169 patwari circles thus obtained has also been supplemented by an analysis, worked out by means of simple ranking technique. The variables considered for the total rank score are as under:

(1) The size of population of the patwari circles (1971).
(2) Percentage of workers in non-primary sector to the total workers in the patwari circles (1971).
(3) Composite functional scores of the patwari circles (1977-78).
(4) Percentage of villages served by pucca roads to the total number of villages in the patwari circles (1975).
(5) Percentage of villages electrified to the total number of villages in the patwari circles (1977-78).
(6) Percentage of villages provided with tap-water facilities to the total number of villages in the patwari circles (1971).
(7) Percentage of net area sown to the total geographical area of the patwari circles (1971).
(8) Percentage of net irrigated area to the net area sown of the patwari circles (1971).
(9) Intensity of cultivation (1971).
(10) Land revenue per acre net cultivated area (1971).

I. Index of Demographic Structure (Figure 21)

The demographic index was made by taking into account the composite scores of 7 demographic variables namely, (1) number of small-sized settlements, (2) population of small-sized settlements, (3) growth rate of population, (4) density of population, (5) scheduled caste population, (6) overall literacy and (7) sex-ratio. It would be observed therefrom (Figure 21) that the variations in the composite score of demographic structure, among 169 patwari circles, are not pronounced much (composite scores range between 8.83 and 26.55). This reflects the relative homogenous character of the demographic structure of the patwari circles in the region. Nevertheless, there are a few patwari circles which possess relatively high score of demographic structure. They are 10 in number, three of them lie in the contiguous tract of the Bhaber plains and the remaining 7 in the upland hills. But an overwhelming majority of them (114 out of 169) fall in the category having low score of demographic structure. Although they are spread over throughout the district, yet their concentration is to be found mostly in the central and eastern parts of the district. The very low score was the characteristic feature of 27 patwari circles lying mostly either in the western part or in the south-eastern part of the district.

II. Index of Occupational Structure (Figure 22)

The index of occupational structure in respect of 169 patwari circles is illustrated in Figure 22. The composite scores have been obtained by considering the five variables together namely (1) the primary sector work-force, (2) non-primary sector work-force, (3) overall work participation, (4) the female work participation and (5) the growth of dependency. The range of composite scores is relatively less pronounced as compared with those of the demographic structure. It would be observed from Figure 22 that most of the patwari circles with the exception of a few, possess low composite scores of occupational structure. They are lying throughout the district. However, patwari circles possessing relatively high composite scores figured 5 only. They are lying mostly in the vicinity of the towns. Another 30 patwari circles have been classified in the medium category. A majority of them lie in the central part of the district. All the 4 patwari circles of Bhaber plains possess either high or medium scores. Of the 6 patwari circles possessing very low composite scores, 5 lie in the western part of the district. The remaining 128 patwari circles possessed low composite scores of occupational structure (the composite scores range between 5.00 and 10.99).

III. Index of Infrastructure Development (Figure 23)

The index of infrastructure development is illustrated in Figure 23. In fact, the existing levels of infrastructure development in respect of different variables are extremely

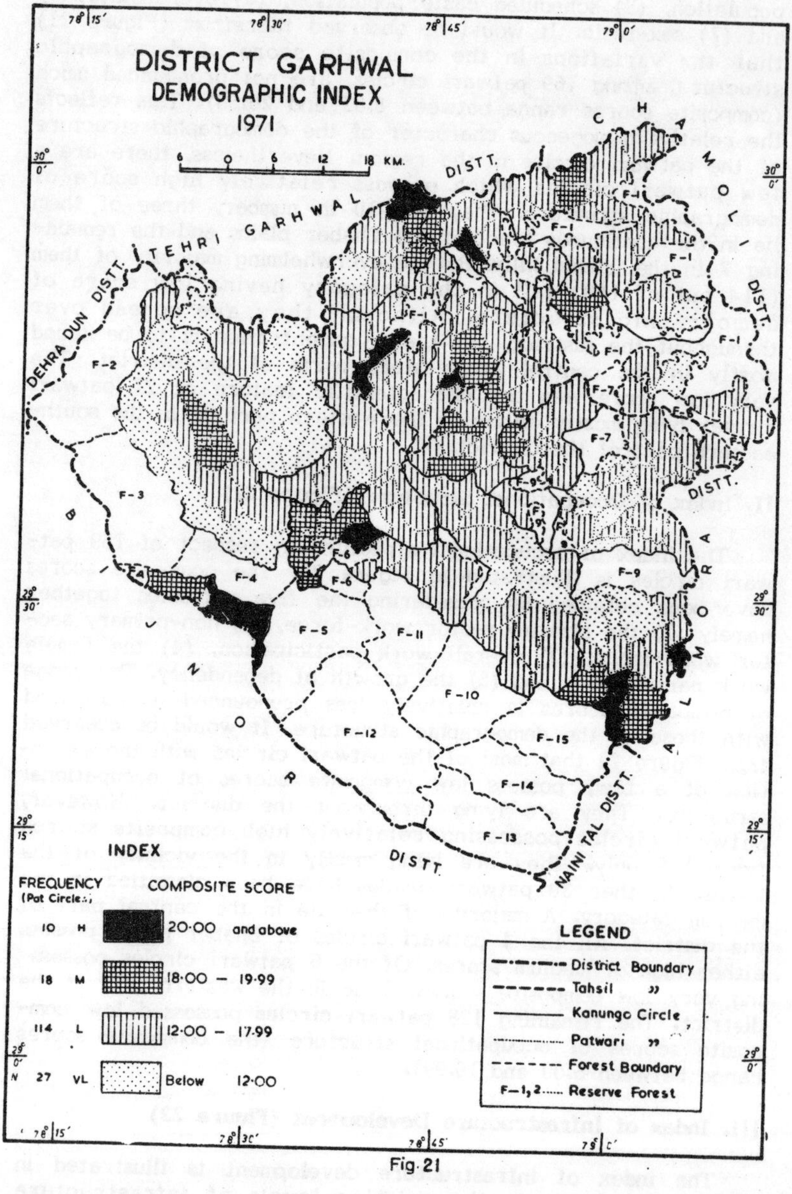

DISTRICT GARHWAL
DEMOGRAPHIC INDEX
1971
6 0 6 12 18 KM.
78° 15'
78° 30'
78° 45'
79° 0'
30° 0'
29° 30'
29° 15'
29° 0'
CHAMOLI DISTT.
TEHRI GARHWAL DISTT.
DEHRA DUN DISTT.
BIJNOR DISTT.
NAINI TAL DISTT.
ALMORA DISTT.
INDEX
FREQUENCY (Pat Circles)
COMPOSITE SCORE
10 H 20·00 and above
18 M 18·00 – 19·99
114 L 12·00 – 17·99
N 27 VL Below 12·00
LEGEND
District Boundary
Tahsil ,,
Kanungo Circle
Patwari ,,
Forest Boundary
F–1, 2...... Reserve Forest

Fig. 21

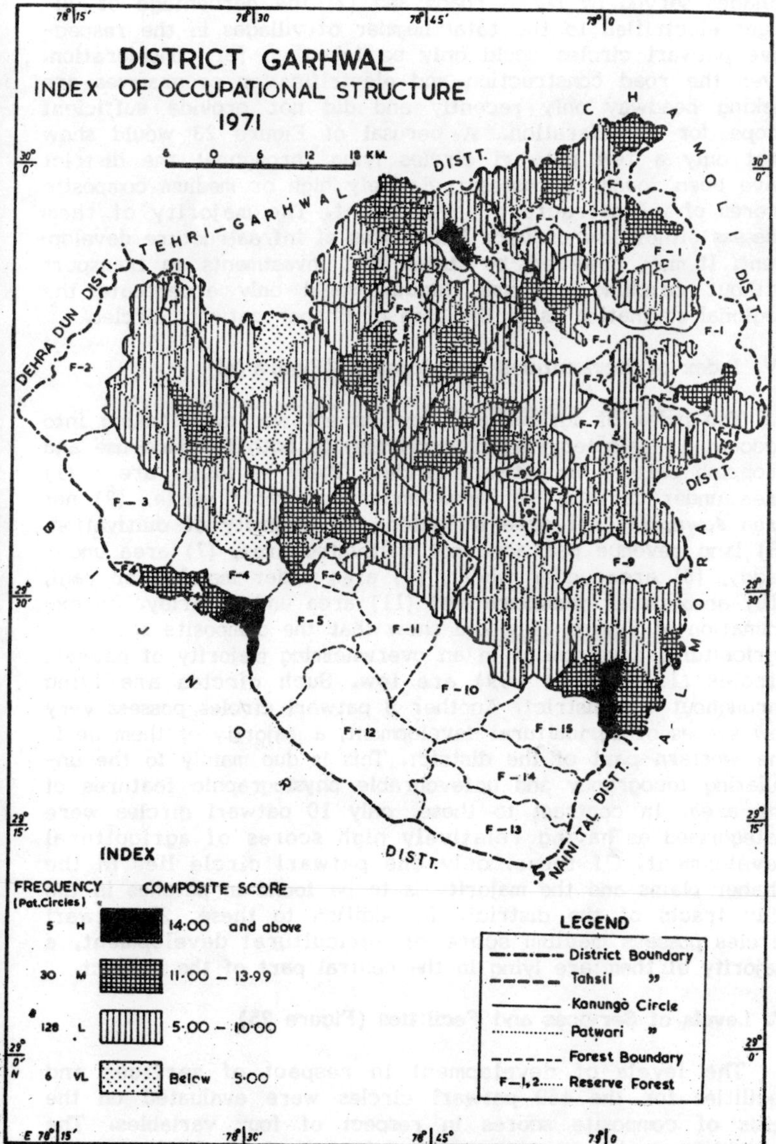
DISTRICT GARHWAL
INDEX OF OCCUPATIONAL STRUCTURE
1971
6 0 6 12 18 KM.
TEHRI-GARHWAL DISTT.
DEHRA DUN DISTT.
CHAMOLI DISTT.
ALMORA DISTT.
BIJNOR DISTT.
NAINI TAL DISTT.
INDEX
FREQUENCY (Pat. Circles)
COMPOSITE SCORE
5 H 14·00 and above
30 M 11·00 – 13·99
128 L 5·00 – 10·00
6 VL Below 5·00
LEGEND
District Boundary
Tahsil "
Kanungo Circle
Patwari "
Forest Boundary
F—1, 2...... Reserve Forest

Fig.22

poor. As such only two variables namely, (1) the percentage of villages served by pucca roads and (2) the percentage of villages electrified to the total number of villages in the respective patwari circles could only be taken up for consideration. Even the road construction and electrification programmes are making headway only recently and did not provide sufficient scope for consideration. A perusal of Figure 23 would show that only a few patwari circles lying throughout the district have been found to possess relatively high or medium composite scores of infrastructure development. The majority of them possess either low or very low scores of infrastructure development. It may, however, be stated that investments on transport without matching economic inputs would only accentuate the regional stagnation as in the case of Bhaber patwari circles.

IV. Index of Agricultural Development (Figure 24)

The index of agricultural development was made taking into account 11 selected variables relating to both the land-use and cropping pattern in patwari circles. These variables are : (1) area under forests, (2) area under culturable waste, (3) net area sown, (4) net area irrigated, (5) intensity of cultivation, (6) land revenue per acre net cultivated area, (7) area under paddy, (8) area under wheat, (9) area under **mandua** or ragi, (10) area under **jhangora** and (11) area under barley. An examination of Figure 24 would show that the composite scores of agricultural development in an overwhelming majority of patwari circles (129 out of 169) are low. Such circles are lying throughout the district. Another 9 patwari circles possess very low scores of agricultural development, a majority of them lie in the western part of the district. This is due mainly to the undulating topography and unfavourable physiographic features of the area. In contrast to these, only 10 patwari circles were categorised as having relatively high scores of agricultural development. Of these, only one patwari circle lies in the Bhaber plains and the majority is to be found in patches in the hilly tracts of the district. In addition to these, 21 patwari circles possess medium score of agricultural development, a majority of them are lying in the central part of the district.

V. Levels of Services and Facilities (Figure 25)

The levels of development in respect of services and facilities for the 169 patwari circles were evaluated on the basis of composite scores in respect of four variables. The variables considered are : (1) primary school facilities, (2) secondary school facilities, (3) postal facilities and (4) health facilities. The levels of services and facilities are illustrated in

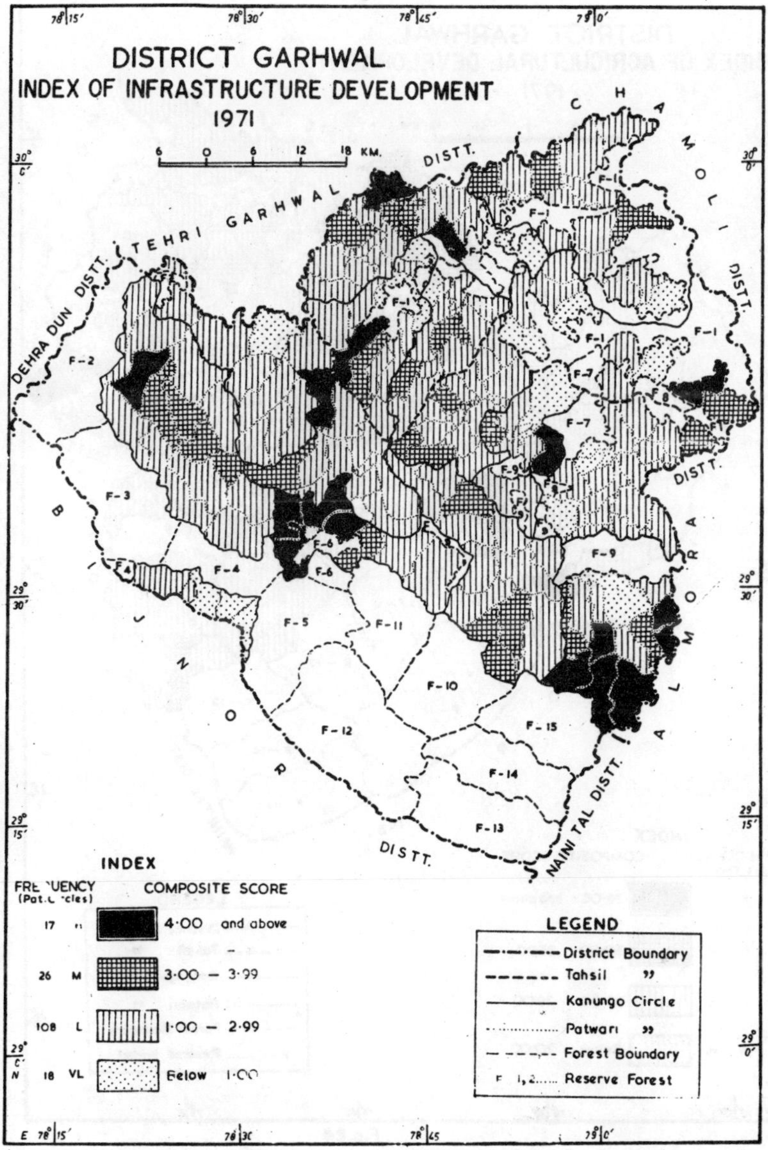
DISTRICT GARHWAL
INDEX OF INFRASTRUCTURE DEVELOPMENT
1971
6 0 6 12 18 KM.
TEHRI GARHWAL DISTT.
DEHRA DUN DISTT.
CHAMOLI DISTT.
ALMORA DISTT.
NAINI TAL DISTT.
BIJNOR DISTT.
INDEX
COMPOSITE SCORE
17 H 4·00 and above
26 M 3·00 – 3·99
108 L 1·00 – 2·99
18 VL Below 1·00
LEGEND
District Boundary
Tahsil "
Kanungo Circle
Patwari "
Forest Boundary
Reserve Forest

Fig. 23

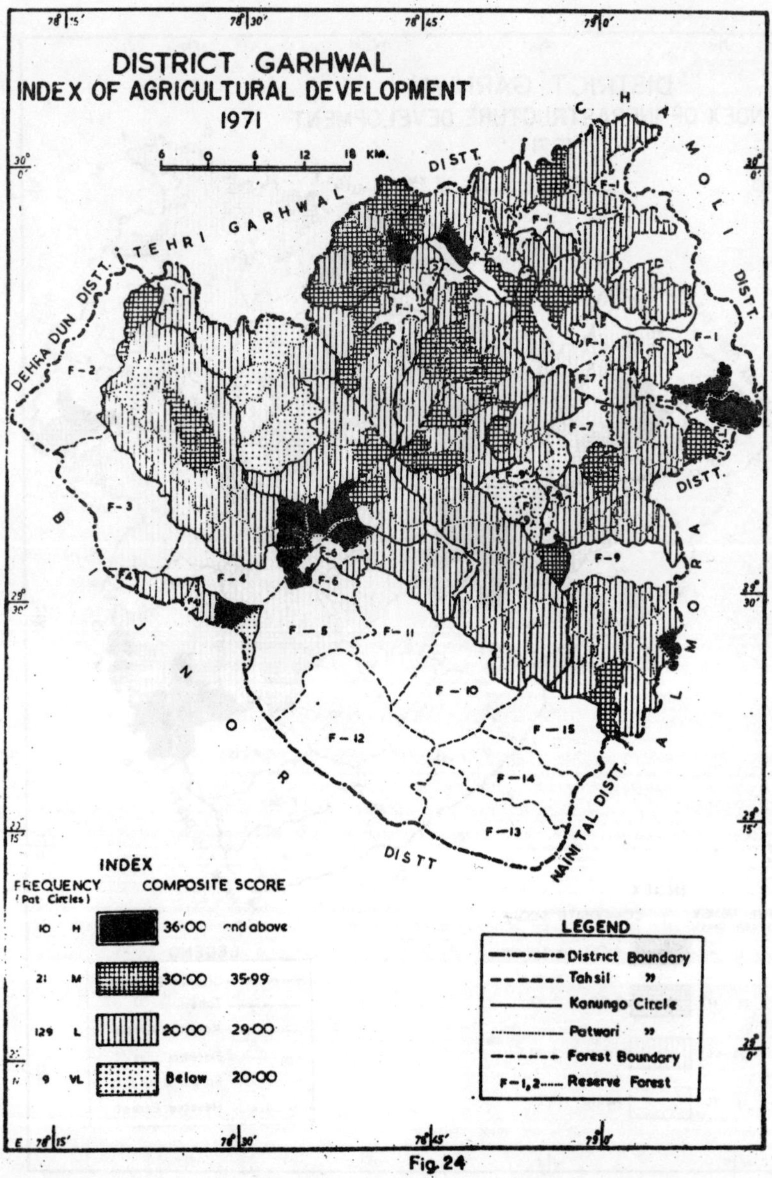
DISTRICT GARHWAL
INDEX OF AGRICULTURAL DEVELOPMENT
1971
6 0 6 12 18 KM.
TEHRI GARHWAL DISTT.
CHAMOLI DISTT.
DEHRA DUN DISTT.
BIJNOR DISTT
ALMORA DISTT.
NAINITAL DISTT.
F-1
F-2
F-3
F-4
F-5
F-6
F-7
F-9
F-10
F-11
F-12
F-13
F-14
F-15
INDEX
FREQUENCY (Pat Circles)
COMPOSITE SCORE
10 H 36·00 and above
21 M 30·00 35·99
129 L 20·00 29·00
9 VL Below 20·00
LEGEND
District Boundary
Tahsil "
Kanungo Circle
Patwari "
Forest Boundary
F-1,2 Reserve Forest
78°15'
78°30'
78°45'
79°0'
30° 0'
29° 30'
29° 15'
29° 0'

Fig. 24

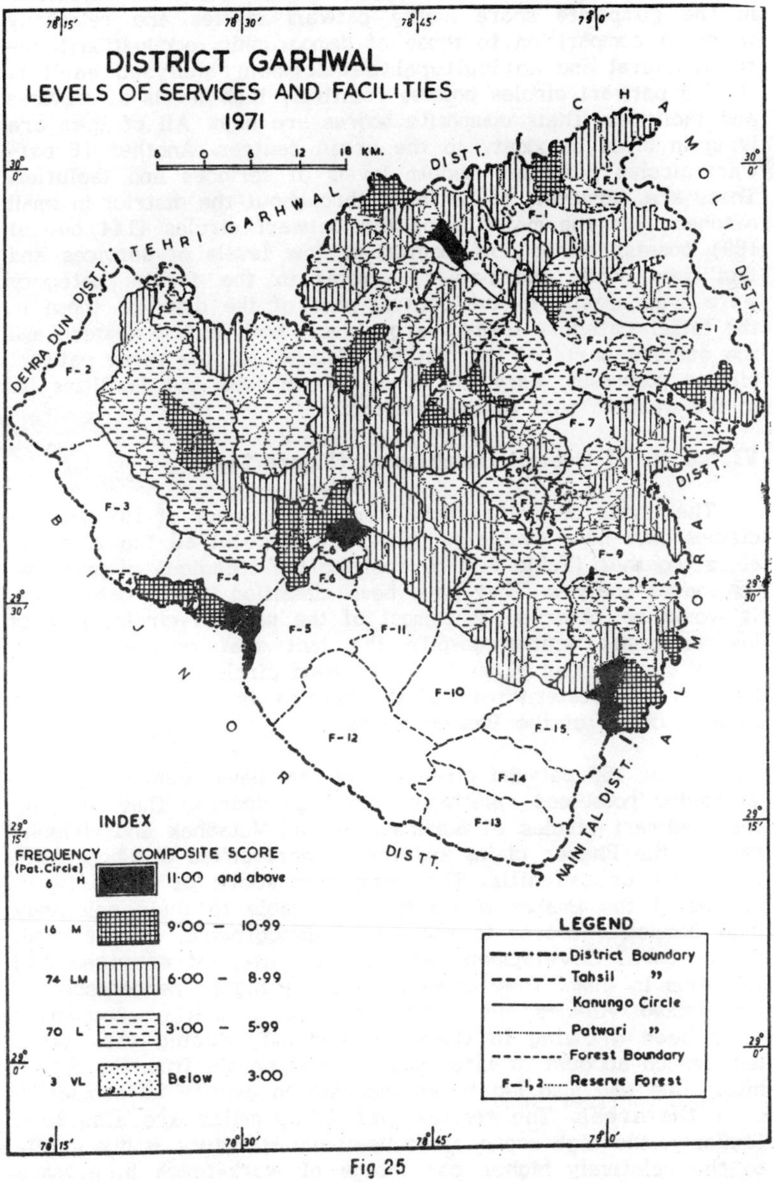
DISTRICT GARHWAL
LEVELS OF SERVICES AND FACILITIES
1971
6 0 6 12 18 KM.
TEHRI GARHWAL DISTT.
CHAMOLI DISTT.
DEHRA DUN DISTT.
ALMORA DISTT.
NAINI TAL DISTT.
BIJNOR DISTT.
INDEX
FREQUENCY (Pat. Circle)
COMPOSITE SCORE
6 H 11·00 and above
16 M 9·00 – 10·99
74 LM 6·00 – 8·99
70 L 3·00 – 5·99
3 VL Below 3·00
LEGEND
District Boundary
Tahsil "
Kanungo Circle
Patwari "
Forest Boundary
F—1, 2...... Reserve Forest

Fig 25

Figure 25. A perusal of the figure would show that variations in the composite score among patwari circles are relatively wider in comparision to those of demographic, occupational, infrastructural and agricultural development analysed earlier. Only 6 patwari circles possess relatively high levels of services and facilities. Their composite scores are high. All of them are lying in close proximity to the urban centres. Another 16 patwari circles possessed medium levels of services and facilities. These are, however, to be found throughout the district in small patches. But the majority of the patwari circles (144 out of 169) possess either low medium or low levels of services and facilities. While the patwari circles in the former category were lying mostly in the central part of the district, those in the latter category formed large tracts both in the western and the eastern parts of the district. Besides, all the three patwari circles possessing very low levels of services and facilities lie in the western part of the district.

VI. Levels of Overall Development (Figure 26)

The levels of overall development in respect of 169 patwari circles have been evaluated taking into account all the 29 variables together (Table 6.1) by applying the technique of principal component analysis. They have been classified into 5 categories. It would be observed that most of the patwari circles possess low composite scores despite the fact that composite score widely varied from 91.00 in the patwari circle of Dabralsyun II lying in the western part of the district to 330.07 in Sukhrao patwari circle of the Bhaber plains.

Out of 169 patwari circles, only five have been categorised as having possessed relatively very high scores. They are the four patwari circles of Sukhrao, Saneh, Motadhak and Haldukhata in the Bhaber plains and the patwari circle of Choprakot-II in the upland hills. The very high score of the patwari circles of the Bhaber plains is attributable to their relatively high composite scores in respect of demographic, occupational, agricultural development and accessibility of services and facilities in them. They possess relatively higher percentages of large-sized villages. Both the size and growth of population have been growing in them tremendously during the last 2 decades on account of large migration of people from the upland hills. This has also led to an increase in density of population over the areas. The females per 1,000 males are also low. Similarly, the high score of occupational structure is due mostly to the relatively higher percentage of work-force in primary sector and higher levels of both the male and female work participation rates. Though agricultural development is low, it pos-

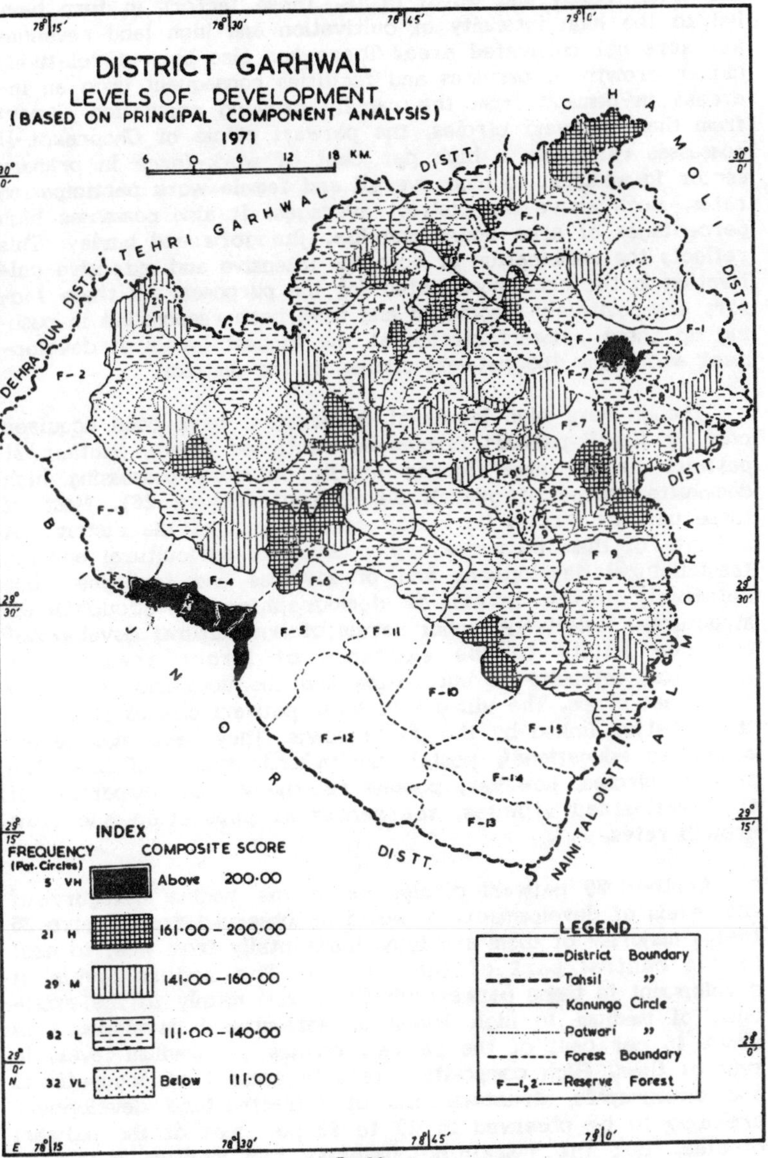
DISTRICT GARHWAL
LEVELS OF DEVELOPMENT
(BASED ON PRINCIPAL COMPONENT ANALYSIS)
1971
6 0 6 12 18 KM.
TEHRI GARHWAL DISTT.
CHAMOLI DISTT.
ALMORA DISTT.
NAINI TAL DISTT
BIJNOR DISTT.
DEHRA DUN DISTT.
78°15'
78°30'
78°45'
79°0'
30° 0'
29° 30'
29° 15'
29° 0'
INDEX
FREQUENCY (Pat. Circles)
COMPOSITE SCORE
5 VH Above 200·00
21 H 161·00 – 200·00
29 M 141·00 – 160·00
82 L 111·00 – 140·00
32 VL Below 111·00
LEGEND
District Boundary
Tahsil "
Kanungo Circle
Patwari "
Forest Boundary
F—1, 2 Reserve Forest

Fig. 26

sesses relatively higher net areas under cultivation, irrigation and under paddy and wheat crops. These factors in turn have led to the high intensity of cultivation and high land revenues per acre net cultivated area. There has also been a relatively higher growth of services and facilities consequent upon an increase in demand from the rapidly growing population. Apart from these patwari circles, the patwari circle of Choprakot-II possesses relatively a high per cent of work-force in primary sector in addition to high overall and female work participation rates, much above the district averages. It also possesses high percentages of area under **mandua, jhangora** and barley. This reflects the combination of both the intensive and extensive cultivation in the area most suited for the purposes. All these factors are positively associated and have been responsible in pushing up these patwari circles at the highest levels of development among the 169 patwari circles of the district.

Though very high levels of development have been acquired only by the 5 patwari circles as mentioned above, another 21 patwari circles have figured in the category possessing high composite scores of overall development (Figure 26). Most of these patwari circles lie in the central part of the district. A majority of them possesses higher levels of agricultural and infrastructural development and of services and facilities but relatively lower levels of demographic and occupational structures. Relatively higher levels of agricultural development are due mainly to the existance of larger areas under irrigation, intensity of cultivation and the dominance of paddy and wheat crops. The villages in these patwari circles are relatively better linked by the pucca roads. They have also better access to educational, postal, health and other facilities. The patwari circles, however, possess relatively high proportion of the small-sized villages, sparseness of population and slow growth rates.

Another 29 patwari circles lie in the medium category of the levels of development. It would be observed from Figure 26 that a majority of them are lying horizontally from west to east in the central part of the district. The medium levels of development in these patwari circles is due mainly to the existence of medium to high levels of agricultural development in about 45 per cent of the patwari circles and medium levels in rest of them. High composite scores in respect of occupational and demographic structure and of infrastructure development are also to be observed in 20 to 25 per cent of the patwari circles. But the remaining majority had medium levels of development in them. In contrast to these, the levels in services and facilities were either low or very low in a majority of the patwari circles.

An overwhelming majority of the patwari circles figuring 82, however, possess relatively low levels of overall development. Their spatial distribution is almost even throughout the hilly tracts of the district. Such a distributional pattern of patwari circles throws light on the existing physiographic conditions and the nature of soils of the hilly tracts of the district under study. The low levels of development of these patwari circles are mainly due to the existence of low levels of agricultural development and of occupational structure in a majority of the patwari circles. Over 80 per cent of the patwari circles in this category possess low levels of agricultural development and the remaining ones possess either medium or very low levels. This is due to the dominance of dry and extensive farming with relatively higher percentages of areas under **mandua, jhangora** and barley crops. A similar situation exists in the case of occupational structure. Due to imbalanced sex-ratio, positive associations exist between the primary sector work-force and overall work participation and also between primary sector work- force and female work participation. Relatively low scores of demographic and infrastructural development are also observed. In each of these, over 50 per cent of the patwari circles posses low scores and the rest either medium or very low. This is on account of the fact that the demographic structure characterises itself by the dominance of small-sized settlements, slow growth rates, low density of population and imbalanced sex-ratio. The low levels of infrastructure development are accounted for by the absence of pucca roads and electrification in most of the villages within those patwari circles. Besides, the levels of services and facilities are also low in over 65 per cent of the patwari circles and very low in the remaining ones.

The lowest levels of development was found in 32 patwari circles, each of whom possessed less than 110.0 as the value of composite score. Although such patwari circles are spatially distributed throughout the district, yet most of them are lying in patches in the western, north-eastern and central parts of the district. The very low levels of development in respect of over 95 per cent of the patwari circles are attributable to the existence of low levels of agricultural development and of demographic and occupational structures and also to the low levels of services and facilities. Lack of irrigation facilities, rugged terrain, dry farming, extensive cultivation and growing of inferior crops are the main features of the agricultural structure. The demographic and occupational factors are similar to those mentioned in the preceding paragraph. All of them have pushed down these patwari circles at the lowest levels of

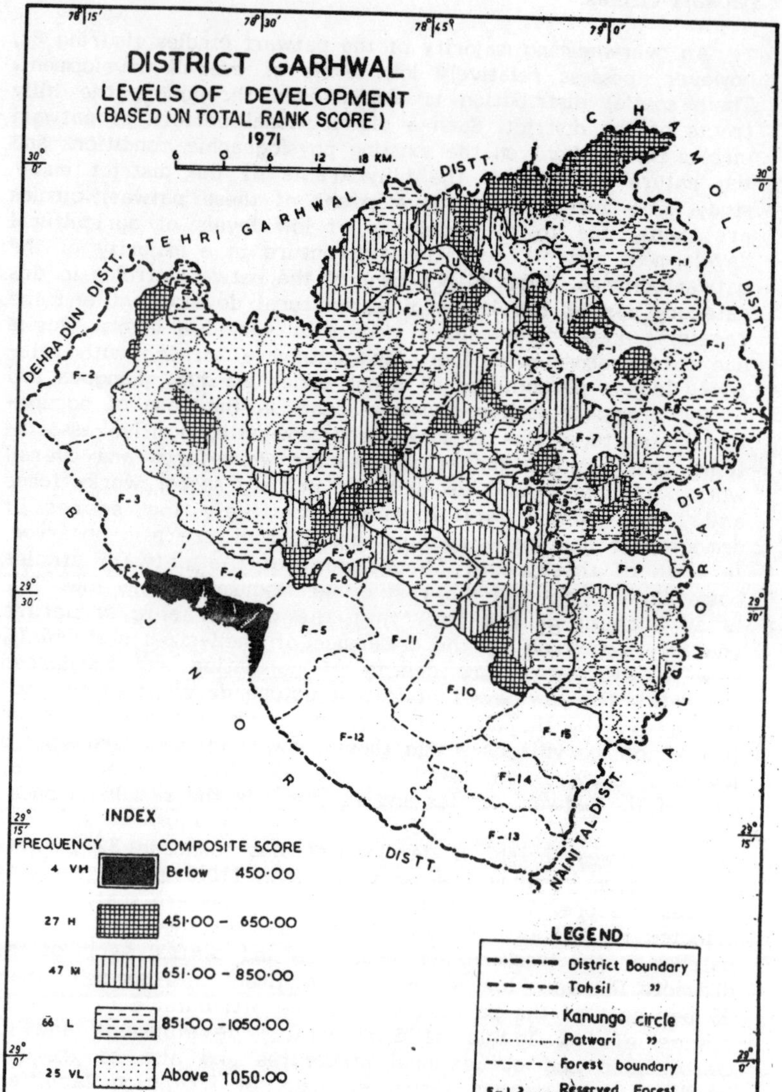

DISTRICT GARHWAL
LEVELS OF DEVELOPMENT
(BASED ON TOTAL RANK SCORE)
1971
6 0 6 12 18 KM.
TEHRI GARHWAL DISTT.
DEHRADUN DISTT.
CHAMOLI DISTT.
ALMORA DISTT.
NAINITAL DISTT.
BIJNOR DISTT.
INDEX
FREQUENCY
COMPOSITE SCORE
4 VH Below 450·00
27 H 451·00 – 650·00
47 M 651·00 – 850·00
66 L 851·00 – 1050·00
25 VL Above 1050·00
LEGEND
District Boundary
Tahsil "
Kanungo circle
Patwari "
Forest boundary
F–1, 2....... Reserved Forest

Fig.27

development.

The foregoing analysis of the different levels of development emerged through the principal component analysis has been supplemented by an analysis of the levels of development worked out by means of simple composite ranking method of 10 selected variables in respect of 169 patwari circles (Figure 27). The range of total rank score lies between 111.0 in Sukhrao patwari circle in Bhaber plains to 1,346.8 in the patwari circle of Ajmer Palla II, in the western part of the district. It would be observed from the perusal of Figure 27 that all the 4 patwari circles of Sukhrao, Saneh, Motadhak and Haldukhata distinctly stand at the highest levels of development. Patwari circles possessing medium, low and very low levels of development numbered 47, 66 and 25 respectively.

Both, the levels of development as emerged through the application of principal component analysis (Figure 26) and the levels of development as worked out by means of simple composite ranking technique (Figure 27) bring out more or less a similar pattern.

SEVEN

Summary & Conclusions

The present study has been an attempt to understand the characteristics of the Hill region in terms of its physiography, demopgrahic and settlement structure, land-use and cropping pattern, levels of productivity and income, functional organisation, infrastructure and other services and amenities. Unlike several studies conducted in the past, the study is essentially spatial, looking at development problems in terms of structure, process and stage in a spatial framework. A micro-level study of Pauri Garhwal District with patwari circles (groups of villages) as the basic units has been made by the use of secondary data supplemented by field enquiry in 218 households of different landholdings distributed in 42 villages. The study reveals the following characteristics.

The overall study of the Hill region and its economy is presented as a backdrop which reveals the characteristics of underdevelopment such as vast potential natural resources; the predominance of subsistence agriculture; low levels of productivity and income and of industrial, infrastructural and functional organisation; low growth rates of population; large proportion of rural population with low level of urbanization; low density of population and high levels of literacy and work participation rates. The settlements themselves are very small with poor accessibility and low levels of interaction. Cultivated land is limited with scarce irrigation facilities. Low levels of social amenities and infrastructure have led to outmigration of male workers resulting in high imbalances in sex-ratio. The Hill region, by and large, has been the supplier of a large variety of major and minor forest products, energy resources and above all, the unskilled working population to the plains in the adjoining regions and in large towns and cities as far as even Bombay and Calcutta.

Physical structure

Analysis of the physical landscape brought out the fact that only 19.27 per cent of the total geographical area of the district is under cultivation and even within this the flat alluvial patches are very rare except in the case of the Bhaber. In other areas, the ungraded rivers have rendered location of settlements and cultivation extremely difficult. The dominance of terraced cultivation and its low level of modernisation have led to environmental degradation. The upper slopes are being denuded and are also subject to intensive soil erosion. Four types of agricultural regions with distinct crop associations have been identified. Tourism and raising of horticulture and grassland economy to the extent it could serve to raise the income of the region and its people are also important to the district's economy.

Spatial Organisation

Analysis of settlement structure and pattern of spatial organisation by using quantitative and cartographic techniques has brought out the typologies in the pattern of organisation in which large settlements both existing and potential could serve as the basic ingredients of the strategy for integrated development of land-uses and settlements. The existing nodal centres both rural and urban, do not provide an optimum linkage pattern due to inaccessibility conditions owing to the lack of transportation and communication on the one hand, and by the existence of large functional gaps resulting from inadequate levels of functions, on the other hand. The small urban centres, lying mostly along the main highway from Kotdwara to Rudraprayag are incapable of generating sufficient growth impulses to the surrounding areas. The large sized settlements occuring mostly in the Bhaber plains are few and hardly show any evidence of nodality around them.

Human Resource structure

The study of human resource structure has brought to light peculiar demographic patterns and intra-district variations among 169 patwari circles. The district recorded a low growth rate of 1.46 per cent per annum. It varied very widely from negative growth rate to highly positive growth rate. Settlements in the patwari circles of Bhaber plains have recorded phenomenal growth of population and density since 1951, mainly due to immigration from the Hill area.

The sex-ratio in 1971 was 1,160 females per 1,000 males with sharp variations within. Patwari circles in the Bhaber plains were the only exceptions where males outnumbered females. This imbalance in sex-ratio was also observed in sample villages with variation from 694 females per 1,000 males in Deolad to 1,475 females per 1,000 males in Birgana.

The district had an average literacy of 31.53 per cent in 1971 with marked variations as between male (50.02 per cent) and female (15.84 per cent) literacy. The literacy rates showed spatial and temporal variations within the district. It was also observed that literacy increased rapidly in areas close to towns and in settlements situated along the main highway from Kotdwara to Rudraprayag and beyond. Incidentally, they are also the areas of high inflow of moneyorder remittances. The sample survey also revealed that educational levels were also high and were in tune with high literacy levels of the people. Males had relatively higher literacy levels than the females.

The district is also characterised by high work participation rate. The female work participation rate varied from 0.32 per cent to 78.14 per cent among different patwari circles against the district average of 45.31 per cent and tended to act independently of male participation in the rural and total but not in urban sector. It was also found that female work participation rates were much higher than male work participation rates in the patwari circles lying in Bhaber plains and along the main axis from Kotdwara to Rudraprayag due to migration of male members of the family. These are also the patwari circles with high intensity of moneyorder remittances.

The livelihood pattern is dominated by work in primary sector, absorbing 85.0 per cent of the total workers. Cultivators formed significantly large segment of the primary activities (78.01 per cent). Agricultural labourers were few (1.30 per cent) and confined mainly to the Bhaber plains. Secondary activities do not show indications of development in terms of growth of income, output and employment. As such dependence of the workers on other occupations outside the region is the characteristic feature of the district.

Levels of Productivity and Incomes

It has been revealed from our sample survey that the yields per hectare of almost all the crops are low except in irrigated lands which accounted for 20.84 per cent of the net area sown. The average yields of paddy in irrigated and unirrigated areas accounted for 15.66 and 10.09 quintals per hectare. The corresponding figures for wheat are 11.42 and 9.14 quintals per hectare respectively. Similarly, in respect of coarser cereals of **mandua, jhangora** and barley, the yields are also low. The district averages in these crops worked out to 8.22, 8.59 and 8.24

quintals per hectare respectively. The variations in productivity per hectare among different size-range of land- holdings are not significant. But they are relatively more pronounced among different sample villages.

Among the 4 crop-combination regions, paddy- wheat crop combination region of Bhaber plains had the highest yield rates. The yields of paddy in irrigated and unirrigated lands were 17.76 quintals and 11.44 quintals per hectare respectively. The corresponding figures for wheat were 13.55 and 9.59 quintals per hectare. The yield of **mandua** or ragi was the highest in the 3-crop combination region (paddy, wheat and **mandua** or ragi) accounting for 8.45 quintals per hectare. Similarly, the yield per hectare of **jhangora** was highest in 5-crop combination region (paddy, wheat, **mandua, jhangora** and barley) and accounted for 9.15 quintals per hectare. The sample study revealed that the net irrigated area for the district was only 20.84 per cent of the net area sown in 1977-78. The district averages for areas under improved seeds and fertilizers accounted for 8.64 per cent and 12.27 per cent of the gross area sown respectively. Similarly, the quantity of fertilisers used was only 11.40 kilograms per hectare of gross area sown. The survey also revealed that there exist potential areas for specialisation in the production of some specific crops such as pulses, vegetables and fruits. The low productivity of crops was found to be attributable to a variety of factors such as climatic conditions, soil differentiations, availability of agricultural inputs and labour-force and the operating expenses involved. As a result of these factors, generation of income from agriculture and its allied activities, at the present moment, is quite insufficient to maintain the existing population. The district, has, therefore, to depend upon to a large extent on the outside incomes.

The low levels of productivity of different crops are reflected in the low levels of income. The net annual income per household from agriculture and its allied activities worked out to Rs.4,431.00 at 1977-78 price level which was 67.64 per cent of the net income from all sources. Among different size-range of land-holdings, the variations were very large. Similarly, per capita income ranged between Rs.510.00 and Rs.3,398.00 among different villages. It has also been revealed that out of the net annual income of Rs.6,550.00 per household in 1977-78, other sources such as wages, salaries, pension, moneyorder remittances and others contributed 32.36 per cent. Amongst these, the contribution of moneyorder remittances was the highest (40.70 per cent).

Consumption Pattern

It has been observed that the bulk of the incomes of the people generated either through agriculture and its allied activities or received through outside remittances are absorbed in meeting the consumption expenditure, leaving little room for savings to accummulate. The total annual expenditure per household at 1977-78 price level was worked out to Rs.6,217.00 or approximately Rs.518.00 per month. The expenditure on food items constituted 69.20 per cent, the expenditure on non-food items 20.79 per cent and remaining 10.01 per cent on items of miscellaneous character such as marriage and other religious functions etc. A sizeable portion of the total expenditure on food items is incurred on cereals and pulses (48.40 per cent) of which rice and wheat are the dominant ones. Similarly, of the total expenditure on non-food items, clothing covered 37.52 per cent followed by expenditure on education (19.96 per cent) and the rest by other items. These patterns of production and consumption have made the consumers to depend heavily on small traders and retailers for both agricultural and non-agricultural goods. They, in turn, depend on the big businessmen and wholesalers at Ramnagar, Kotdwara and Rishikesh. The large inflows of outside remittances consequently drain out of the region immediately in the form of consumption expenditure.

Pattern of Outmigration

The cummulative impact of low levels of productivity and income and of low standard of living of the people has been on the working population who are perforce to migrate outside the district for gainful employment. An analysis of the migration streams revealed that there existed a strong tendency on the part of the migrants to move to areas of similar environment. As such the inter-district migration within the Hill region constituted 46.40 per cent of the total. Next in importance is the relatively rich agricultural plains of Western Uttar Pradesh which accounted for 44.16 per cent of the inter-district migration. Other regions shared the rest (9.44 per cent). Similarly, the inter-state migration showed that migration to the adjoining areas was relatively much more than to the areas farther away. The Northern region comprising the states of Himachal Pradesh, Jammu and Kashmir, Haryana and Punjab and the Union Territory of Chandigarh, recorded the highest percentage of 30.75 to the total migrant population. The Metropolitan City of Delhi though much smaller in respect of its geographical area seems to be the most attractive area for the migrants (27.02 per cent of the total). Next to Delhi region was the Eastern region comprising of the states of Bihar,

Orissa, West Bengal, Assam and other eastern states of India (18.76 per cent). The other regions covered the rest.

Our sample study revealed that 8.59 per cent of the households in 42 sample villages had permanantly migrated to various places particularly in the neighbouring towns of the district during the last 3 decades. Besides, 112 households (51.38 per cent) out of 218 households where field enquiry was conducted, reported cases of outmigration. In these households, there were, on an average, 4 workers and 45 per cent of them were migrant workers. The percentage variations of migrant workers to the total workers among different villages ranged from 20 per cent to as high as 100 per cent; though in different size-range of holdings, the percentage variations ranged from 40.35 per cent to 50.50 per cent.

Of the total migrant workers, intra-district migration was 6.47 per cent, inter-district migration 23.38 per cent and 68.66 per cent had moved out of the state of Uttar Pradesh. Among the various regions of India, Delhi region topped with 30.90 per cent, followed by Central region (13.93 per cent), Northern region (11.94 per cent), Westerm region (8.96 per cent), Eastern region (9.95 per cent) and Southern region (2.99 per cent) to the total migrant workers for the district.

The pattern of outmigration from the district also reveals that it is not highly localised but is diffused spatially. The magnitude of outmigration is greater in settlements and areas which had the initial advantage of educational facilities, traditional routes of tranportation and communication providing accessibility conditions and above all the initiative and drive of the educated rural elites who motivate these migrants to shift to the urban centres. Thus, the city's pull factor has been more dominant than the push factor of the region.

The sample study also showed that the occupational pattern of the migrants varied widely. They were engaged in various tertiary activities but dominantly in defence services. Their educational levels were high and were in tune with the high literacy levels of the district. Most of them lay in the younger age-groups. This is an important factor as the exodus of energetic people of younger age-group leads to retardation of the development of the region. A majority of the migrants (63.88 per cent) visited their home places in a year and the remaining ones made visits monthly, quarterly or even beyond a year.

The levels of incomes of outmigrants were relatively low. Over 55 per cent of the migrants were in the income ranges of less than Rs.5,000.00 per annum or Rs.415.00 per month. The average annual income of the outmigrants was Rs.7,000.00 per annum (Rs.583.00 per month). The range varied widely among different income groups from Rs.743.00 per annum in the lowest income group to Rs.27,850.00 per annum in the highest income group. The average annual remittances of outmigrants worked out Rs.1,069.00 per annum or Rs.89.00 per month. The variations of remittances was, however, between Rs.30.00 per month in the lowest income group to Rs.170.00 per month in the highest income group. A majority of the outmigrants (71.97 per cent) remitted by way of moneyorders and the remaining by other media.

Patterns and Variations in the inflow of Moneyorder Remittances

Analysis of the magnitude of outmigration and money flow to the households and its variations led us to confirm that the district economy depends to a large extent on outside incomes chiefly by way of moneyorder remittances. This dependence has, over the years, increased steadiy but gained momentum during the recent years. In 1972-73, the inflow of moneyorder remittances in the district amounted to Rs.41,131,000 (or Rs.3,431,000 per month). It increased to Rs.70,445,000 (Rs.59 lakhs per month) by 1980-81 indicating an overall growth of 71 per cent or approximately 8 per cent per annum. The monthly inflow of moneyorder remittances of Rs.34 lakhs are disbursed by way of 37,000 moneyorders among 123,240 households in 43 Postal regions.

The moneyorder remittances into the district come from all the Regions of India and their intensity vary from region to region. Of the total monthly remittances of Rs.34.31 lakhs, Uttar Pradesh's share was the highest (32.65 per cent) strongly suggesting the relative importance of migrant population in the areas within the state. This was sharply followed by the Western region, accounting approximately 28.81 per cent of the aggregate flow. Delhi region stood third with 13.07 per cent of the total inflow of moneyorder remittances in the district. The other regions namely, the Eastern region, the Northern region, the Central region and the Southern region contributed 9.92 per cent, 9.66 per cent, 3.79 per cent and 2.10 per cent respectively.

The inflows of moneyorder remittances are widely dispersed spatially among the 43 Postal regions of the district. The range of variations among them lay between Rs.12,591 (0.37 per cent) in Kanskhet Postal region to Rs.225,784 (6.58 per cent) in Pauri Postal region. The average monthly value of moneyorder remittances per household worked out Rs.27.84 for the district and ranged between Rs.5.53 per household in Kalagarh Postal region to Rs.50.20 per household in Jaharikhal Postal region. It has been observed that the Postal regions showing high intensity of the inflow of moneyorder remittances are linked by the main transport lines from Kotdwara and Rishikesh reflecting better accessibility conditions, linkage effects and greater interactions among people. This indicates pull factor rather than push factor in respect of outmigration of the people.

Impact of Outmigration and Moneyorder Remittances

The study highlights that outmigration has deprived the economy of its best managerial skills and entrepreneurial ability. There is a rapid deterioration of population structure; progresssive underuse and decline of private and social assets; exploitation of industrial potentials by the outsiders; and expropriation of abnormal profits by leading businessmen and the wholesalers. All these have been detrimental to the growth of the economy and would continue to be so in future for lack of formulation of a spatial development strategy close to the regional structure, processes of development over time and its diffusion in space.

It has also been observed that the district economy is caught up in a spiral pattern, ever increasing in height and radius as it were. The sequence of factors leading to such a phenomenon is as follows. The initial nature and character of spatio-economic and socio-cultural dimensions of the district under study, have so far constrained the development of its actual and potential resources to a very low level. The low level of underdevelopment in turn, led to low levels of productivity, output, incomes and employment. Existing inaccessibility conditions have maintained the geographical immobility and isolation intact and have not permitted much interaction of the people with the outside world. Push factors could only motivate outmigrants to a very limited extent. Consequently, the district has in the past remained economically backward, rurally stagnated, socially isolated and cut off from the main streams of modernisation. In the subsequent stage and in recent times, however, the advent of development and planning have facilitated better accessibility conditons, wider linkages and greater interactions of greater amplitude, so stepping up the process of outmigration of the people. As an overwhelming majority of outmigrants left their parents, wives and children at their respective homes, their subsistence and maintenance inevitably necessitate frequent remittances of income from outside. This has led to the pheonomenon of inflow of remittances mainly by way of moneyorders. These remittances canalised chiefly towards the purchase of consumers' goods rather than producers' goods. In course of time, the structure of demand underwent a change, accentuated further by demonstration or emulation effects in the consumers' behaviour patterns on the one hand and on the other the structure of supply remained more or less static because of the low levels of savings, investments, capital formation, output, income and employment. Increasing demand for consumers' goods without a corresponding increase in producers' goods led to a further increase in demand for moneyorder remittances from still further outmigration of working population, aggravated further by increasing pressure of population and accessibility conditions due to development of transportation. Thus the vicious circle of outmigration→inflow of moneyorder remittances→increasing demand for consumers'→goods without corresponding increase in producers'goods outmigration spirals at every subsequent stage. The increasing spiral as revealed by our analysis is accounted for more by the pull factors than by the push factors. This is especially so in areas within the district which had the initial advantages of urbanisation, infrastructure development, accessibility conditions, interactions and outside contacts of the people and above all the leadership of rural elites equipped with knowledge and information providing motivation for outmigration to the working population.

Identification of Typologies of Development

The analysis of the spatial process at work led us to examine the areal differentiations of the development process leading on to the identification and characterisation of typologies of development within the district. The patwari circles are found to fall in five types by applying the technique of the principal component analysis supplemented by simple composite ranking technique.

The Development Strategy

The foregoing analysis has focussed in detail the spatial processes operating in the district economy and in turn in the Hill region as a whole. The development strategy for the Hill region, as it emerges from this study is as follows. The most important consideration is the physical planning of landuses in accordance with the drainage and topographical conditions. The recent legislation of the Government of Uttar Pradesh banning the felling of trees for the next ten years in the Hill region following from the "Chipko" movement could as well be the first in this direction. Afforestation of slopes subject to erosion would be a complementary step. Some of the lands not suitable for tilling could be brought under grassland and horticulture to supplement the meagre income from agriculture. Gul practice of irrigation offers scope for bringing more area under irrigation. For this purpose there is a need to map out the spatial distribution of cultivated lands and to prepare a water use plan tapping minor drainage channels. The strategy of small watershed planning envisaged by the Planning Commission as a strategy in integrated environment with development should be applied in selected areas. This is particularly suited to the area because of the small and scattered nature of the settlements. Such a strategy would also form the basis for stabilising the local population. The region's resource base does provide some insight into the setting of industrial and other activities. The experiences of Himachal Pradesh since becoming a separate state would be of help in preparing such a dvelopment framework in quantitative terms. The two situations though not comparable as between the preparation of a development plan for a state and of a sub-region within a state are similar in so far as the regional structure and development norms are concerned. The concept of a spatial organisation based on nodality has a limited application even where it is applicable as for instance in integrated development of land use, settlements and economic activities in the Bhaber area and in the elongated stretch linking Kotdwara, Lansdowne, Pauri, Srinagar, Rudraprayag etc. It has to be made complementary to the dispersed pattern of development aimed at providing certain minimum levels of facilities and activities to support the livelihood of the local population dwelling in small and scattered hamlets.

APPENDICES

Appendix I

List of Patwari Circles Containing their Geographical Area, Population and the Number of Settlements.

Code No. (as in Figure 1)	Name of the Patwari Circle	Geog. Area (Km.^{2})	Population (1971)	Number of settlements		
				Inhabited	Uninhabited	Total
(1)	(2)	(3)	(4)	(5)	(6)	(7)
1	Dhanpur I	16.33	3,926	21	-	21
2	Dhanpur II	21.35	3,924	16	2	18
3	Bachhansyun I	10.71	2,663	14	1	15
4	Bachhansyun II	9.69	3,130	23	3	26
5	Bachhansyun III	12.86	3,801	31	-	31
6	Chalansyun I	12.20	2,999	20	6	26
7	Chalansyun II	16.87	3,016	27	-	27
8	Chalansyun III	20.05	3,287	30	6	36
9	Kandarsyun I	18.09	2,885	14	3	17
10	Kandarsyun II	8.55	2,557	19	-	19
11	Kandarsyun III	9.36	2,547	14	3	17
12	Kandarsyun IV	11.23	2,521	15	1	16
13	Dhaijuli I	14.86	2,711	14	1	15
14	Dhaijuli II	6.33	3,209	16	1	17
15	Dhaijuli III	11.60	3,075	12	2	14
16	Chauthan I	19.49	3,310	21	4	25
17	Chauthan II	11.28	1,663	15	4	19
18	Chauthan III	21.51	3,044	27	1	28
19	Choprakot I	21.15	2,422	10	1	11
20	Choprakot II	15.54	2,955	10	-	10
21	Choprakot III	15.17	3,133	15	1	16
22	Balikandarsyun I	16.56	2,327	15	2	17
23	Balikandarsyun II	13.78	3,226	19	-	19
24	Balikandarsyun III	17.83	3,806	16	-	16
25	Ghurdorsyun III	12.54	4,367	21	4	25
26	Ghurdorsyun IV	11.02	3,176	14	1	15
27	Ghurdorsyun Bidolsyun I	24.00	3,514	11	2	13
28	Ghurdorsyun Bidolsyun II	17.19	3,923	21	-	21
29	Katulsyun I	15.59	4,175	29	4	33
30	Katulsyun II	18.29	3,471	19	5	24
31	Nandalsyun I	1.78	315	7	-	7

32	Nandalsyun II	9.07	3,239	32	4	36
33	Edwalsyun I	20.61	3,253	23	12	35
34	Edwalsyun II	13.27	2,483	25	2	27
35	Edwalsyun III	8.82	2,210	16	3	19
36	Rawatsyun Bangarhsyun I	12.45	3,691	42	6	48
37	Bangarhsyun II	11.67	2,042	15	3	18
38	Bangarhsyun III	20.57	2,398	25	3	28
39	Kandwalsyun I	19.30	3,815	26	9	35
40	Kandwalsyun II	16.52	3,329	23	5	28
41	Sitonsyun I	9.70	2,585	15	6	21
42	Sitonsyun II	6.75	1,814	8	-	8
43	Sitonsyun III	10.90	1,959	12	1	13
44	Sitonsyun IV	8.19	1,925	15	1	16
45	Banelsyun I	10.83	1,829	17	6	23
46	Banelsyun II	30.42	2,730	22	6	28
47	West Maniyarsyun I	23.02	3,085	29	5	34
48	West Maniyarsyun II	20.28	3,020	27	6	33
49	East Maniyarsyun I	18.27	2,667	19	6	25
50	East Maniyarsyun II	16.71	2,773	19	1	20
51	Gagwarsyun I	9.68	2,297	8	4	12
52	Gagwarsyun II	9.07	2,224	10	3	13
53	Gagwarsyun III	14.62	1,670	8	3	11
54	Gagwarsyun IV	11.80	1,905	13	-	13
55	Gagwarsyun Patwalsyun V	11.59	2,406	7	-	7
56	Aswalsyun I	17.40	2,123	15	5	20
57	Aswalsyun II	8.80	2,479	16	1	17
58	Aswalsyun III	18.08	2,874	19	8	27
59	Aswalsyun IV	16.29	2,812	25	2	27
60	Paidulsyun I	11.77	2,588	10	1	11
61	Paidulsyun II	10.25	2,974	14	3	17
62	Paidulsyun III	13.16	3,659	14	5	19
63	Paidulsyun IV	18.24	3,584	14	2	16
64	Kapolsyun I	14.08	3,112	23	4	27
65	Kapolsyun II	16.26	3,673	29	-	29
66	Kapolsyun Khatsyun III	17.93	3,834	16	2	18
67	Mawalsyun I	6.22	3,279	20	5	25
68	Mawalsyun II	5.92	2,678	23	6	29
69	Mawalsyun III	5.71	2,958	16	5	21
70	Ringwarsyun	5.68	3,262	18	6	24
71	Jaintolsyun	10.24	2,290	19	3	22
72	North Maundarsyun I	13.34	2,605	19	3	22
73	North Maundarsyun II	7.66	2,097	15	7	22
74	South Maundarsyun I	6.66	1,697	15	1	16
75	South Maundarsyun II	8.67	1,919	15	-	15

76	South Maundar-syun III	8.67	2,009	15	-	15
77	Gurarsyun I	12.10	2,429	17	1	18
78	Gurarsyun II	8.38	2,138	20	2	22
79	Gurarsyun III	14.83	2,627	20	-	20
80	Kimgadigad I	8.76	5,109	14	-	14
81	Kimgadigad II	15.76	2,803	14	1	15
82	Pingla Pakha	2.76	2,558	17	1	18
83	Saindhar	11.50	2,270	12	1	13
84	Talain I	9.85	2,082	19	-	19
85	Talain II	9.72	3,359	18	-	18
86	Talain III	7.61	2,761	17	8	25
87	Kolagad	19.73	4,031	26	1	27
88	Sabli I	12.25	4,018	12	-	12
89	Sabli II	11.58	3,145	10	-	10
90	Sabli III	8.97	2,044	8	1	9
91	Sabli IV	3.20	2,366	13	-	13
92	Sabli V	13.28	2,604	18	-	18
93	Bangarsyun	10.50	3,532	24	2	26
94	Dhoundiyalsyun I	21.18	2,436	13	3	16
95	Dhoundiyalsyun II	5.65	2,303	19	6	25
96	Meldhar	11.26	2,015	15	2	17
97	Khatli Palla I	16.46	4,136	20	1	21
98	Khatli Palla II	14.31	5,252	21	-	21
99	Khatli Palla III	21.55	3,541	23	-	23
100	Khatli Walla I	6.78	2,061	14	2	16
101	Khatli Walla II	8.62	2,350	13	-	13
102	Khatli Walla III	11.90	3,335	14	-	14
103	Iriyakot Malla I	13.65	2,786	18	-	18
104	Iriyakot Malla II	9.69	2,719	18	1	19
105	Iriyakot Malla III	16.45	3,284	17	-	17
106	Badalpur Malla I	12.43	2,561	18	5	23
107	Badalpur Malla II	16.28	1,944	15	4	19
108	Badalpur Malla III	11.27	3,827	27	1	28
109	Badalpur Bichla I	9.50	3,573	16	2	18
110	Badalpur Bichla II	20.30	3,044	16	-	16
111	Badalpur Bichla III	30.49	3,409	25	-	25
112	Paino I	16.91	2,362	25	3	28
113	Paino II	27.48	3,273	26	-	26
114	Paino III	32.16	3,286	21	2	23
115	Gujru I	13.63	2,546	20	-	20
116	Gujru II	14.29	3,147	25	-	25
117	Gujru III	8.43	2,112	33	3	36
118	Gujru IV	11.10	1,666	21	-	21
119	Iriyakot Talla I	21.30	3,420	18	-	18
120	Iriyakot Talla II	20.45	3,121	18	1	19
121	Iriyakot Talla III	20.48	2,168	17	2	19
122	Bijlot I	14.29	1,965	14	-	14

123	Bijlot II	16.84	2,413	21	1	22
124	Bijlot III	12.93	2,635	16	-	16
125	Bungi I	23.91	2,799	30	3	33
126	Bungi II	19.22	2,021	31	1	32
127	Bungi III	21.82	2,728	30	-	30
128	Badalpur Talla I	17.13	3,061	31	-	31
129	Badalpur Talla II	18.64	2,768	25	6	31
130	Badalpur Talla III	45.58	4,557	33	3	36
131	Seela I	11.59	3,750	44	8	52
132	Seela II	17.71	3,433	43	4	47
133	Seela III	19.11	2,258	22	1	23
134	Kaudiya I	10.63	3,203	22	2	24
135	Kaudiya II	13.79	3,344	21	1	22
136	Kaudiya III	17.14	3,012	22	-	22
137	Langoor Walla I	7.51	2,645	25	-	25
138	Langoor Walla II	19.55	2,510	20	1	21
139	Langoor Walla III	7.85	2,958	13	-	13
140	Langoor Palla I	9.33	2,973	24	1	25
141	Langoor Palla II	16.73	3,104	21	2	23
142	Langoor Palla III	20.36	3,552	22	1	23
143	Dabralsyun I	4.93	2,262	16	2	18
144	Dabralsyun II	5.27	2,469	13	-	13
145	Dabralsyun III	15.24	2,861	16	-	16
146	Dhangu Malla I	16.76	2,750	14	-	14
147	Dhangu Malla II	22.47	2,848	14	-	14
148	Dhangu Bichla I	33.65	2,449	12	-	12
149	Dhangu Bichla II	21.36	2,700	17	-	17
150	Dhangu Talla I	24.73	2,079	11	-	11
151	Dhangu Talla II	15.06	2,153	16	-	16
152	Udaipur Malla I	27.07	2,818	18	2	20
153	Udaipur Malla II	31.02	3,083	22	3	25
154	Udaipur Talla I	23.25	5,211	23	-	23
155	Udaipur Talla II	30.55	2,600	18	-	18
156	Udaipur Walla I	17.45	3,174	22	-	22
157	Udaipur Walla II	17.25	2,930	28	4	32
158	Udaipur Walla III	23.26	2,763	21	-	21
159	Udaipur Palla I	29.36	2,374	24	2	26
160	Udaipur Palla II	29.27	3,355	21	1	22
161	Ajmer Walla I	29.77	3,391	19	1	20
162	Ajmer Walla II	29.65	2,639	21	-	21
163	Ajmer Walla III	17.45	3,097	23	1	24
164	Ajmer Palla I	28.95	3,213	17	2	19
165	Ajmer Palla II	22.54	2,405	18	-	18
166	Sukhrao	11.66	7,458	13	-	13
167	Saneh	8.02	19,267*	18	-	18
168	Mota Dhak	9.90	5,392	14	-	14
169	Haldukhata	12.42	6,811	30	1	31

*inclusive of Kalagarh

Appendix II

Village Schedule

IDENTIFICATION

(a) Village .... (b) Block ....
(c) Patwari Circle .... (d) Kanungo Cirlce ....
(e) District .... (f) Area (sq. Kms.) ....
(g) Height above sea level ....

Q.1. Population

Age Range	Males	Females	Total
0 - 9			
10 - 19			
20 - 29			
30 - 39			
40 - 49			
50 - 59			
60 - 69			
70 +			
ALL RANGES			

Q.2. Occupation

CATEGORIES	Age 0-14	Ranges 15-34	35-59	60 +
(a) Primary Sector				
(i) Cultivators				
(ii) Agricultural Labourer				
(iii) Mining, Forestry etc.				
(b) Secondary Sector				
(i) Household Industry				
(ii) Manufacturing				
(iii) Construction				

(c) Services Sector

(i) Trade & Commerce
(ii) Transport, Storage etc.
(iii) Other services

All Categories

Q.3. No. of Literates

Literates	Male	Female	Total
(i) Literates without educational level.			
(ii) Primary or Junior Basic level.			
(iii) High School/Higher Secondary level.			
(iv) University Degree or Postgraduate level.			
(v) Technical and others			
ALL CATEGORIES			

AGRICULTURE

Q.4. What are the important crops grown in the village?

0.5. Agriculture Calendar

S.No.	Crops	Time grown	Months when they occur		
			Sowing	Harvesting	Marketing
1.					
2.					
3.					
4.					
5.					
6.					
7.					
8.					
9.					
10.					
11.					
12.					
13.					
14.					
15.					

Q.6. Are irrigation facilities available? Yes/No.

(i) If Yes, mention the sources: 1. Canals 2. Guls 3. Fountain 4. Tank 5. Others 6. Reservoir

(ii) If not, mention the reasons:
1. Lack of water source.
2. Government's neglect.
3. Lack of people's consciousness.
4. Others.

Q.7. What are the Agricultural Financial Institutions in the village?
1. Moneylenders
2. Co-operative Society
3. Both
4. Any other

(i) What rates of interest do they charge?

(ii) Is debt servicing satisfactory? Yes/No

(iii) If not, what are the main defects?
1. Lack of funds.
2. Lack of management skills.
3. Public neglect.
4. Government's apathetic attitude.

Q.8. Are the following available in the village?

(i) Seed Stores Yes/No.

(ii) Co-operative Store Yes/No.

(iii) Fertilizer Depot Yes/No.

Q.9. Accessibilities to services and amenities:

(A) Administrative, Educational, Medical facilities etc.

Facilities	Within Village	Between 1-3 Km.	Between 3-5 Km.	Between 5-10 Km.	Above 10 Km.
(1)	(2)	(3)	(4)	(5)	(6)
(1) Administrative					
(i) District Headquarter					
(ii) Block Headquarter					
(iii) Tahsil Headquarter					
(iv) Kanungo Circle Headquarter					

(1)	(2)	(3)	(4)	(5)	(6)
(v) Patwari Circle Headquarter					
(vi) Police Station					
(2) Educational					
(i) Primary School					
(ii) Middle School					
(iii) High School/ Inter-mediate College					
(iv) College					
(3) Medical					
(i) Hospital					
(ii) Dispensary					
(iii) Maternity & Child Welfare Centre					
(iv) Health Centre					
(v) Family Planning Centre					
(4) Postal					
(i) Branch Post Office					
(ii) Sub-Post Office					
(iii) Bank					
(5) Livestock					
(i) Veterinary Hospital					
(ii) Stockman Centre					
(iii) Artificial Insemination Centre					

(B) Shops

Name of the shop	No. of shops	If outside the village, its location in order of preference	
(i) Grocer	.....	1.	2. .....
(ii) Tea	.....	1.	2. .....
(iii) Utensils	.....	1.	2. .....
(iv) Clothing	.....	1.	2. .....
(v) Tailoring	.....	1.	2. .....
(vi) Haircut	.....	1.	2. .....
(vii) Medicine	.....	1.	2. .....
(viii) Others (specify)	.....	1.	2. .....

(C) Small Industrial Establishments

Name of the Establishment	No. of Establishments	If outside the village, its location in order of preference	
(i) Flour Mills	.....	1.	2. .....
(ii) Oil Press	.....	1.	2. .....
(iii) Potteries	.....	1.	2. .....
(iv) Shoe making	.....	1.	2. .....
(v) Blacksmith	.....	1.	2. .....
(vi) Carpentry	.....	1.	2. .....
(vii) Khadi	.....	1.	2. .....
(viii) Others (specify)	.....	1.	2. .....

<u>Q.10 Felt Needs of the villagers</u>

(1) What are the felt needs of the villagers?

1. ....
2. ....
3. ....
4. ....
5. ....
6. ....

(2) Accessibility to felt needs.

	Felt needs	Within village	1-2 Km.	2-3 Km.	Above 3 Kms.
1.	Drinking water				
2.	Fuel				
3.	Grass and Fodder				
4.	Timberwood				
5.	Transport				
6.	Others				
7.	....				
8.	....				

(3) What are the problems connected with the accessibility of felt needs.

Facilities	Available in the village	If not, places and frequency of visit					
		Ist Preference			2nd Preference		
		Place	Distance	Frequence	Place	Distance	Frequence
1. Hospital/ Dispensary							
2. Maternity & Child Welfare							
3. Family Planning/Health Centre							
4. Transport & Communication							
5. Educational							
6. Postal							
7. Veterinary							
8.							
9.							
10.							
11.							
12.							

Q.11. Marketing

Items		Local	Outside (name of the place)
(1)	Commodities sold	1.	
		2.	
		3.	
		4.	
(2)	Commodities purchased	1.	
		2.	
		3.	
		4.	

(3) What are the villages which are dependent on your village for various transactions?
1. ......
2. ......

(4) What are the villages on which your village depends on others?
1. ......
2. ......

Q.12. Social Problems

(1) Is village community socially stratified? Yes/No

(2) If yes, what are the stratified groups?
1. Brahmins
2. Rajputs
3. Scheduled Caste
4. Any others

(3) Does caste discrimination persist among different caste groups? Yes/No

(4) What is the position of Scheduled Castes among different groups?
1. Better off
2. At par
3. Worse off

(5) What is the social status of women in the village community

1. Superior
2. At par
3. Inferior

(6) Is there equitable division of labour between sexes? Yes/No

(7) Is there any change in social and cultural conditions of village community?

Q.13. Is there any change in consumption pattern in both agricultural inputs and items of personal consumption?

Q.14. Is there any change in cropping pattern, yields and agricultural practices?

Q.15. Is there any change in transportation and communication?

Q.16. What are the developments in the villages? Since when they have taken place?

Q.17. What are the development problems of your village?

Household Questionnaire

1. Particulars of Sample Villages:

   Block -
   Kanungo Circle -
   Patwari Circle -

2. Name of the Head of the family/others. If others, respondent's relationship to the Head of the family.

3. Composition of the Household:

S.No.	Members of the Household and their relationship	Sex	Marital status	Age	Occupation		
					Agri.	Industry	Service
1.							
2.							
3.							
4.							
5.							
6.							
7.							
8.							
9.							
10.							
11.							
12.							

Q.1. : Agriculture and allied activities

S.No.	Particulars	Area in local units(specify)		
		Irrigated	Unirrigated	Total
A.	Net Area cultivated			
B.	From the Total area of holding:			
	(i) Owned			
	(ii) Leased in (specify)			
	(iii) Uncultivated			
C.	(i) Area under Kharif crop			
	(ii) Area under Rabi crop			
	(iii) Area under other crops			
	Gross Area i+ii+iii			
	Area under Plantation			
	Area under Forest			

Q.2 : Did you or any member of your house lease out/rent out any land?

If yes,
Area in local units.

Q.3 : Source of Irrigation

Source and means of irrigation	1974-75	1975-76	1976-77
(i) Canal			
(ii) Gul System			
(iii) Others			

Q.4 : Development

S.No.	Particulars	1974-75	1975-76	1976-77
(i)	Area under improved seeds			
(ii)	Quantity of Fertilizer distributed			
(iii)	Area under Fertilizers			
(iv)	No. of improved implements			

Q.5 : Livestocks

Animal	No.	Value in Rs.	Purchased		Sold		Total Exp-enses of gra-zing	Veteri-nary
			No.	Value in Rs.	No.	Value in Rs.		
(1)	(2)	(3)	(4)	(5)	(6)	(7)	(8)	(9)
Bulls								
He Buffalloes								
Bullocks								
Cows								
She Buffalloes								
Sheep								
Goats								
Horse/ponies								
Others (specify)								

Q.6 : Agriculture Production - Crops (Kharif)

Particulars	Crops							Total
(1)	(2)	(3)	(4)	(5)	(6)	(7)	(8)	(9)
A. Name of variety of crops								
B. Total Area								
(i) Irrigated								
(ii) Unirrigated								
C. Total Quantity produced.								
(i) Irrigated								
(ii) Unirrigated								
D. Average Yield per Hect.								
(i) Irrigated								
(ii) Unirrigated								
E. Total Quantity sold								
F. Price per local Unit Rs.								
G. Total Quantity sold X F								
H. Total Quantity of bye products produced								
I. Value of bye products sold in Rs.								
J. Total Quantity of product and bye-products (Rs.)								
K. Operational Expenses due to								
(i) Seeds								
(ii) Manures								
(iii) Fertilizer								
(iv) Repairs/ Maintenance								
(v) Labour charges								
(vi) Water charges								
L. Total								

Income from Kharif Crop = J. - L.

Q.7 : Agriculture Production - Crops (Rabi)

Particulars	Crops							Total
(1)	(2)	(3)	(4)	(5)	(6)	(7)	(8)	(9)
A. Name of variety of crops								
B. Total Area								
(i) Irrigated								
(ii) Unirrigated								
C. Total Quantity produced.								
(i) Irrigated								
(ii) Unirrigated								
D. Average Yield per Hect.								
(i) Irrigated								
(ii) Unirrigated								
E. Total Quantity sold								
F. Price per local Unit Rs.								
G. Total Quantity sold X F								
H. Total Quantity of bye products produced								
I. Value of bye products sold in Rs.								
J. Total Quantity of products and bye-products Rs.								
K. Operational Expenses due to								
(i) Seeds								
(ii) Manures								
(iii) Fertilizer								
(iv) Repairs/ Maintenance								
(v) Labour charges								
(vi) Water charges								
L. Total								

Income from Rabi Crop = J. - L.

Q.8 : Vegetables/Fruits/Plantations

Items	Vegetables	Fruits	Plantation	Total
(1)	(2)	(3)	(4)	(5)
A. Vegetables/Fruits/Plantation crops by growth (specify)				
B. Total area in local units or number of trees				
(i) Irrigated				
(ii) Unirrigated				
C. Value of Quantity sold (at sale price)				
D. Value of quantity retained (at harvest price)				
E. Value of product of plantation crop sold				
F. Value of bye-product retained (at harvest price)				
G. Total value of product and bye-product produced C+D+E+F				
H. Total Operating Expenses				
I. Income from Vegetables/ Fruits/Plantation (G - H)				

Q.9 : Receipts from livestock & poultry

Items	Quantity/No. produced	Sold	Consumed	Total (3+4)
(1)	(2)	(3)	(4)	(5)
(i) Milk				
(ii) Milk product (Ghee etc.)				
(iii) Meat				
(iv) Skin				
(v) Wool				
(vi) Eggs				
(vii) Others				

Income from Livestock/poultry = Q.9 col.5 - Q.5 col.6

Q.10 : Income from other sources

Details	Amount received	Remarks
Salaries		
Wages		
Pension		
Rent of land/building		
Others		

Q.11 : Summary of Income from Agriculture and Allied Activities from -

(i)	Kharif Crop	Q.6
(ii)	Rabi Crop	Q.7
(iii)	Vegetables/Fruits/Plantation	Q.8
(iv)	Livestock	Q.9 col.5 - Q.5 col.8

Q.12 : Borrowing

Source	Amount Borrowed		Amount repaid	
	Principal	Interest	Principal	Interest
1.				
2.				
3.				

Q.13 : Lending

Source	Amount lent		Amount got back	
	Principal	Interest	Principal	Interest
1.				
2.				
3.				

Q.14 : Consumer Expenditure

Items	Monthly Average				Amount (Rs.)
	Total		Home produced		
	Qty.	Value Rs.	Qty.	Value Rs.	
(1)	(2)	(3)	(4)	(5)	(6)
A. Food Items					
Rice					
Wheat					
Maize					
Pulses					
Oil					
Milk					
Milk Product					
Sugar					
Spices					
Veg. & Fruits					
Meat					
Fish					
Egg					
Pan, Tobacco, Bidi etc.					
Others					
Total Food Items					
B. Non-Food Items					
Fuel & Lighting					
Clothing					
Footwear					
Toilet					
Education					
Medicine					
Services (barber, dhobi)					
Conveyances					
Entertainment					
Total Non-Food Items					
C. Others					
Marriages					
Religious					
Functions					
Unexpected travel					
Total					
Grand Total A+B+C					

Q.15 : Outmigration Pattern

1. Has any of the members of your family migrated outside the village? Yes/No
   If yes,

   Number of migrants. ....

2. Year of outmigration.

3. Give the following details:

S.No.	Place of outmigration	Occupation	No. of dependents at his home place	No. of dependents at his place of work	Reasons of out-migration
1.					
2.					
3.					
4.					
5.					

3. Income & Remittances
   (a) Average annual income of the outmigrant(s). Rs. .....

   (b) Average annual remittances

Mode	Value
Moneyorder	Rs. .....
Insured Posts	Rs. .....
Relatives/ Friends	Rs. .....
Others	Rs. .....
Total	

   (c) Frequency of remittances
   (i) Monthly
   (ii) Quarterly
   (iii) Half-Yearly
   (iv) Yearly

   (d) Purposes of remittances
   (i) ......
   (ii) ......
   (iii) ......
   (iv) ......
   (v) ......

4. Does he frequently visit the home place? (a) Yes/No.

(b) If yes, the frequency of visits in a year. (b) ......

(c) Reasons of visits. (c)
1. ......
2. ......
3. ......
4. ......
5. ......

(d) If no visits, reasons (d)
1. ......
2. ......
3. ......
4. ......
5. ......

(e) Has he acquired any property? Yes/No.

(i) Outside the village,
(ii) If yes, nature of property
1. ......
2. ......
3. ......
4. ......
5. ......

Q.16 : Objective Questions

(1) As compared to your earlier conditions of living 10 years back, how do you feel about your present conditions.
1. Better off
2. Same
3. Worse off

(2) Do you agree that your village is backward?
1. Agree
2. Not agree

(3) If yes, what are the causes of backwardness?
1. ......
2. ......
3. ......
4. ......
5. ......

(4) What suggestion would you give to remove the backwardness?
1. ......
2. ......
3. ......
4. ......
5. ......

(5) Do you agree that during the last 30 years no progress has been made by your village under the impact of Five-Year Plans?

1. Agree
2. Not agree

(6) If No, what lapses have been responsible in the implementation of Five-Year Plans by the Government?

(7) What are the main developments in the village? Since when they have taken place?

(8) What are the development problems of your village?

Bibliography

Abel, Martin E. and Easter, K. William: "Agricultural Planning and Programme - Evaluation - Focus on Regional Restraints;" **Economic & Political Weekly,** July 1971, pp.1572-1596.

Baer, Warner: "Regional Inequality and Economic Growth in Brazil"; **Economic Development and Cultural Change,** Vol.XII, April, 1964, pp.268-285.

Balakrishna, R.: "Limitations of the Deductive Theory of Industrial Location"; **Indian Journal of Economics,** October, 1946, pp.117-121.

Benjamin, Higgins: "The Dualistic Theory of Underdeveloped Areas"; **Economic Development and Cultural Change,** No.4, January, 1956, pp.99-115.

Berry, B.J.L. and Garrison, W.L.: "The Functional Basis of Central Place Hierarchy": **Economic Geography,** Vol.34, 1958, pp.145-154.

Berry, Brien J.L.: **Geography of Market Centres and Retail Distribution,** Prentice Hall, Inc. Englewood Cliffs, NJ. 1967.

Bhargava, Gopal: "Scope, Objective and Strategy of Regional Planning for India": **A.I.C.C. Economic Review,** June 1, 1966, pp.32-38.

Bhat, L.S.: **Regional Planning in India,** Statistical Publishing Society, Calcutta, 1972.

Bhat, L.S. et.al.: **Micro Level Planning,** K.B. Publications, New Delhi, 1976.

Bhatia, Shyam S.: "Changes in Cropping Pattern - A Study of Uttar Pradesh"; **Economic Weekly,** August, 1963, pp. 1413-1424.

Bhattacharyya, A.N.: "Effect of Tribal and Caste Factor on Rural Settlements in U.P."; **Indian Geographical Journal,** Vol.31, Nos. 3 & 4, 1956, pp.94-102.

Blaut, J.M.: "Micro-geographic Sampling : Quantitative Approach to Regional Agriculture Geography"; **Economic Geography,** Vol. 35, 1959, pp.79-88.

Blunt, E.A.H.: **The Caste System of Northern India;** Oxford University Press, London, 1931.

Boudeville, J.R.: **Problems of Regional Planning,** Edinburg, 1966.

Brahme, S.: "Approach to Rural Area Development"; **Indian Journal of Regional Science;** Vol.IV, No.1, 1972, pp.6-11.

Christaller, W.: **Central Places in the Southern Germany;** (Translated by C.W. Baskin), Prentice Hall, Englewood Cliffs, New Jersey, 1966.

Cohen, R.L.: **Economics of Agriculture,** James Nishet & Co., London, 1954.

Cunningham, A.: **The Ancient Geography of India,** Indological Book House, Varanasi, 1963.

Dale, E. Herman: "The Population Question in N.E. Brazil; Its Economic and Idealogical Dimensions"; **Economic Development and Cultural Change;** Vol.18, No.4, July, 1970, pp.536-574.

Dalton, G.: "Traditional Production in Primitive African Economies", **Quarterly Journal of Economics;** Vol.76, No.3, 1962, pp.361-378.

Darwent, D.F.: "Growth Poles and Growth Centres in Regional Planning - A Review"; **Environment and Planning;** No.1, 1969.

Dasgupta, Biplab: "Socio-economic Classification of Districts; A Statistical Approach"; **Economic & Political Weekly,** Vol. VI, No.33, 1971, pp.1763-1774.

Deshpande, C.D., Bhat, L.S. and Arunachalam, B.: **Impact of Metropolitan City on the Surrounding Region;** Concept Publishing Company, New Delhi, 1980.

Drewnowaski, J.: **Social and Economic Factors in Development;** United Nations Research in Social Development (UNRISD), Report No.3, Geneva, 1966.

Dunn, E.S.: **Location of Agriculture Production;** Gainsville, Florida, 1954.

Economic & Statistical Division, Government of Uttar Pradesh: **Statistical Diary,** 1980.

Fox, Karl A.: "The Study of Interaction between Agriculture and Non-Farm Economy"; Local, Regional and National"; **Journal of Farm Economics,** Vol. 44, No.1, February, 1962.

Friedman, John: **Regional Development Policy : A Case Study of Venezuela,** The M.I.T. Press, Combridge, 1966.

Friedman, J. and Alonso, N.: **Regional Development & Planning - A Reader** ; The M.I.T. Press, Cambridge, Mass., 1964.

Friedman, John, R.P.: "The Concept of a Planning Region"; **Land Economics,** Vol.32, No.2, February, 1956, pp.1-13.

Friedman, John R.P.: "Locational Aspects of Economic Development"; **Land Economics,** Vol. 32, No.3, August, 1956, pp.213-227.

Furtado, C.: **Development & Underdevelopment,** Los Angeles, 1967.

Ganseer, A.: **Geology of the Himalayas;** Interscience Publishers, London; A Division of John Wiley & Sons, Ltd., 1964.

Graham, Douglas H.: "Divergent and Convergent Regional Economic Growth and Internal Migration in Brazil - 1940-1960"; **Economic Development and Cultural Change,** Vol.18,

No.3, April, 1970, pp.362-382.

Grigg, D.: "The Logic of Regional Systems"; **Annals of the Association of American Geographers**; Vol.55, No.3, September, 1965, pp.465-491.

Government of Andhra Pradesh: **Planning and Development of Backward Region: A Case Study of Rayalaseema**, Vol.I, Hyderabad, 1971.

Gulati, Leela: "Female Work Participation : A Study of Inter-State Differences"; **Economic and Political Weekly**, January 11, 1975, pp.35-42.

Gulati, Leela: "Female Work Participation : A Study of Inter-State Differences - A Comment"; **Economic and Political Weekly**, June 7, 1975, pp.1215-1218.

Hagerstrand, T.: **Innovation Diffusion as a Spatial Process**; Chicago Press, Chicago, 1967.

Hagget, P. & Chorley, R.J.: **Models in Geography**; Methuen, London, 1967.

Hazari, R.K.: **Industrial Planning and Licensing Policy Final Report**, 1967.

Higgins, Benjamin: **Economic Development**, W.W. Norten Co., New York, 1959.

Hilhorst, J.G.M.: **Regional Development Theory - An Attempt to Synthesize** ; The Hague, 1967.

Hirschman, A.O.: **Strategy of Economic Development**; New Haven, 1969.

Hingorani, B.H.: **Forest Industries in U.P.**; One Hundred Years of Forestry (1861-1961), Lucknow, 1962.

Hoselitz, Bert F.: "Generative and Parasitic Cities," **Economic Development and Cultural Change**; Vol.VIII, No.3, April, 1955, pp.278-294.

Hoselitz, Bert F.: **Sociological Aspects of Economic Growth**; Free Press, New York, 1966.

Indian Society for Agricultural Economics: Readings in Land Utilisation; **Indian Journal of Agricultural Economics**; Bombay, 1957.

Isard, Walter: **Location of Space Economy**, 1956.

Isard, Walter: **Methods of Regional Analysis**, Cambridge, M.I.T. Press, 1962.

Isard, Walter & Cumberland, J.H.: **Regional Economic Planning - Techniques of Analysis for Less Developed Areas** ; Organisation for Economic Co-operation and Development (O.E.C.D.), Paris, 1961.

Jhingran, A.G.: **Himalayan Geology**, Wadia Institute of Himalayan Geology, Delhi, Vol.I, 1971.

Joshi, P.C.: "Economic Pressure in U.P. Village"; **Agricultural Situation in India**, Vol.XVI, No.2, 1961, pp.127-131.

Joshi, P.C.: **Changing Class Structure of Rural U.P.**, An unpublished Doctoral Dissertation, Lucknow University,

Lucknow, 1955.
Klassen, L.H.: **Area, Economic & Social Redevelopment;** Organisation for Economic Co-operation and Development (O.E.C.D.), Paris, 1968.
Klassen, L.H.: **Social Amenities in Area Economic Growth;** Organisation for Economic Co-operation and Development (O.E.C.D.), Paris, 1968.
Krutilla, John V.: "Criteria for Evaluating Regional Development Programme"; **American Economic Review,** Vol.45, May, 1955, pp.1-28.
Lahiri, T.B.: **Balanced Regional Development;** Oxford & I.B.H. Co., Calcutta, 1972.
Leff, Nethaniel, H.: "Economic Development and Regional Inequality: Origins of the Brazilian Case"; **Quarterly Journal of Economics,** Vol.86, May, 1972, pp.255-286.
Leibenstein, Harvey: "The Theory of Underdevelopment in Backward Economies"; **Journal of Political Economy,** April, 1957.
Lewis, Arthur W.: **Development Planning : The Essentials of Economic Policy;** George Allen & Unwin, Ltd., London,1966.
Losch, A.: **The Economics of Location,** New Haven, 1954.
Mckee, D.L.: **Regional Economics - Theory & Practice;** Free Press, New York, 1970.
Mellor, John, W.: "The Process of Agricultural Development in Low Income Countries"; **Journal of Farm Economics,** August, 1962, pp.700-716.
Meyer, John R.: "Regional Economics - A Survey"; **Surveys of Economic Theory - Growth and Development;** Vol.II, St. Martin's Press, New York, 1965.
Misra, S.D.: "Agricultural Geography of Himachal Pradesh"; **Oriental Geographer,** Vol.VII, No.1, 1963.
Misra, S.D.: "Population and Settlements in Himachal Pradesh"; **Deccan Geographer,** Vol.III, No.1, 1965, pp.31-53.
Misra, R.P.: (Ed) **Regional Planning - Concept, Techniques Policies & Case Studies,** Mysore University Press, 1969.
Misra, R.P. **et.al: Regional Development Planning in India - A New Strategy;** Vikas Publishing House, Delhi, 1974.
Mitra, A.: **Levels of Regional Development** ; Census of India, 1961, Vol.I, Part I(i) and (ii), 1965.
Myrdal, Gunnar: **Economic Theory & Underdeveloped Regions;** Gerald Duckworth & Co. Ltd., London, 1957.
Myrdal, Gunnar: **Asian Drama - An Inquiry into the Poverty of Nations;** Penguin, Mass., Vols. I, II, III, 1968.
National Council of Applied Economic Research (N.C.A.E.R.): **Market Towns & Spatial Development in India,** New Delhi, 1965.
N.C.A.E.R.: **Techno-Economic Survey of U.P.,** New Delhi, 1965.
N.C.A.E.R.: **Inter-district and Inter-state Income Differentials,**

Occasional Paper No.6, New Delhi, 1955-56.
North, Douglas C.: "Location Theory and Regional Economic Growth"; **Journal of Political Economy**, Vol. 63, No.3, June, 1955, pp.203-258.
North, Douglas C.: "Agriculture in Regional Economic Growth"; **Journal of Farm Economics**, Vol. 41, No.5, December, 1959, pp.943-951.
Nurkse, Ragnar: **Problems of Capital Formation in Underdeveloped Countries**, Oxford, 1953.
Organisation for Economic Co-operation and Development (O.E.C.D.): **Multidisciplinary Aspects of Regional Development**, Paris, 1969.
O.E.C.D.: **Regional Factor in Economic Development**; Paris, 1970.
O.E.C.D.: **Issues of Regional Policies**, Paris, 1973.
Okun, Bernard and Richardson, R.W.: "Regional Income Inequality and Internal Population Migration"; **Economic Development and Cultural Change**; Vol.9, January, 1961, pp.128-143.
Pal, Indra: "Forest Wealth of U.P."; **The Geographer**, Vol.3, No.1, Aligarh, 1950, pp.16-21.
Pal, M.N. & Subramaniam C.: "Indian Planning: The Need for greater Emphasis on Regional Development"; **A.I.C.C. Economic Review**, Vol. 18, No.3, August, 1966, pp. 33-39.
Pascoe, E.H.: A **Manual of Geology of India**; Government of India Press, Calcutta, Vol.III, 1956.
Perroux, F.: "Economic Space : Theory and Applications"; **Quarterly Journal of Economics**, Vol.64, February, 1950, pp.89-104.
Philbrick, Allen K.: "Principles of Areal Functional Organisation in Regional Human Geography"; **Economic Geography**, Vol.33, No.4, October, 1957, pp.299-336.
Planning Commission, Government of India: **Report of Industrial Licensing Policy Inquiry Committee**, July 1969.
Planning Commision, Government of India: **Five Year Plans** (I to VI).
Planning Commission, Government of India: **Resource, Development Region and Divisions of India**; New Delhi, 1965.
Planning Commission, Government of India: **Regional Variations in Social Development and Levels of Living**, New Delhi, Vol.I & II, 1967.
Planning Commission, Government of India: **Report of the Working Group (N.N.Wanchoo)** to recommend Fiscal and Financial Incentives for starting Industries in Backward Areas, New Delhi, 1969.
Planning Commission, Government of India: **Identification of Backward Areas** - Report of the Working Group (B.D. Pande Group), New Delhi, 1969.
Planning Research & Action Institute, Government of U.P.:

Scheme for the Development of Backward Areas, Lucknow, 1956.

Puri, G.S.: **Indian Forest Ecology,** Volumes I & II, New Delhi, 1960.

Rao, V.L.S.P.: **Regional Planning in India,** Asia Publishing House, Bombay, 1963.

Rao, V.L.S.P.: **Growth Promoting and Growth Retarding Factors in Development - Muzzaffarnagar District - A Case Study ;** R.P.C. Project, Delhi University, 1969.

Rao, V.L.S.P. & Bhat, L.S.: "A Regional Framework for Resource Development;" **Bombay Geographical Magazine,** No. 1, 1962, pp. 35-50.

Raza, Moonis: "Land Forms and Land-use in U.P.", **Geographer** Vol. 15, 1968, pp. 1-15.

Reddy, D. Narasimha: "Female Work Participation: A Reply"; **Economic and Political Weekly,** June 7, 1975, p. 702.

Richardson, Harvey W.: **Regional Economics ;** Weidenfold & Nicolson, London, 1969.

Ronald Abler **et. al.: The Spatial Organisation;** Prentice Hall, Inc. The Englewood Cliffe, New Jersey, 1971.

Rostow, W.W.: **The Process of Economic Growth ;** W.W. Norton Company, Inc., New York, 1953.

Rostow, W.W.: **The Stages of Economic Growth ;** Cambridge, Mass., 1960.

Sāgreya, K.P.: **Forests & Forestry ;** National Book Trust, India, New Delhi, 1967.

Sen, Lalit K.: **Planning Rural Growth Centres for Integrated Area Development;** A Study in Miryalguda Taluq, N.I.C.D., Hyderabad, 1971.

Sen, Lalit K.: **Readings on Micro-level Planning and Rural Growth Centres,** N.I.C.D., Hyderabad, 1972.

Sen, Lalit K. & Mishra, G.K.: **Regional Planning for Rural Electrification - A Case Study of Suryapet Taluq,** Nalgonda District, Andhra Pradesh, N.I.C.D., Hyderabad, 1974.

Sen, Lalit K.: **Growth Centres in Raichur - An Integrated Area Development Plan for a District** in Karnataka, N.I.C.D., Hyderabad, 1975.

Sengupta, P. & Sdasyuk, Galina: **Economic Regionalisation of India - Problems and Approaches,** Census of India, 1961 (Monograph No. 8).

Shafi, M.: "Forests in the National Economy of India", **The Geographer,** Vol. 3, No. 1, December, 1950, pp. 8-15.

Shah, S.M.: "Agriculture Pattern in relation to Irrigation"; **Indian Journal of Agricultural Economics ;** Vol. XVIII, March, 1963, pp. 154-160.

Sharma, A.N.: **Spatial Approach for District Planning;** Concept Publishing Company, New Delhi, 1981.

Sharma, A.N.: "Road network Planning for Rural

Development"—"**Scientific Management of Transport Systems (Ed.)**" by N.K. Jaiswal) ; North Holland Publishing Co., Amsterdam, 1981, pp. 151-160.

Sharma, A.N. & Bhat, D.R.: "Pattern of Urban Development in Karnal District"; **Geographical Viewpoint**, Vol. V, No. 1, 1974, pp. 1-18.

Sharma, P.N.: "Integrated Area Development"; **Economic Times**, November 25, 1975.

Sharma, S.R.: "Conceptual Framework of Regional Planning"; **Economic Weekly**; Vol. XIII, No. 36, September, 1961 pp. 1413-1424.

Singh, Baljit: "Economic Stagnation and Prospects", **Indian Economic Journal**, Vol. VIII, March, 1963, pp. 301-316.

Singh, Daulat **et. al.**: "Dynamics of Integrated Area Development in India", **Indian Journal of Agricultural Economics**, Vol. XXVIII, No. 4, October/November, 1973, pp. 32-38.

Singh, R.L.: **India - A Regional Geography** (Ed.); National Geographical Society of India, Varanasi, 1971.

Sinha, J.N.: "Female Work Participation - A Comment"; **Economic and Political Weekly**, April 1975, pp. 672-674.

Sinha, J.N.: "Rational View of Census Economic Data"; **Indian Journal of Industrial Relations**; October, 1972, pp. 126-139.

Spate, O.H.K, and Learmonth, A.T.A., **Indian & Pakistan**, Methuen, 1967.

Srivastava **et.al.**: **Demographic Trends in India** (Ed.); Sunlight Printers, Delhi, 1975.

Town & Country Planning Organisation (T.C.P.O.), Government of India: **South East Resource Region, India**; New Delhi, 1969.

U.N.O.: **Regional Planning - Report of the Sixth Inter-regional Seminar on Development Planning**; Quito, Ecuader, 1973.

United Nations Research in Social Development (UNRISD): **Regional Development**; A Review of Concepts and Theories of Growth Poles and Growth Centres, Geneva, 1970.

Vender Kroef, J.M.: "Economic Development in Indonesia - Some Social and Cultural Impediments"; **Economic Development and Cultural Change**, No. 4, January, 1956, pp. 116-133.

Wanwali, Sudhir: **Regional Planning for Social Facilities**; An examination of entire plan concepts and their application; A Case Study of Eastern Maharashtra, N.I.C.D., Hyderabad, 1970.

Weaver, John C.: "Crop Combination Regions in the Middle West," **The Geographical Review**, Vol. 44, 1954, pp. 175-200.

Weaver, John C.: "Crop Combination Regions for 1919 and 1929 in the Middle West"; **The Geographical Review**, Vol. 44, 1954, pp. 560-572.

Williamson, Jeffrey G.: "Regional Inequality and the Process of National Development"; **Economic Development and Cultural Change**, Vol. XIII, No. 4, Part II, July, 1965, pp. 3-84.

Yeates, Maurice H.: **An Introduction to Quantitative Analysis in Economic Geography**; McGraw Hill, New York, 1968.

BIBLIOGRAPHY PERTAINING TO STUDY AREA

Anas, M.: "Rural Settlements in the Sub-Himalayan Region"; **Geographer**, Vol. 6, No. 2, 1954, pp. 23-34.

Atkinson, E.T.: **The Himalayan Districts of North West Provinces of India**, Volumes 1 - 3, Goverment Press, Allahabad, 1882, 1884, and 1886.

Atkinson, E.T.: **Economic Mineralogy of the Hill Districts of N.W.P.**, Allahabad, 1882.

Auden, J.B.: Traverses in Himalayas; **Records of Geological Survey of India**, Vol. XIX, 1935.

Auden, J.B.: "The Structure of the Himalayas in Garhwal"; **Records of Geological Survey of India**, Vol. XXI, 1937.

Auden, J.B.: General Report of the Geological Survey of India; **Records of the Geological Survey of India**, Vol. XXIII, 1938.

Backett, J.B.O.: **Report on the Settlement Operations in Garhwal District**; Government Press, Allahabad, 1886.

Batten, J.H.: **Official Report on the Province of Kumaon**; Government Press, Agra, 1841.

Barthwal, M.S.: **Garhwal Mein Kaun Kahan (in Hindi)**; Maya Hindustan Press, New Delhi, 1951.

Berreman, Gerald D.: **Hindus of the Himalayas**, Oxford University Press, Bombay, 1963.

Berreman, Gerald D.: "Caste and Economy in the Himalayas"; **Economic Development and Cultural Change**; Vol. 10, 1962, pp. 386-394.

Berreman, Gerald D.: "Pahari Polyandry - A Comparison"; **American Anthropologist**, Vol. 64, 1962, pp. 326-342.

Bhakt Darshan: **Garhwal Ki Diwangat Vibhutian** (in Hindi); Saraswati Press, Dehradun, 1980.

Bhatnagar, P.P.: **Census Handbook Garhwal District - 1961**; Superintendent, Printing and Stationery, Allahabad, 1966.

Bhat, Hari Datt: **Garhwali Bhasha Aur Uska Sahitya** (in Hindi), Hindi Samiti, Government of U.P.; Lucknow, 1976.

Blunt, E.A.H.: **Census of India. 1911**, Vol. 15, Part I, Government Press, Allahabad, 1912.

Board of Revenue, Government of U.P.: **Agricultural Census in U.P.**, 1970-71.

Bose, S.C.: **Land and People of the Himalayas**; Indian Publications, Calcutta, 1968.

Bose, S.C.: "Nomadism in High Valleys in Uttarakhand and Kumaon; **Geographical Review of India**, Vol. XXII, September, 1960, pp. 34-39.

Bose, S.C.: "Some Geomorphological features near Kedarnath and Badrinath"; **Geographical Review of India**, Vol. XII, No. 3,

1960, pp. 17-26.

Bose, S.C.: "Optimum belt in Western Himalayas"; **The Decan Geographer**, Vol. II, No. 1, July, 1966.

Bryant, T.B.: **Working Plan for Forests of Kumaon and Garhwal Forest Divisions**, 1896.

Budhi Sagar: **Kurmanchal Kahawatein** (in Hindi); An unpublished Doctoral Dissertation, Lucknow University, 1964.

Burn, R.: **Census of India, 1901**, Vol. 16, Part I, Government Press, Allahabad, 1902.

Burrard, S.G. & Hayden, H.H.: "A Sketch of the Geography and Geology of the Himalayan Mountains and Tibet," Part IV; **The Geology of the Himalayas**, Government of India Press, Calcutta, 1907.

Corbett, Jim: **Man Eaters of Kumaon**; Oxford University Press, New York, 1946.

Corbett, Jim: **Man Eating Leopard of Rudraprayag**; Oxford University Press, London, 1953.

Dabral, M.P.: **Land Utilisation in Garhwal Himalayas**; An unpublished Ph.D. Thesis, Vikram University, Ujjain, 1970.

Dabral, S.P.: **Uttarakhand Ke Bhotantik** (in Hindi); Veergatha Publications, Dogadda, Garhwal, 1964.

Dabral, S.P.: **Alaknanda Upatyaka** (in Hindi); Veergatha Publications, Dogadda, Garhwal, 1964.

Dabral, S.P.: **Shepherds and Graziers of Uttarakhand** (in Hindi); Veergatha Publications, Dogadda, Garhwal, 1965.

Dabral, S.P.: **Uttarakhand Ka Itihas** (in Hindi); Veergatha Publications, Dogadda, Garhwal, Volumes 1 to 8, 1966-76.

Day, H.C.: **Forest Administration in Kumaon**; One Hundred Years of Forestry (1861-1961), Lucknow, 1962.

Dhoundiyal, S.P.: **The Economic Life of Garhwal**; An unpublished Doctoral Dissertation, Agra University, Agra, 1945.

Dhyani, R.P.: **Economic Problems & Planning of Garhwal Himalayas** (in Hindi); Arvind Press, Kotdwara, Garhwal, 1974.

Dobhal, G.L.: **Pauri Garhwal - A Regional Study**; An unpublished M.Phil. Dissertation, Centre for the Study of Regional Development, School of Social Sciences, Jawaharlal Nehru University, New Delhi, 1972.

Dobhal G.L.: "Moneyorder Remittances and Outmigration - A Case Study of Pauri Garhwal District"; **Annals of the National Association of Geographers, India**, Vol. I, No. 2, December, 1981, pp. 75-97.

Eyde, E.H.H.: **The Depressed Classes of the Kumaon Hills**: Census of India, 1921, Vol. 16, Part I, Appendix C, Government Press, Allahabad, 1923.

Gairola, T.D.: "The Castes and Sub-castes in Garhwal"; **Journal of U.P. Historical Society**, Lucknow, Vol. 15, 1922, pp. 41-64.

Government of India: "Development of Tribal Areas in the Hill Districts of North-Western U.P."; **Journal of Lal Bahadur Shastri National Academy of Administration**, Mussoorie, Vol. XX, No. 2, 1975.

Government of U.P.: **Schemes for the Development of Backward Areas**, Lucknow, 1958.

Government of U.P.: **Report of the Sub-group on Hills, U.P.**; Working Group for National Commission for Agriculture, 1970.

Grierson, G.A.: **The Linguistic Survey of India**, Vol. 9, Part IV, Government of India Press, Calcutta, 1916.

Himalaya Seva Sangh: **Problems of the Northern Frontiers**; Report of the Discussions at the National Conference on the Himalayas, Himalaya Seva Sangh, Rajghat, Delhi, 1972.

Ibbotson, A.W.: **Pargana Settlement Reports** - Ganga Salan (1928), Talla Salan (1929), Barahasyun (1929), Bhaber (1930), Choundkot (1930), Dewalgarh (1930), Chandpur (1931) and Malla Salan (1931).

Ibbotson, A.W.: **Final Report on the 11th Revenue Settlement of Garhwal District**, Government Press, Allahabad, 1933.

Johri, Pratap Chand: **Tribal Economy in Kumaon**; An unpublished Doctoral Dissertation, Agra University, Agra, 1959.

Joshi, L.D.: **Khas Family Law in Himalayan Districts of U.P.**; Government Press, Allahabad, 1929.

Joshi, S.C.: **Settlement Pattern in Kumaon**; An unpublished Doctoral Dissertation, Agra University, Agra, 1968.

Kanaujia, L.R.S.: "The Terai Region of U.P. - A Study in Human Geography"; **The National Geographer**, Vol. I, No. 1, 1958, pp. 1-10.

Kaushic, S.D.: "Types of Human Settlements in Jaunsar Himalayas"; **Geographical Review of India**, Vol. 21, No. 2, 1959, pp. 1-18.

Kaushic, S.D.: "Human Settlement and Occupational Economy in Garhwal Bhot Himalayas"; **Journal of Asiatic Society**, Calcutta, 1959, pp. 23-42.

Kaushic, S.D.: "Agriculture in the Himalayas"; **National Geographical Journal of India**, Vol. VIII, Part 3-4, 1962, pp. 22-41.

Kaushic, S.D.: "Climatic Zones and their related socio-economy in Garhwal Himalayas"; **Geographical Review of India**; Vol. XXIV, Nos. 3 and 4, 1962, pp. 17-26.

Kaushic, S.D.: "Agriculture in Himalayan Ganga Basin"; **National Geographical Journal of India**; Vol. VIII, Nos. 3 & 4, 1962, pp. 270-283.

Kaushic, S.D.: "A glaciological study of the Garhwal-Kumaon Himalayas"; **Proceedings of National Academy of Sciences, India**, Vol. XXXV, Section B, Part IV, Allahabad, 1965.

Kaushic, S.D.: "Hydro-electric Power Potential in the Himalayan districts of U.P., Himachal and Punjab"; **Agra University Journal of Research**, No. XIII, Part II, 1965, pp. 75-92.

Kaushic, S.D.: "Geomorphological features and their evolution in Uttarkashi-Bhatwari Area of Garhwal Himalayas"; **21st International Geographical Union Congress**, New Delhi, 1968.

Kharkwal, S.C.: "**Land Forms and Settlements in Nainital and its environs;**" An unpublished Doctoral Dissertation, Banaras Hindu University, Varanasi, 1969.

Madhava, Ashish: "Agricultural Economy of Kumaon Hills"; **Economic and Political Weekly**, Vol. XIV, No. 25, June 23, 1979, pp. 1958-1964.

Maithani, B.P.: "Garhwal's Economic Paradox"; **Mainstream**, New Delhi, January, 1971.

Majumdar, D.N.: **Himalayan Polyandry**; Asia Publishing House, Bombay, 1962.

Majumdar, D.N.: "Some aspects of cultural life of the Khasas of the Cis-Himalayan Region"; **Journal of Royal Asiatic Society of Bengal**, Vol. VI, No. 1, 1940, pp. 60-82.

Majumdar, D.N.: "Racial and Serological Survey of U.P.": - **1941 Census : Sankhya**, Vol.IX, 1941.

Majumdar, D.N.: "Racial Composition of the Polyandrous People of Jaunsar Bawar in Dehradun District, U.P.; "**Journal of U.P. Historical Society**, Vol.XVIII, Part II, December, 1940, pp.34-60.

Mathur, R.S.: **Working Plan for the Kalagarh Forest Division**; Western Circle, U.P. (1970-71 to 1979-80), Volumes I and II, Nainital, 1971.

Mountaineer: **A Summer Ramble in the Himalayas (Ed.)**; Hurst & Blackett, London, 1960.

Mukandi Lal: "Garhwal School of Paintings"; **Illustrated Weekly of India**, June 3, 1973.

Naithani, R.C.: **Water Resources in Kumaon**; An unpublished Doctoral Dissertation, Agra University, Agra, 1971.

National Council of Applied Economic Research (N.C.A.E.R.): **Survey of Hilly & Backward Areas of Punjab**; New Delhi, 1966.

National Industries Development Corporation: **Survey of Industrial Programming in Hill Districts of U.P.**; 1969-70.

Nautiyal, Shivananda: **Garhwal Ke Lok Nritya** (in Hindi), Amit Publications, Ghaziabad, 1974.

Negi, B.S.: "The Mineral Resources of the Kumaon and Garhwal"; **Geographical Review of India**. Vol.XXII, No.3, 1960, pp.40-48.

Negi, B.S.. "Soils of Uttarakhand Division of U.P."; **Geographical Observer**, Vol.V, 1969, pp.75-80.

Negi, B.S.: "Agricultural Regions of Garhwal District": **Geographical Observer**, Vol.VI, 1970, pp.27-32.

Negi, B.S.: "Land-use Pattern and Suggestion for Development in

District Garhwal", **The Geographical Observer**, Vol.II, 1971, pp.8-16.

Oaklay, E.S.: **The Holy Himalayas**: Oliphant, Anderson and Ferrier, Edinburg, 1903.

O'smaston, A.E.: **A Forest Flora for Kumaon**; Government Press, U.P., Allahabad, 1935.

Painuli, Paripurnanand: **The Valley of Gods**, Tehri, 1959.

Painuli, Paripurnanand: "Backward Regions: Diagnosis and Remedies"; **Hindustan Times** December 12, 1972.

Pande, B.D.: **Kumaon Ka Itihas** (in Hindi) : Almora Shakti Press, 1937.

Pande, G.C.: **Economy of Kumaon Division - A Field Survey**; An unpublished Doctoral Dissertation, Lucknow University, Lucknow, 1968.

Pande, T.: **Kumaon Ka Lok Sahitya** (in Hindi); Almora Book Depot, Almora, 1962.

Pande, Y.D.: "Agriculture in Nainital and Bhaber"; **Geographical Review of India**, Vol.13, No.2, 1961, pp.19-39.

Pande, Y.D.: "Forest Resources of Kumaon"; **Indian Geographical Journal**, Vol.XXXVI, No.2, April and June 1961, pp.64-80.

Panna Lal: **Hindu Customary Law in Kumaon**; Government Press, Allahabad, 1942.

Pant, M.M.: **Working Plan for the Garhwal Forest Division**; Garhwal Circle, U.P. (1971-72 to 1980-81), Volumes I & II, Nainital, 1971.

Pant, S.D.: **The Social Economy of the Himalayans**"; George Allen & Unwin Ltd., London, 1935.

Pascoe, E.H.: **A Manual of Geology of India and Burma**; Volume III, 1950.

Pate Ram: **Garhwal - Ancient and Modern**; Army Press, Simla, 1917.

Pauw, E.K.: **Report on the 10th Settlement of Garhwal District**; Government Press, Allahabad, 1896.

Planning Commission, Government of India: **Development of Tourism in Hill Areas of U.P.** - Report of the Working Group, June, 1973.

Planning Department, Government of U.P.: **Hamara Parvatiya Chhetra**, 1965.

Plowden, W.C.: **Census of N.W. Provinces, 1865 - General Report**, Government Press, Allahabad, 1867.

Prasad, Rajeshwari: **Census Handbook, Tehri Garhwal - 1951**; Government Press, Allahabad, 1953.

Prasad, Rajeshwari: **Census Handbook, Pauri Garhwal - 1951**; Government Press, Allahabad, 1953.

Prasad, Rajeshwari: **Village Directory, Garhwal**, 1953.

Ramsay, H.: **Report on the Revision of Settlement in the Kumaon District**; Government Press, Allahabad, 1874.

Raturi, Hari Krishna: **Narendra Hindu Law**; Government Press, Allahabad, 1917.

Raturi, Hari Krishna: **Garhwal Ka Itihas** (in Hindi); Garhwali Press, Dehradun, 1928.

Ruskar Nath: "Agriculture in Hills"; **Indian Farming**, Vol.XIII, No.3 and 4, 1963, pp.15-17 and pp.15-19 respectively.

Sankrityayan, R.: **Himalaya Parichay (1)**, Allahabad Law Journal Press, Allahabad, 1953.

Sankrityayan, R.: **Kumaon** (in Hindi), Gnan Mandal, Banaras, 1959.

Sanwal, R.D.: "Agricultural extension in a Kumaoni Village"; **Journal of Development Studies**; Vol.I, 1965.

Sanwal, R.D.: **Social Stratification in Rural Kumaon**"; Oxford University Press, Bombay, 1976.

Sapru, H.N.: **Industrial Survey Report, Garhwal District**; Government Press, Allahabad, 1914.

Sapru, H.N.: **Industrial Survey Report, Almora District**; Government Press, Allahabad, 1925.

Saxena, R.N.: **Social Economy of a Polyandrous People**; Agra University Institute of Social Sciences, Agra University Press, Agra, 1955.

Sen, Lalit K.: **Regional Planning for a Hill Area**: A case study of Pauri Tahsil in Pauri Garhwal District; N.I.C.D., Hyderabad, 1976.

Shah, Shanker Lall: **"Economic Life in Kumaon Region"**; An unpublished Doctoral Dissertation, Agra University, Agra, 1954.

Sinha, D.M.: **Census Handbook, Garhwal District, 1971**; Parts I and II, Onkar Press, Allahabad, 1976.

Srivastava, S.S.: **Working Plan for the Lansdowne Forest Division** : Western Circle, U.P. (1964-65 to 1973-74), Parts I and II, Nainital, 1964.

State Bank of India: **Lead Bank Scheme on Garhwal District, U.P.**; 1971.

Stowell, V.A.: **A Manual of Land Tenures of the Kumaon Division (Hill Tracts)**; Government Press, Allahabad, 1953.

Swaroop, R.: **Himalayan Region of U.P.**; An unpublished Doctoral Dissertation, Agra University, Agra, 1960.

Tewari, A.K.: "Land Utilisation in Jaunsar Bawar"; **Deccan Geographer**, Vols.III & IV, July 1966 and January, 1967.

Traill, G.W.: **Statistical Sketch of Kumaon**; Asiatic Researches, Vol.16, 1828.

Turner, A.C.: **Caste in the Kumaon Division and Tehri Garhwal State**; Census of India, 1931, Vol. I, Government Press, Allahabad.

Tyson, J.: "Himalayan Traders"; **Geographical Magazine**; Vol.XXVI, No.3, May, 1953, pp.33-41.

Upreti, Ganga Datt: **Proverbs and Folklores of Kumaon and**

Garhwal; Ludhiana Mission Press, Ludhiana, 1894.

Vaishnava, Saligram: **Uttarakhand Ka Rahasya** (in Hindi); Garhwali Press, Dehradun, 1926.

Vaishnava, Saligram: **Garhwali Pakhana** (in Hindi); Garhwali Press, Dehradun, 1938.

Walton, H.G.: **British Garhwal : A Gazetteer**; Vol.XXXVI of the District Gazetteer of United Provinces of Agra and Oudh; Allahabad, 1911.

Walton, H.G.: **Almora : A Gazetteer**; Vol.XXXV of the District Gazetteer of the United Provinces of Agra and Oudh; Allahabad, 1911.

Walton, H.G.: **Dehradun : A Gazetteer**; Vol.XXXVII of the District Gazetteer of the U.P. of Agra and Oudh, Allahabad, 1911.

Williams, G.P.C.: **Historical and Statistical Memoirs of Dehradun**; Government Press, Roorkee, 1874.

INDEX